D1351271

RACERS

The Inside Story of Williams Grand Prix Engineering

RACERS

The Inside Story of Williams Grand Prix Engineering

DOUG NYE

General Editor: David McDonough

Arthur Barker Limited London

A subsidiary of Weidenfeld (Publishers) Limited

Published in Great Britain by
Arthur Barker Ltd
91 Clapham High Street
London SW4 7TA

Designed by Behram Kapadia

ISBN 0 213 16815 4

Printed in Great Britain by
Fakenham Press Limited, Fakenham, Norfolk

Contents

Acknowledgements

Of the many people who have helped us in the preparation of this book, we would like to thank, in particular, the entire Frank Williams team at Didcot, all of whom have shown characteristic co-operation and enthusiasm in making *Racers* an accurate reflection of their endeavour.

To sponsors of the team, too, we owe a debt of gratitude for their support and encouragement.

Lastly, special thanks are due to Kathy Ager, of LAT Photographic, whose efforts in researching photographs for the book have gone far beyond the call of duty.

D.N.
D. McD.

The photographs in this book are reproduced by kind permission of the following:

Behram Kapadia: pages ii, 144, 155(l).
LAT Photographic: 2, 21(l), 25, 27(b), 31, 33, 35, 41, 45, 49(b), 55, 56, 58, 65, 71, 81, 83, 91, 94, 97, 98, 101, 103, 111, 113, 121, 123, 125, 129, 133, 137, 141, 142, 160.
Leyland Vehicles Ltd: 67, 92, 126, 135, 155(r).
Lynton Money: 11(b).
Williams Grand Prix Engineering Ltd: x, 5, 11(a), 21(r), 27(a), 29, 49(a), 87.

Colour Section:

Geoff Goddard: p.1, p.2, p.3(a).
Behram Kapadia: p.6(r), p.7(a), pp.6–7(b), p.8.
LAT Photographic: p.3(b), p.4, p.5, p.6(al), p.7(al).

Foreword by Frank Williams

Millions of people follow Grand Prix racing – through television, radio, newspapers, motor racing magazines, and at the circuit. They are drawn to the sport – as I have been all my life – by a compelling and fascinated interest in risk and danger. To the historic attractions of wealth, favour and glamour motor racing adds speed and the chance to win for one's country.

It is a fact of life that the fine sporting tradition of good-humoured, competitive amateurism in motor racing has been eased out by constant demands – partly imposed by overcomplex rules – for faster, more sophisticatedly engineered cars, costing ever more vast sums of money to develop, build and race.

Consequently, running a team today is just as much concerned with seeking out and striking business deals, as it is with understanding the technicalities of the sport itself. I am glad *Racers* has been written with the commercial world as much in mind as the devotees of motor racing. Our sport will not survive unless these two worlds understand each other and actively co-operate.

I am grateful to Doug Nye and David McDonough for making possible this definitive record of my efforts in the sport I love, and that is my life.

Most of all, this book enables me – albeit indirectly – to offer my most sincere thanks to everyone who has helped me fulfill my lifetime's ambition to run a winning team; and most particularly, to thank everyone at Williams Grand Prix Engineering, without whom the accolades of the last two seasons would not have been possible.

FRANK WILLIAMS
November, 1981

Preface

What follows is a record of immense enterprise and endeavour. It is a motor racing story, but one played out against a wide and dynamic backdrop. Grand Prix racing for the Formula One Constructors' Cup and Drivers' World Championship titles exists as a massive iceberg, of which only the glamorous and spectacular tip is normally visible. It attracts huge media coverage all over the world, and while its technology has become extremely sophisticated, it also provides many commercial interests outside racing with a powerful promotional tool.

This is the story of a grittily determined Englishman who set out to build a life in Grand Prix racing, helped by staunch friends and diverse skills, surviving years of crushing adversity to create the dominant Formula One team of recent years.

We see boyish enthusiasm mature undiluted into worldly-wise business acumen. We see how dedication and commitment to a dream reaped its own reward. The business of Grand Prix racing is also examined – what it offers its commercial sponsors, and how it can be put to work for them. And more . . .

Behind each and every driver on a Grand Prix grid there is a devoted and highly skilled industrial unit, men committed to their cars' development and preparation to race-winning standard, irrespective of the time and effort their job demands. The infrastructure of Formula One, the hidden mechanism which puts the great show on the road, is also examined in these pages.

Above all this is a British success story. British Formula One teams have dominated the World Championship series since 1958. The Constructors' Cup competition was instituted that season and it fell immediately to Vandervell Products' Vanwall team. Mike Hawthorn took the drivers' crown, driving an Italian Ferrari, and he became the first British World Champion.

In the twenty-four series from that time to 1981, British constructors have won seventeen World titles, compared to Ferrari's six for Italy, and Matra's lone success for France, which in any case required British engines, a British driver – Jackie Stewart – and the very English Tyrrell team to do the job. Ten of those titles were achieved using the British-financed, British-made Cosworth DFV engine which, with well over 150 World Championship race victories to its credit, is by far the most successful Grand Prix power unit in the sport's seventy-five year history.

During long years of at best patchy British achievement in all other professional sports, our domination of Grand Prix motor racing and our ability to accept the complex technological challenge it offers are too often overlooked.

One of the aims of this book is to set the record straight, studying the personalities and complex problems involved without shirking the necessary technology which makes this great business-sport so very special. This is the story of Frank Williams and the Williams Grand Prix Engineering team, its personnel, and its World Championship successes. It is the comprehensive story of what makes a Racer.

Piers and Frank, friends
with problems at
Clermont-Ferrand in
practice for the 1969
French Grand Prix.

I · FRANK WILLIAMS, RACER

'There's always room at the top, and it's damned crowded down below.
Why shouldn't one get there? It only needs a little more push and a little
more attention to detail than the average fellow is prepared to give . . .'

Sir Henry Segrave: *The Lure of Speed*, 1928.

The Man

Frank Williams is dapper, brisk and faultlessly articulate. He fizzes with energy. Turning forty, he sometimes feels he looks older, with his prematurely receding well-cropped hair, but he is very fit. His only intense recreational interest outside motor racing and racing cars is running, and that term is chosen carefully. He is no flabby city-slick jogger trying to look good in a track-suit and running shoes. For ten years or more he has run seriously, relentlessly – a minimum of five miles a day, sometimes eight.

He is a non-smoker, and teetotal. Almost superstitiously he will not touch even a cup of coffee or a cold drink while his cars are in action. At a Grand Prix meeting he eats nothing, and will eat nothing until far into the evening when he may unwind enough to tackle just the lightest of light snacks. With his drivers at work, his cars running, he is totally absorbed, clicking watches, taking times, watching the opposition's latest ploys and performance, analysing all that is going on around him. Part of his mind is always out there with his drivers in those form-hugging tailored cockpits, willing speed into their cars and problems out . . .

Frank had entered Formula One with Piers Courage as his driver. They had grown up together in racing – friends first, entrant and driver second. When Piers was killed in Frank's car, the entrant was left to struggle on, a small figure, alone but strong.

He would never grow so close to another driver. He never forgot Piers and his widow Sarah. He kept in close touch with their small sons, Jason and Amos. Frank was never to forget, but through the low years of uncompetitiveness into more recent years of immense success his attitude to drivers became harder, colder and more clear.

He worries endlessly – as do his partner Patrick Head and Patrick's engineering team – over the constructional integrity of their cars, and is quietly proud of the safety record they are building. But a world-class driver's instinctive insistence upon speed and power rests uncomfortably with his more intellectual need for a margin of safety. Everybody involved understands that, and appreciates the inevitably fine balance between the two.

It would be understandable if the race weighed heavier on Frank than the practice and qualifying periods which precede it. He says not. Latterly he has felt more relaxed. 'After years of fully expecting my cars to fail before the finish, now retirement has become a rarity.'

Reliability is not luck. With proper organization, proper engineering disciplines and proper team systems, nothing on those cars is going to break unless a mistake has been made, somewhere. There is always a reason for race failure, and experience, ability, technique and fore-thought can usually cover all the options, short of a race accident. Frank had been a long time learning that lesson, and he had to foot the bill for every mistake made along the way.

And between practice periods and the race, late into the evenings in garages at Buenos Aires or Montreal, Kyalami or Monte Carlo, every team principal is usually long gone to his hotel for dinner while Frank Williams is still hovering, close to his cars.

He cites two reasons for his presence. First, he simply loves those cars, he is fascinated by them: '. . . They mesmerize me, I think it's truly powerful to see a Formula One car sitting on its stands, at rest, with its suspensions hanging down at full droop. I get a tremendous charge out of it – just like seeing a really potent, charismatic warplane sitting on the ground . . .'. And secondly?

He has discovered the hard way that reward is truly proportionate to the effort put in. Since his own intensely competitive nature demands the highest rewards, he has to invest, personally, intense effort. As his team developed, so he became aware that he could of course leave the circuit at six, like so many of his peers, and his two cars would still be running the following day. But all night '. . . I would have been thinking of all the snags and hitches I've known in twelve years of Formula One.' His presence could apply just one more experienced mind's input to his team's effort. Around midnight Saturday his men would have already put in ferocious hours – hours that would shock to death any conventionally unionized blue-collar worker on the factory floor. His team counts intensely on its artisan tradesmen back home at the Didcot factory, but the crunch comes on-circuit, and the race-team mechanics are the company's front-line troops.

Wryly Frank will sometimes contend they all believe they are effing superstars and will nod sage acknowledgement as Patrick's ringing naval officer tones occasionally bring them crashing back to earth. But open management and concerted effort, virtually as equals, is the accepted way of business in the team. Once a ballooning ego has been pricked – and they are shot on sight – the air is cleared for another maximum effort by all concerned, Frank and Patrick leading from the front.

Come the gathering dusk on-circuit and Frank changes his perhaps dusty team uniform for tee-shirt, tracksuit trousers and running shoes. He warms up vigorously, purging an inevitably tired mind and body. Then he sets off, running fast, usually around the race circuit unless it is somewhere like Österreichring, where rowdy camping crowds can sometimes pose a very real threat. He's a six-minute miler. Sometimes back home he drives the eight miles or so from his Goring-on-Thames home to the Didcot works, and runs the eight miles back. He even runs on his visits to his sponsors in Saudi Arabia – setting out through the streets around 1 a.m. when the temperature has fallen. He admits that after a full practice day he feels mentally and physically exhausted: '. . . but a run leaves me purged, ready to sleep and

recharge. If it hurts, it's doing you good.' There's some rough sports psychology involved there too. Most opposing teams' principals are older men; men who never bothered to keep so fit. Should any of them still be around the circuit, perhaps they might be just a little chastened to see him bouncing round, arms and legs pumping, mile after mile . . . If the Williams cars had been leading the pack as well, it might just get to them, a tiny victory in the wider war and a further tiny boost to his own competitiveness . . .

Outside motor racing and his running Frank's family means much, his wife Ginny and their two young children, Jonathan and Claire; he is a doting father. While other principals proudly invest in the expensive toys of successful business life – executive aircraft, helicopters, fashionable town and resort houses, flashy home gadgetry – Frank has a beautiful but compact country house, and seems to get a similar charge from investing in the very latest thing from Cosworth, the engine suppliers, or funding some marvellous computer-controlled machine tool for the factory; anything to help the team win . . .

He admits to 'a huge interest in all forms of aviation', enjoying the experience of flying but without any great drive to become a pilot himself. The running of major airlines fascinates him. He takes *Flight* magazine every week and keeps abreast of who is buying what, or opening up which new route, and why. In 1979 he began logging every flight he made, partly for tax purposes but largely as an interest. Boarding an airliner at Heathrow, Riyadh, Rio or Johannesburg he notes its type and registration number, the class and flight-time to destination. Typed out at the end of the year, his flight log fills several foolscap pages.

He is a naturally self-disciplined man who sets the highest standards for himself and for his team. He can object fiercely if a team-member's car isn't cleaned often enough. Even in the lowest years of his team, when a county court order came to be regarded as the ultimate extension of credit, he would never save money by making do with old engines. The best was barely good enough.

And unusually for Formula One he reached the World Championship through the good times and the bad, accumulating real friends and never making a real enemy. 'Tread on nobody on the way up, you might need them on the way down . . .' As an

The worrier – Frank Williams,
team chief.

habitually courteous, well-mannered man, he is impeccably businesslike, supremely well-informed where would-be sponsors are concerned. He does his homework. With old friends, his 'blokes' at the works, or journalists, the innate courtesy seldom falters as Williams the articulate talker becomes a ready, habitually salty-tongued wit, an equal – the effervescent enthusiast, the motor racing fan . . . He did change with success. He became less ready to see the funny side, more intense, the responsibilities of eighty-plus employees and a major business weighing quite heavily. His threshold of boredom had always been low, and now he rationed his time more sparingly than ever, wasting none on what he saw as non-essentials.

The pressures of modern Formula One are so intense, and can become so personal, that it is difficult to persuade many of Williams' rivals to talk objectively of him and his team's recent successes. But Bernard Ecclestone, boss of Brabham, readily admits, 'There's no doubt he surprised a lot of us by coming good. For years and years he scratched around in Formula One. But he gets the job done and he's worked hard to get where he is now . . .'

And Gordon Murray, the Brabham designer, who had some very poisonous things to say about his adversaries when they considered his pneumatically adjustable suspension system illegal on the 1981 Brabhams, could still observe of Frank: 'He had some pretty awful cars for years in Formula One, but he always used to say "I'll do the job properly the day I get the big money." A lot of people used to laugh when he said that. But he was *absolutely* right – and he defied a lot of his critics. Good luck to him . . .'

Teddy Mayer of McLaren – a team whose organization during the mid-seventies impressed Frank deeply: 'He's done a great job to get it all together after years of trying – you have to admire him for his staying power . . .'

The Italian Ferrari team are famous for their occasional tirades against the British Formula One establishment. While most British specialist teams, like Williams, build chassis to carry proprietary Cosworth engines and – albeit highly modified – proprietary transmissions, Ferrari like Renault and Alfa Romeo make the whole car – engine, transmission and chassis alike. The legendary and now octogenarian Mr Ferrari himself describes

these three great marques as the *Grande Costruttori*, while Williams and their ilk are mere *Assemblatori* in comparison! Nonetheless, his *Capo Ingegnere*, *Commendatore* Mauro Forghieri says: 'Formula One is supremely competitive – no matter which way one approaches it. From that point of view you have to admire Frank Williams and the amount of sheer hard work he puts into this business. He has probably worked harder over the past ten years than anybody else getting where he is today.

Jean Sage – director of the mighty Régie Renault team and one of the chief rivals of the often trenchantly Francophobic Frank Williams: 'Frank's team are good competitors and a very fine team indeed. They are very patriotic too – sometimes even more than the Renault team?'

Early in 1980 Frank had the idea of waving a Union Jack and the green Saudi flag to greet his cars, should they win, in honour of the sponsors. At the French Grand Prix at Ricard that year, which Alan Jones won by homeric effort, beating the Ligiers and Renaults on their home ground, salt was rubbed into French wounds as Alan drove his *tour d'honneur* with the red-white-and-blue fluttering from his car's cockpit . . .

Frank Williams has harboured a life-long ambition to become a wealthy man – having set out with little beyond enthusiasm and his competitive nature. 'I had a real wish to become a wealthy, successful person – not so that I can indulge in aeroplanes and boats and other toys, because I genuinely don't want that. I find myself looking at other blokes my age who started at around the same level, and I like to see where they have got to – how far they have climbed up their particular ladder, relative to me. Some have done better, some worse – it's important to me . . .'

When pressed on ambitions beyond a thirty-year future in Grand Prix racing he will admit to two: one is deadly serious, the other he confesses is childish, but genuine just the same: 'I am devoted to England. I believe deeply that it is the best country in the world to live in, and a beautiful country too, and some time I would love to own a couple of thousand acres of prime English farmland with a beautiful house on it, and be able to leave it in my family for generations.

'Ideally I would like it to be on the Kent coast, so I could put concrete blocks across the beach and be the first to keep the Russians out ... or the French! That's heritage. That's what I would like to found ...'

And the second? 'Stupid really – but when I'm gone and they put me in the ground and the old will is published in *The Daily Telegraph*, people will step back and say, "Coo, look what old Frank Williams left, he must have been a clever boy!" That's all.'

When away for a Grand Prix race meeting, Frank Williams is usually awake in his hotel room around seven. He's alert and on the balls of his feet the moment they touch the floor. He does not take breakfast. He shaves carefully, is washed and dressed in his crisp team uniform by 7.45, and waits downstairs in the hotel foyer, ready to leave for the circuit.

He may glance briskly at his special Saudia Airlines Rolex watch, tetchy at the delay. The rugged figure of his partner and Chief Engineer, Patrick Head, similarly uniformed, at last appears. He seems usually to be late, Frank knows and expects it and Patrick is aware it irritates him. These are men of very different yet complementary skills, but both are Racers, no holds barred.

With team manager Jeff Hazell and team engineer Neil Oatley in the back of their BL loan car, they may drive up to the circuit, Jeff and Neil probably wondering what's going to happen – will Frank's irritation at being delayed erupt? But there's no serious 'needle'; they are a happy team, self-possessed and self-contained, unlike so many less successful teams, their people seem to need no close contact with personnel outside their own tight-knit organization. To outsiders the Williams team seem distant and remote, almost cloistered. But they work ferociously hard and are self-sufficient. They need no outside contact to enjoy their work and their racing – but at any race there is a level of pressure, a level of tension, which stretches the most equable and fulfilled temperament until it can snap.

Back in 1969 when Frank first entered Formula One, he operated one car, built by Brabham the previous year and since modified to his own requirements, which was maintained and run by five mechanics. The driver, Piers Courage, was Frank's closest personal friend. They followed the eleven-race World Championship series through most of its course around the world, and added a sprinkling of the minor non-Championship Formula One races which were still being run at that time. By modern standards the atmosphere was relaxed, the financial stakes were modest and calendar pressures light. Frank was a private entrant, an owner of an ex-works car which he operated under his own team banner. In essence the private owner was a dying breed, but Frank was different. Historically the private entrant in Grand Prix racing had been a wealthy man indulging his enthusiasm, like a race-horse owner with a string of thoroughbreds. Many had been owner-drivers, men like Count Villapadierna, 'Paco' Godia-Sales and Baron de Graffenried, who are still around the sport in organizational capacities. Others ran true private teams, most notably the immensely successful British entrant Rob Walker, who had run Cooper and Lotus cars for drivers like Stirling Moss, Maurice Trintignant, Jo Bonnier and Jo Siffert.

But all of them were privately wealthy enthusiasts. When Frank Williams came to Formula One he was just an enthusiast – with minimal private means beyond what he could earn through his racing car dealership business, and what he could attract from sponsors increasingly eager to find exposure in Grand Prix racing. Effectively Frank was the first of a new breed, a private entrant who made Formula One his business, and had to make it pay simply to survive. By 1971 he too was having his own car built and became a Formula One constructor. Now he was following a different path, one well-trodden by drivers like Bruce McLaren, Jack Brabham and Dan Gurney, and by team managers like Ken Tyrrell before him.

It was this path which led him to found Williams Grand Prix Engineering Ltd in 1977, after losing control of his original company the previous year. And it was WGPE which brought the Williams name to World Championship prominence in 1980–81.

The Early Years

Francis Owen Garbett Williams was born on 16 April 1942, at South Shields in England's industrial north-east. It was wartime. Mother was a schoolteacher and father an RAF pilot, flying Wellington bombers. He left Frank's mother at about the time of his birth, and she had to raise her child alone.

They lived in Jarrow-upon-Tyne, a name etched into British social history by the Jarrow Crusade of the unemployed during the Great Depression. Frank's mother worked hard, his childhood was by no means deprived but pennies had to be hard-earned, and were spent with caution . . .

He was cared for by his grandparents much of the time, until at three-and-a-half he was sent to a Roman Catholic convent school at Blundell Sands, near Liverpool. He stayed there for three years before spending a year in day-school in Jarrow. In May 1949 Mother found him a boarding place at the Roman Catholic Marist Brothers' school in Dumfries, Scotland. He stayed there for nine years and completed a good classical education, while Mother '. . . really struggled to earn sufficient to pay the fees.' She won a headship, and specialized in teaching sub-normal and backward children. She was good at it, but Frank was isolated from her. They never grew close, and after leaving home to become 'a Racer' in 1962 he hardly saw her again.

The Marist Brothers ran a hard regime with a fiercely demanding syllabus. They emphasized attainment. It was a lesson the determinedly competitive Frank Williams learned well.

Being close to the English border, the school was split roughly sixty-forty between Scots and English. As a seven-year-old in his first three weeks there Frank was dismayed to hear 'those funny accents' – he couldn't understand a word.

School holidays were spent in Jarrow until 1953, then at Broadstairs in Kent until 1956, as her job took Mother to the south-east. 'I think I was happiest at Broadstairs,' Frank will say in a rare look back. 'I loved the sea . . . had a small boat which I'd row around the harbour for hours on end, occasionally walk across to Ramsgate, where I'd made friends . . . we had lovely times there in the holidays . . .'

Mother was appointed headmistress of a school for educationally sub-normal children outside Calverton, a small village some ten miles north of Nottingham in the Midlands. During holidays from Dumfries Frank would find it '. . . not half so interesting as Broadstairs, but by that time I was really into motor racing . . .'

He had developed a consuming passion for motor cars. Before he was ten he was memorizing car specifications from the pages of magazines like *The Motor* and *The Autocar*, not with any real understanding but with compulsive interest.

'At that time in the mid-fifties there was a lot of motor racing rivalry between England and Scotland, and our school split into a Scots faction supporting Ecurie Ecosse and their private Jaguars, and an English faction rooting for the works Jaguar team. That introduced me to the racing side of motoring . . .'

One of his school-mates had parents friendly with David Murray, patron of Ecurie Ecosse. Several others were relatively well-heeled and their families would arrive to take them out in shiny new cars. Frank's mother was rarely able to take him for a day-trip, and when she did it was always by train.

'I never felt deprived because of that, but it did make me intensely aware of motor cars and of their prestige value in the world . . .

'One boy came from a family which owned a string of betting shops in Glasgow, and one day he arrived with a brand spanking new Jaguar XK150S – not just a 140 or standard 150, but a 150S! He took me for a ride in it and I was virtually speechless. I was fascinated by cars and determined to have one, some day. I would come to school not by train but hitch-hiking, just so that I could ride in cars. Cars really mattered to me, deeply. I was and still am a complete nut for motor cars . . .'

One school-friend, Francis Holmes, had a father who was a wealthy motor trader in England's north-east. Mrs Holmes virtually adopted Frank Williams, taking him on trips with her son at half-terms. The family had many cars and were based in Newcastle on Tyne. The business bought some of its stock from car auctions in Glasgow, across the Scottish border. The Holmeses would drive from Newcastle to Glasgow with a number of spare drivers, buy cars and drive them back in convoy. Frank would tag along, 'for the joy of three hours in the passenger seat of a 3.4 Jaguar. I'd ride in the most interesting of the cars they bought. I never drove myself, but I'd snatch a seat behind the Jaguar's wheel and make all the right noises . . .'

During the school holidays he would hitch-hike from Nottingham to Newcastle on Tuesday nights, purely to make that Glaswegian pilgrimage. 'I'd arrive at Newcastle Station at around four or five o'clock in the morning – never late – I became quite well-known there. The baths would open at six, so I'd have a shave and clean-up, present myself at the Holmes's at seven, and off to Glasgow. That Wednesday night I'd be back on the road, hitching home to Nottingham . . .'

His hitch-hiking also took him to motor racing circuits anywhere in England, distance no object. One of the first races he saw was the 1958 British Grand Prix at Silverstone, in which Peter Collins and Mike Hawthorn finished first and second for Ferrari.

Twenty-one years later two white-and-green cars ran first and second in that race, and one of them won it, driven by Clay Regazzoni. The cars belonged to Frank Williams.

For several years he never missed a Boxing Day Brands Hatch meeting. It was a long and arduous hitch-hike, down the A1 from Nottingham to Brands Hatch in Kent. 'And there'd be no traffic at all on the A1 come ten o'clock on Christmas Night. Boxing Day Brands '59 was bitterly cold and wet, I was soaked and frozen to the core. I had to change all my clothes in the little hut beside what is now the Competitors' Entrance to Brands Hatch. Several times I took refuge there just to keep warm, and I always started hitching home from there . . .' Twenty-one years later a white-and-green car won the British Grand Prix at Brands Hatch. It was Alan Jones' Williams . . .

By his late teens Frank was pondering his future. He had a flair for languages, taking excellent passes in Latin, French, Italian and German. 'But mathematics was a different matter. I gave it up at thirteen, pretty early to start specializing, eh?' He thought of studying medicine, or of joining the Army. At seventeen he knew for certain he did not want to enter University. 'I'd been at boarding schools since the age of three. I wanted out!'

His motoring interest won. In 1960 he left school to begin a management trainee course with Cripps Bros of Nottingham, the local Rootes Group car and commercial vehicle distributor. They also had a franchise for International Harvester agricultural and earth-moving machines. Frank was set to work on commercials; '. . . hard and filthy work, lying under dripping cattle trucks with the back axle in your lap – or under caterpillar tractors, where there were a million ways of losing your fingers . . .'

And he had begun to drive, first with Mother's Morris Minor 1000 around the grounds of her school, before passing his test first time in Nottingham. Mother chipped in with some cash to help him buy his first car. It could be no ordinary family saloon. It was a racer.

Two prominent club drivers named Mick Cave and Simon Pilkington had been running an ex-Graham Hill Austin A35, tuned by Graham's Speedwell Conversions company. They wanted to graduate to an A40, and advertised the 'tea-pot' for sale. Frank went down to London to collect 'UVX 930' and was 'thrilled-to-bits' with it. 'It was quick and noisy, and everyone turned to look at it. At twenty I loved all that! I brought it out at weekends and drove it round Nottingham, and entered it for my first races...'

At that time British club racing offered numerous classes catering for street-legal tuned cars. Frank entered 'UVX' for a minor clubbie at Oulton Park in Cheshire. It was April 1961 – 'The track was nice and dry and I had a good day, I didn't crash. But on the way home the car broke a half-shaft, so instead of returning to Nottingham in triumph I had to hitch, which was rather ignominious. We towed the car home next day...'

He raced perhaps six times that year, sometimes taking along a friend named Johnny Middleton. The story of his development from occasional club racer to Formula One constructor comes best in his own words:

'I was earning about £3 10s a week then, living at home free and spending all my spare money on the car. I bought used racing tyres from Mick Cave for ten bob each and went racing with a handful of spare spark plugs, two spare wheels and tyres and no clue. In only my second or third race at Mallory Park in July I rolled the car in the wet. I clambered out and up on to the top of the safety bank to watch the rest of the race. That was where I met Jonathan Williams, whose Mini had gone off at the same place a few laps earlier. He had been watching me get more out of shape as every lap went by, until I joined him on the bank. We got talking, and were to become good friends. Back in the paddock he introduced me to a tall, well-spoken friend of his who had come up to help for the day, and his name was Piers Courage...

'The A35 was soon straightened out. I took it to the Downton tuning company in Wiltshire for a Weber carburettor to be fitted. I invested all my spare cash in this demon tweak, collected the car one Saturday morning and set off immediately for a race that afternoon at Oulton Park in Cheshire. I had four hours to get there from south of Salisbury, it was raining and there was no way I was going to manage it. Sure enough, I was delighted the way the car went on its new Weber and in the middle of Salisbury I gave it too much throttle, the bald Dunlop R5 racing tyres at the back came unstuck and she spun backwards straight into a lamp-post. The tail was split open right down the middle, and the back-axle was pushed about four inches out of line at one end. Feeling very sorry

for myself I drove home to Nottingham with the car crabbing sideways.

'It was evidently a write-off, and over the winter of 1961–62 Johnny Middleton and I broke it up, rescued the Downtonized engine and all other usable bits and built them into an A40 bodyshell for the new season.'

Then he was fired from Cripps. Part of their training course entailed one day a week studying at the local Technical College. 'The technical side fascinated me, but they insisted upon taking us through rudimentary English first. I had A-level English, so this niggled me intensely and I would just take the day off instead. Cripps found out and I was instantly dismissed...'

He joined a company delivering crumpets around England and Wales, driving ancient Commer vans which were desperately unreliable. Meanwhile he had cemented his friendship with Jonathan Williams and Piers Courage. 'Obviously at first I was just some guy from the north to them, but around November '61 they called me at home from a nearby coinbox. Piers had just completed building a Lotus 7 from a kit and to run it in they had driven up from London. Could they stay the night? First thing next morning Piers was up and away in the Lotus to go to work in London. He was a trainee chartered accountant at the time.'

During the 1962 club season, Jonathan raced a black-painted Austin A40 similar to Frank's pale-blue version. Jonathan's was ex-Doc Shepherd and had been the car to beat. He drove it well and won more than Frank, '... but we had several very good hard races together at circuits like Brands Hatch, Cadwell Park, Mallory Park and Silverstone. At the Whitsun Crystal Palace meeting in London my car went very well and I shared a new 1-litre class lap record with Mike Young's Anglia before stuffing the nose in. That record stood for about three years.'

He would hitch-hike down to London quite regularly to see Jonathan and Piers. They were sharing a flat in Lower Sloane Street with Sheridan Thynne, who club-raced a Mini, and Mark Fielden, who was tragically killed soon after in an accident at Silverstone when he was sitting in his car on the pit apron, and another car spun into it out of Woodcote Corner. They were all,

Cadwell 1962 – Williams' day: Frank
spins, Jonathan wins.

Frank leads the pack at Crystal Palace,
where he broke the lap record, 1962.

except Piers, supposedly studying at the Chelsea College of Aeronautical and Automobile Engineering in Sydney Street.

Sheridan – who was to become responsible for liaison between the Williams team and their Leyland Vehicles co-sponsors in 1980–81 – recalls how each of the flat's inmates had some form of private allowance on which to live: 'But there was a cafe in Pimlico Road which did a three-course supper, plus bread and margarine, for 5s a head, and we ate there religiously – enjoying a far lower standard of living than our parents perhaps expected – purely to save money so we could go racing. When Frank came on the scene in 1962 he was different, because he was working. One night after a meeting at Brands Hatch we all came back to London for a meal and I vividly recall our surprise at Frank parking his A40 outside the flat, then leaping up straight after the meal to hitch-hike back to Nottingham because he had to go to work...'

Frank had filled in briefly at a filling station, and then landed a job as a trainee salesman for Campbell's Soup. 'I was twenty-one. I got the job for ten pounds a week plus a brand-new Ford Anglia company car, and they posted me to Yorkshire where I lived in digs. I had to wear a bowler hat and try to sell soup to hard-headed storekeepers in little Yorkshire villages. I was reasonably successful. I saw a lot of Yorkshire, but I didn't have much self-confidence, and if a bloke said, "Push off, and take your soup with you," then I would just turn to jelly, and push off...'

Deep inside he must have looked covetously at the life-style of his London friends, and in 1963 '... I finally became *a Racer*' – he says it like that, emphatically – 'I left home for good, moved to London, and became Jonathan Williams' mechanic.'

Jonathan had decided to invest in a Merlyn Formula Junior car and a VW pick-up truck on which to transport it. Formula Junior was the international cadet class of single-seater racing at that time, demanding miniature Grand Prix cars with production car-based engines of no more than 1100cc, with push-rod valve gear rather than the more sophisticated overhead camshaft type which could produce more power. At Monaco Jonathan had misjudged a corner and crashed very heavily, destroying the Merlyn and suffering a bad knock on the head. He had bounced back, bought himself a Lotus 22FJ car which was sprayed jet-black, and Frank

joined him as mechanic to follow the Formula Junior circus on its gypsy wanderings around Europe.

'We lived in the pick-up, and one night a week would share a hotel room so that we could have a proper meal, bed, breakfast and a shower. Essentially the Formula Junior circus was on the move around Europe from the start of May to the end of September, travelling on to a new circuit every weekend, living on start money and prize money earned along the way...

'Our first meeting was a hill-climb in Trieste, but with my mechanicking Jonathan didn't reach the top in practice. The car caught fire and we had to rebuild it frantically to make the start because we had no money and were relying on the start money to survive. He did actually make it to the top in the event itself and we collected about 60,000 *Lire* for our trouble.

'In those genteel days there would be a proper prize-giving dinner in the evening after the event, at which you were expected to present yourself and collect your start money and winnings. No show, no pay-out. The party that night was in the castle overlooking Trieste, and I vividly remember standing beside the VW's cab, parked by the Trieste–Venice road, looking in the driving mirror and shaving with soap and water and a piece of tin snipped from a petrol can as a blade. You had to be nice and fresh for the party... I must have smelled faintly of petrol, but we were paid and travelled on...

'That year was an eye-opener for me. We travelled and raced all over Europe, from deep into the leg of Italy across the Iron Curtain to places like Schleiz, the Sachsenring and Halle-Salle in East Germany.

'It was at one of those East German tracks that I met Charlie Crichton-Stuart. I was acutely aware of all the very latest Formula Junior machinery, and there he was standing in immaculately shiny Dunlop racing overalls beside a gleaming latest-mark car with special Mark 11 Cosworth engine and all the best bits. He asked me if I could possibly undo a union and change the oil for him. Of course I could. I jumped at the chance.'

Other vivid memories of that season are of losing his passport in East Germany, and Geoff Duke – the great former World

Champion motor-cyclist – finding it for him; of being paid six hundred crisp new Deutschmarks as start money for a race at the Solitude circuit outside Stuttgart despite the Lotus catching fire again; of seeing the Dolomites for the first time, so jagged and looking so much older than the Alps . . . 'Climbing some of the grades there Jonathan and I had to jump out of the little Volksie and run alongside, reaching into the cab to steer and holding one hand down on the throttle, otherwise it wouldn't have made the summit.

'It carried the car on the back under a canvas tilt with its nose poking out behind. We used to sleep in there on either side of the car with our heads against the rear wheels and our feet snuggled around the fronts. I used to make myself comfortable with a leg either side of the front wheel. On one occasion we were fast asleep like this, parked in a German layby, when a *Polizei* decided he wanted to see what this little racing car was all about, poking out through the Volksie's tilt. He yanked the flap open and as the light flooded in so Jonathan awoke with a start and rose from the waist, staring-eyed, mumbling 'Wazzamadder – who is it?' He frightened the life out of the policeman, like a body rising from the grave . . .'

Frank had gone off on this tour with high hopes for Jonathan, but the Monaco accident seemed to have de-tuned him for the remainder of the year. Then at Wunstorf – a West German airfield with a temporary race circuit marked-out by straw bales and oil drums – he saw Jochen Rindt for the first time.

'I proudly claim the title of having become Jochen's first fan. Piers later recalled Jochen in those days as being 'all pink trousers and white E-Type', which was right, but out on circuit, in his ex-Kurt Bardi-Barry Cooper, he was magnificent.

'There was a very fast fifth-gear curve on Wunstorf airfield, and I can still vividly picture Jochen simply flying through there in beautiful four-wheel slides. I thought it was splendid, I was sure he had a great future, and it's not putting it too strongly to say I worshipped him from then on . . .'

Meanwhile Jonathan had run short of money and returned home to make some. Frank stayed in Europe and went to the inaugural meeting of the new Zolder circuit in Belgium with a

Swedish FJ driver named Picko Troberg. Frank acted as his mechanic, and admits that at one stage in practice he succeeded in supplying him with four reverse speeds and one forward. 'I thought I could change ratios, and I couldn't . . .'

But because he could speak languages he was approached by an increasing number of Continental drivers anxious to buy parts for their predominantly British-made and British-engined FJ cars. 'I would fix them up, put a tenner on top of the price as a handling charge-cum-profit, and from those small beginnings a wheeler-dealing business began to grow . . .'

One of the regular FJ gypsies was a Parisian taxi-driver named Gabriel Aumont. He towed his ageing Lotus 20 around on a trailer hitched behind a Peugeot 404 Paris taxi. 'We used to pull his leg terribly because he was a Frog, but he was a good chap and took it all in good part. Late that season he lent me his car for the Eifelrennen FJ race on the *Sudschleife* circuit at Nürburgring . . .' This is a four-mile loop using the same pits area as the majestic 14.2-mile *Nordschleife* Grand Prix course; '. . . and I loved it. It was my first single-seater race and my first in Europe. I was doing quite well amongst the also-rans at the back of the field until the car inevitably broke down.

'I amused myself by watching Jochen's progress thereafter, slithering by on opposite lock, smoke puffing from the hard-pressed little Cooper's tyres and his foot hard down the whole way. Of course, he fell off into the ditch eventually, and I walked up after the finish and helped him hoike it out and back on to the road.

'He immediately climbed in to drive it back to the pits and told me to hop on the back, astride the engine, hanging on to the roll-over bar behind his head, for a lift. The trouble was that once he set off he seemed to forget the wheels were all buckled and pointing in different directions, and secondly that I was on the back! He drove faster and faster, steam was puffing out of the ruptured radiator and I was soon reaching over and tapping frantically on his helmet just to remind him I was there. Luckily it was only about half a mile to the pits, but it was a ride I'll never forget, typical Jochen . . .

'I also went to Zandvoort as a mechanic to David Prophet, from

Birmingham, who was running a Lotus 23 and Brabham F3, good equipment, which he towed on a double-deck trailer behind a Wolseley 6/99. He was a good bloke, competitive and aggressive. I liked him. He finished in both Zandvoort races and on the way home, rushing to catch the boat, we were held up by somebody on a dual-carriageway through a built-up area. It was about one o'clock in the morning, and the carriageway was divided down the middle by a reservation, with gaps every so often. David suddenly yanked the Wolseley and the two-car trailer hard left through one of these gaps, whizzed down the opposite carriageway in the wrong direction to pass this bloke in front, and then pulled back through the next gap into the right carriageway once more.' David Prophet was killed in a helicopter accident at Silverstone early in 1981, while these words were being written.

Around October that year, 1963, Frank moved into the flat in Pinner Road, Harrow, which Charlie Crichton-Stuart was then sharing with Jonathan, Piers, Charles Lucas and a Rhodesian racer named Louis Jacobz. For a short period Innes Ireland was to live there as well. It was an hilarious place to be.

'One day I rolled a Fiat 500 on to its side just turning into the drive. On another occasion Piers came whistling in at the wheel of Charlie's car, lost control and hurtled straight into the garage. The shock freed the door which neatly clanged shut behind him. We were most impressed.

'I was the last in, and the poorest, so I couldn't afford a whole room of my own. I actually rented the sofa, and slept on that. Even so, I was always behind with the rent.'

Frank would do almost anything to earn some money. On one occasion Charlie bet him a fiver he wouldn't dare go down to the railway line at the bottom of the garden stark naked. Frank took him on, sprinted down the garden nude – only to find that Charlie had timed it perfectly and a stopping train was coming along. He shot back to the house like a frightened rabbit, and found they had locked him out...

The new season of 1964 saw a new racing Formula replacing Formula Junior. It was called Formula Three, and it used similar single-seater cars to the old FJs, while restricting their engines to just 1000 cc and to one single-choke carburettor in place of the two

twin-chokes used before. If you restrict the engine's ability to draw in fuel-air mixture you restrict its power output. This was the case with Formula Three, but it was to prove a very successful class.

Where Frank was concerned, this was the season which brought Anthony 'Bubbles' Horsley into the picture. He had bought a 'rather evil' Ausper FJ for himself with a small legacy, and added a crashed Brabham which Frank would be allowed to drive on a Continental tour in return for his services as mechanic on both cars. Bubbles added an ex-Hoover company 1½-ton Morris diesel van and a very good Don Parker two-car racing trailer to tow behind it. Living in the back of the Morris was untold luxury after a season sharing the back of a Volkswagen pick-up with Jonathan and his Lotus 22.

While Bubbles and Frank shared the Morris van, the Ausper and the rebuilt Brabham, Jonathan and Piers Courage had teamed up for the new year as the Anglo–Swiss Racing Team, running a pair of Lotus 22s. The Swiss connection came from Chuck Graemiger, who maintained the cars, based in Vevey. This was Piers' introduction to single-seater racing after spending his first season with the Lotus 7 in 1962, and then running a black Merlyn 1100 sports car through 1963. 'Like the rest of us, his technical knowledge was strictly limited. He once shunted his 22 – I think it was at Monza – and straightened the twisted chassis by standing it against a wall and backing his Ford Zephyr into it. Crude, perhaps, but it put him back on the grid to earn some more start money.'

According to Bubbles the Morris van worked well enough in the early-season tour but the inevitable traces of diesel oil which infected their 'living quarters' gave them both a form of dermatitis. Frank recalls: 'After leaving England with a "healthy" 15 psi oil pressure, it clanked back with only three or four. We couldn't get enough money together for a Gold Seal exchange engine, but coincidentally the big Sicilian F3 race was due at Enna. It's a very long way from London, about two thousand miles by road, but to attract a good field the Sicilians always offered good starting money, about a hundred pounds a time.

'This proved a magnetic attraction for us and we set off, towing the cars behind an ancient 1955 Plymouth which Bubbles had acquired from Piers. It became an epic trip.

'Going down the Brenner Pass we ran out of brakes. You had to pump the pedal like fury to make anything happen, then they locked on and we stopped with smoke pouring off them and a dreadful smell. We had to stop every few miles to bleed and re-bleed the system to find some pedal. Then air would get in again and we had to pump repeatedly on the slightest down-grade. With the two-car trailer on the back and a boot full of spares, the always dubious Plymouth brakes were stretched beyond their abilities.

'We stopped for a bite, and when we got back into the car and drove off I managed to leave Bubbles' wallet on the roof, and we lost it. We turned back when we realized it was missing, but it was long gone. We were well down the leg of Italy, about three hundred miles from the ferry at Reggio di Calabria. We had no money to speak of, and in those days there was no Autostrada, just mile after mile of climbs and swoops. We would sprint the Plym across the valley floors, then grind up the hills and pussy-foot down them, brakeless of course. I rode on the trailer draw-bar, heaving the trailer brakes on by hand.

'We arrived in the hills above Reggio hoping we'd just be in time to catch the ferry to Messina and meet some of our pals in the F3 circus who could cash a cheque for us. No such luck. Bubbles drove the Plym downhill into the square by the docks with the right-side tyres rubbing the kerb and me heaving on the trailer-brake to prevent a runaway.

'The square was deserted, the ferry had gone. We weren't going to get to Enna. We had three days to live through before the circus would return, and about 150 *Lire* to live on. That would just about buy a bottle of pop and three bread rolls.

'So we lived in the Plym for three days while the locals got used to us. They put up market stalls around us one morning, ran the market, struck camp and moved away again while we just sat there, in the middle of it all. I was starving. But there was no way out, we just had to wait. Bubbles was furious.

'Finally, late on the Monday afternoon, Eddie Fletcher came through on his way home. We had never been so pleased to see a friendly face, and he cashed a hundred-pound cheque for us. We celebrated with a meal and a bath in a hotel . . . but now we had to get home, and the Plym was jiggered . . .

'It was absolutely on its last legs. There were no more worth-while race deals going and we headed back to England. I had raging toothache and couldn't sleep because of it, and Bubbles was just totally demoralized and fed up with the whole business, and furious with me for losing our money. We drove up the Adriatic coast because it promised to be flatter than the way we had come, and while Bubbles slept in disgust I drove for hours on end. I eventually had to stop and have a tooth pulled, which was a relief, but now Bubbles refused to drive. As we climbed into the first range of mountains the Plym rebelled and shed its entire exhaust system below the manifold. We just rumbled on, deafening the peasants and nearly gassing ourselves. Then at night the dynamo flaked out, so we were on the battery for lights and ignition. We were always in trouble with the brakes.

'Onto the Autobahns in Germany we were running with the two tiny Varley batteries from the F3 cars wired into the Plym's circuit to give us some sidelights – and then came the fog . . .

'It was so thick that headlights wouldn't have made any difference, and I was charging along, grimly determined to make it home. We thundered along at probably 40–45 mph, with a great procession of Germans behind us, happy for someone to follow.

'After a stop to refuel we had to borrow a battery to restart, and after another five miles or so the power-steering packed up. Now we had no lights, no brakes, rock-solid steering and still miles to go. This F3 racing around Europe really was glamorous . . .

'Finally we made it to the boat and at last had a slice of good luck as Ron Harris – who had run the works Lotus FJ team – was on the same ferry with his E-Type Jaguar. He helped restart the Plym using jump-leads, so at last we drove into the Customs Hall at Dover, deafening everybody with the open exhausts. The officers merely waved us to one side and deliberately ignored us while they cleared the tourists first. But we didn't dare switch off, and after sitting there for ten minutes or more with the Plym at its deafening tick-over the entire Hall was filling with smoke and fumes. Bubbles lay slumped in the back with his beard and tiny specs, thoroughly demoralized and refusing point-blank to leave the car. When the Customs demanded we switch off before they all asphyxiated we had to refuse, for there was no way we could restart.

'They did finally clear us through, and we abandoned the rig in the car park. It had taken three days to drive back from Calabria. Ron Harris gave me a lift back to London in the E-Type, and I literally broke into a friend's flat to find some shelter, curled up, and slept like the dead . . .'

It was the 1964 season which brought Jochen Rindt to prominence in Formula Two and gave him his true Formula One debut. Frank was running the first car he had ever bought with his own money at that time, a 1951–52 Ford Consul registered LFG 385. It had first gear and top, no second, and above 40 mph the front suspension would shudder uncontrollably. Neither door on the driver's side would open. Frank had bought it from the racer's friend, 'Tom the Weld', Roy Thomas, whose retreat in Shepherd's Bush, West London, was a mecca to impecunious racers with broken motor cars. 'He charged me twenty-five pounds for it. I finally sold it back to him for forty-five . . .' He was learning!

Jochen was running a Formula Two Brabham with backing from Ford Austria and BP, and he leapt to fame virtually over-night when he beat Jim Clark, Graham Hill, Jack Brabham and the other stars over Whitsun at Mallory Park and Crystal Palace. Frank had actually delivered the new Brabham to Jochen for his first race early in the year, driving the Austrian's new twin-rear-wheeled Ford van from London to Vienna in twenty-three hours. 'That trip has caused a lot of trouble at my team ever since, because if a truckee moans that he's only got two days in which to drive to Vienna I trot out this story, and that really stirs them up. Jochen was a hard man, though, I wasn't used to driving a longish vehicle with twin rear wheels, and by the time I pulled up in triumph at his place both outside tyres had blown where I had crushed them over kerbs. It was very deflating. He was furious. It cost twenty quid for new tyres. Jochen always counted every penny . . .'

During that historic drive at Crystal Palace Frank was giving Jochen his pit signals: 'It was fantastically exciting to see him win in such company.' But the new-found superstar image was dented a little by the transport Frank provided for him: 'Here I was picking up one of the world's most promising racing drivers at Heathrow Airport, and we had to climb in the passenger side of my Consul because the driver's side doors wouldn't open. The day after the Palace I drove him through London to see Dennis Druitt of BP about his contract. He hated being a passenger, and even though you can't get into much trouble in London traffic he was on his feet most of the way shouting 'Slow down, slow down!'

'It was a different matter when he was driving. Coming back from the F2 race at Oulton Park in a Peugeot he suddenly just let go of the wheel and climbed into the back, saying 'I'm tired, now you drive,' and you had to grab the wheel, clamber over and take control; there was no question of stopping.

'He could do anything in a motor car. When he began driving F2 Brabhams for the Roy Winkelmann team in 1965 they were based in Slough, and there's a never-ending climbing left-hand slip road there which takes you up off the M4 motorway and over to Slough on the other side. Jochen would take his Alfa Romeo into that slip road at 116 mph from the fast lane of the motorway, and go screaming round there with the front tyres scrubbing off speed and the inside rear wheel clear of the road. Of course he'd scrub off so much speed he'd only be doing about 74 mph at the exit, but it was a pretty fantastic experience if you were his passenger. He was magic in a car, he could make it do anything he wanted . . .'

Frank had developed a deep-seated ambition to become a successful International F3 driver, while enjoying life and learning all the time, trading more parts and tyres with the Continentals. 'My first race that season was actually at Sachsenring in the Brabham, but its gear-linkage fell apart and I didn't qualify for a place at the start. We went to Wunstorf again, this time in the Morree van. There I whizzed into a straw-bale chicane far too fast, hurtled off course, and shot over a raised runway light with a terrible bang under the footbox. It was terribly irresponsible driving, because it could easily have ripped off my heel, or worse.'

Frank and Bubbles would rent out sleeping space in the van, playing host to Charlie Crichton-Stuart, Piers and Jonathan: 'We'd each climb into a sleeping bag and sleep nose to toes across the van with the shortest bloke between the wheel-arch humps. One time, I think it was at Wunstorf, Piers raised a laugh by driving into the camping field late at night, and as his headlights swept across the grass they suddenly illuminated Bubbles who had crept out for a squat, trousers round his ankles, blinking in the sudden light like a startled rabbit.'

They raced at many varied circuits. At Caserta, well into Italy, Piers arrived sleepless. He ran a handsome Ford Zephyr Zodiac with a four-speed gearbox and all the trimmings. 'He had perfected the art of reading a book while driving alone, just to keep himself interested on the Autobahns and Autostrada. I think it was on this trip to Caserta that the police saw him trundle by, book on the steering wheel, eyes glazed over.

'At that time they stopped you by the observer sticking his arm out waving a lollypop stick to indicate you should pull over. Their patrol car cruised past Piers, slowed to his speed and out went the lollypop. Piers dozily wondered what they were playing at, pulled out and smartly overtook them. They tried again, and he overtook them again.

'The third time they were really serious, and the driver also stuck his arm out clutching a lollypop sign. With an arm and a lollypop projecting from both sides of the patrol car, Piers suddenly came to with a start, thought "God Almighty, he's a big bloke!" and stopped immediately.'

Piers was a six-footer and he developed his own method for sleeping in the Zodiac. He would open both doors if the night was dry, stand a suitcase either side (he was never short of clothes) and that formed a bed just long enough for his lanky frame.

Eddie Fletcher, who had bailed out Bubbles and Frank in Reggio, was another F3 character when it came to sleeping habits. He always insisted upon wearing pyjamas wherever he found himself, and early in the morning beside a German Autobahn one

might see Eddie's green Zephyr with a racing car hitched behind, the door would open and Eddie Fletcher would emerge, splendidly pyjama'd, stalking off to the gents clutching his toothbrush.

In retrospect Frank admits that he and his friends were groping in the dark against their own ignorance of racing and racing cars. The finer points of chassis tuning and preparation were black magic to them; spare engines were a luxury afforded only by the most professional teams; for many of them even spare tyres and an adequate choice of gear ratios were a rarity.

Frank has always been teetotal and does not smoke. Bubbles recalled one Monza meeting after which he had persuaded him to 'drink a few', then they set out for Austria with Frank driving and Bubbles – as usual – stretched out asleep in the back. As Frank's eyelids drooped he stopped and told Bubbles he could go no further, it was his turn to drive. 'He took over and I fell asleep in the back . . .' Bubbles continues the story: 'I drove literally four hundred yards down the road, stopped and climbed into the back to resume my kip . . . Frank woke up fresh and ready to go. "Where are we Bubs?" he asked. "I don't know really, just drive." Off he went, and as soon as he saw the first road sign he just went maaad!'

They ended their season at the Nürburgring *Sudschleife*, where Frank had had his ride with Jochen Rindt the year before . . .

'I was quite quick there in the Brabham, it was a great circuit for the foolhardy: bravery or recklessness could give you quite a good time. But then I made a bad start, and was very put out at being so far down the field. Eventually I fell off out on the back of the circuit and put the Brab up the bank.'

Bubbles: 'I was charging round in the Ausper, only to see my Brabham mangled in all directions projecting from the forest with Frank dangling from a tree grinning from ear to ear and waving. I was so incensed at that oafish grin when he'd obviously just destroyed half my worldly wealth that the next corner caught me out and I flew into the trees as well . . .'

Frank: 'Bubbles winded himself badly on the steering wheel and he was scooped up into the ambulance and despatched to hospital. Bubbles lay in the back thinking that medical aid in Germany was expensive, and when the ambulance stopped at a junction he burst open the doors and ran off! He was eventually tracked down in the paddock by some worried *Polizei*, who rollocked him for wasting everybody's time.'

The Brabham was beyond economic repair and the partnership dissolved. Bubbles went off to share a flat with American FJ/F3 driver Roy Pike, in Chiswick, West London. Frank was on his uppers, intent on making enough money to continue in racing. Bubbles could find no buyer for the Morris van and it lay abandoned in Shepherd's Bush. 'Nobody even wanted to pinch it – it just lay there for months and I slept in it when I couldn't afford Pinner Road's sofa any more. In the afternoons, when Bubbles, Roy and Roy's girlfriend – who was the only worker among the four of us – were out, I used to nip into their flat for a cup of tea, wolf down some bread and cake, and live on that. They probably knew what I was up to, but they never complained . . .'

During the winter of 1964–65 Frank helped Guy Horsley, Bubbles' brother, renovate a couple of old houses which he had just bought, in return for a roof over his head at night and breakfast each morning in a transport café across the road. Frank used the Morris van for personal transport, regularly eking out a pint of diesel fuel in a round-trip to Harrow and back to see Charlie – he would admit, 'The Mobil Economy Run has nothing on me when money's short . . .'

But his trading business was beginning to boom. He returned to Pinner Road around Christmas and lived there in relative comfort for seven pounds a week, with his own telephone installed to deal on. Johnny Middleton was working as Charlie's mechanic and he rented Frank a two-year-old red Austin-Healey Sprite for another six pounds or so a week. Frank was selling parts and equipment in considerable volume all over the Continent, and nothing was too much trouble. If there was a trailer for sale in Lancashire he would drive up to collect it, tow it down to the Sussex coast where he knew a customer was waiting, perhaps take a gearbox in part-exchange and promptly deliver that to a customer in East Anglia. 'I was a voice on the phone finding stuff that people wanted to sell and customers who wanted to buy it. I became friendly with guys like Harry Stiller, who accumulated a great volume of Formula Three equipment and didn't necessarily know what to do with it at the end of the season. Harry's garage was like an Aladdin's cave to me, packed with perhaps twenty part-used Dunlop R5 tyres, shelves of gear ratios, Lotus steering racks, Brabham parts . . . I would stand there thinking, 'There's five hundred pounds' worth here," and say, "Well Harry, how about one hundred for the lot?" If a young Frank Williams came into our stores at Didcot today and saw our stock he would have a heart attack on the spot.'

Frank enjoyed his trading, but it was all a means to the end of buying a competitive Formula Three car for himself. He wanted to win an International F3 race and did not look far beyond that. One problem was that Bubbles was back at Pinner Road and he was intercepting some of Frank's would-be customers on the telephone extension. 'He was much shrewder than I,' Frank will admit. 'He struck better deals, but my advantage was that nothing, but nothing, was too much trouble . . .'

By April 1965 he had scraped together sufficient money to buy a year-old F2 Cooper chassis, which had belonged to the professional Normand team. An ex-Normand mechanic named Colin Bennett assembled the car for him, fitting a Formula Three engine.

'I took it to Belgium for its first race at Zolder and rented it for three hundred pounds to a local ace named Taf Gosselin, who had a lot of Ferrari experience. He flew straight off the road and destroyed it completely. I charged him a thousand pounds for the damage, collected the debris and went home. It was a lot of money, but now I had to buy another car with it or I would be out of racing . . .'

John Coombs, the Guildford Jaguar dealer, had run his own team for many years, usually with Graham Hill as driver. He had an ex-Graham F2 Cooper for sale, and one Saturday afternoon Frank told Charlie that he'd be away from the flat for a couple of hours, he was going down to Guildford to buy a car from John Coombs.

'I was completely overawed at the prospect of dealing with him, and he saw me coming, with my bag full of cash. I couldn't get out of him how much he wanted for the car, but he got out of me how much I had in the bag. He invited me to dinner, then put me up overnight, and I finally returned to Harrow after twenty-four hours, with the car and about twenty quid left in my bag ...'

Frank did perhaps ten races in that ex-Coombs car, being assisted by a rather strange ex-Harrovian named Paddy Allfrey. He was a very wealthy, fiercely independent young man from Malvern, who seemed to want nothing more from life than to be an F3 mechanic and occasional driver. He had a bank account. Frank was mesmerized. He was not to have a bank account of his own until 1975 ... Allfrey offered to run the Cooper for Frank, and they towed it around behind a half-ton Morris Oxford van.

After Jackie Stewart's fantastic rise to fame through Formula Three in 1964, several major teams entered the class the following year. Charles Lucas, the Pinner Road inmate whose father ran a pre-cast concrete business and who had access to considerable private means, established his own team running three of the previous season's works F2 Brabhams, re-engined to Formula Three form. They were to be driven – on occasion – by Luke himself, and regularly by Piers Courage, Jonathan Williams and Peter Gethin. Charlie was driving a beautifully prepared metallic-green Brabham under the Stirling Moss Automobile Racing Team banner, the Chequered Flag sports car dealership ran Brabhams, notably for Roy Pike, and so on. They were all very professional, there were many more well-financed British and Continental one-car outfits, and somewhere at the bottom of the entry lists and the back of the grid were the privateers with obsolete cars and no real hope.

The Zolder shunt was in May, and the first weekend in June saw F. O. Williams driving the grey and blue ex-Hill Cooper at Chimay on the borders of Belgium, France and Luxembourg. It felt awful and a front suspension ball-joint broke, luckily in the 30 mph hairpin; anywhere else, and Frank would have been up above 100 mph on narrow country roads lined by ditches, trees and telegraph poles. The car felt evil. Roy Pike tried it at Silverstone and spun, announcing his opinion that Frank would kill himself in it. At Goodwood in a general practice session Graham

Hill tried it, and spun. Jonathan tried the car one day at Monza, and told Frank simply, 'Sorry mate, I can't help you.'

Frank: 'All I thought about was winning in F3, but I was obviously a long way from it, lacking experience, equipment and talent. To win you had to have the latest Cosworth MAE engine, which in those days was fabulously expensive at six hundred pounds. And they were virtually unobtainable, with a long waiting list. A fellow driver-dealer named Robs Lamplough then sold me his for five hundred, and that was real power, a superb engine. I was absolutely thrilled to bits with it – then Harry Stiller offered me a hundred pounds' profit – and it was his ...'

Frank finally got his name in the record books at Skarpnack aerodrome outside Stockholm, Sweden, on 5 September 1965, by diplomatically finishing just behind Harry Stiller's Brabham, fourth in an International Formula Three race. 'By that time I was inured to the Cooper's peculiarities and it was proving quite a quick car. My driving had improved and I felt I was getting in the groove ... We drove down to Monza the following weekend, which is an enormous trip, only to overheat the engine. I sat in the paddock for a day, lapping in the warped cylinder head by hand ... Back in Scandinavia at the end of that month I finally sold the Cooper to a Swedish motor trader and came out ahead on the deal. He painted it yellow. It went worse ...'

Frank worked flat-out during that winter to start 1966 with really competitive equipment. He was deeply into the whole Formula Three scene. He knew who was buying what, what he had to sell, who wanted it, and who could afford it. He was storing parts and cars in four lock-ups around Harrow, and his fluency in French, Italian and German made him an ideal contact man for the many Continental racers.

'Ron Tauranac of Brabham gave me a good price on new F3 cars and I sold fourteen of them that winter, showing a profit of about a hundred pounds on each. I took old cars in part-exchange, and was reasonably successful in finding homes for them as well, plus new owners for Lola's total production of just four F3 cars, which I spotted one day standing unsold in a corner of their factory at Slough. I borrowed five thousand pounds from Jonathan Williams' father to buy them, and in time sold them all for two thousand apiece . . . I was able to pay back Mr Williams with a little interest on top, and show a profit. After all these deals I wound up with a brand-new F3 Brabham of my own plus two good Cosworth engines, a VW pick-up transporter and my own mechanic, a nice guy named John Batley, who helped me in the business as well as in preparing and transporting the F3 car.'

His first race with the new Brabham was in Italy, where he admits he felt he was 'a real hot-shot with all the latest equipment. After just one lap I decided it was run in and went barrelling into the first corner after the pits and turned right in spirit while the car just understeered straight on into the straw bales and turned over.

'Soon after, at Vila Real in Portugal, I was really in the groove. That is a fantastic public road circuit and the Brabham was about third or fourth quickest in practice when I lost control over a railway level crossing out on the back-stretch and spun into the gate-post. It cut the front off the car and I was very lucky to emerge unscatched – I could easily have lost my legs. It was a super circuit, though – I regret I couldn't get the hang of the downhill section there – John Fenning, one of the circus' front-runners, was taking it flat. He was braver than I.'

John Batley contrived to capsize Frank's Volksie transporter on the way home from Portugal, falling asleep over the wheel and toppling down an embankment, but miraculously damage was light. In August Frank ran a new Brabham at Enna, having sold the old car in Rome, and then on 28 August 1966, at the tiny little kart-type track at Knutstorp in Sweden, Frank Williams actually won an International F3 race at last, beating Freddy Kottulinsky, Karl von Wendt, Lars Lindberg, Picko Troberg and Reine Wisell – all familiar names at that time.

'Now I wanted to build up my business, buy really good equipment, and win some more . . . It was around this time that I really "fell out" with Bubbles Horsley. He had been building up an F3 Brabham from a bunch of bits in a garage about half a mile from Pinner Road. He had gone off somewhere, and he had some seven-inch and nine-inch Brabham wheels which I needed desperately. I reckoned he owed me for pinching my deals on the telephone so I took his wheels. . . . As it happened he then sold the Brabham and when his customer arrived to collect the car it was standing there on bricks! The customer was livid and Bubbles never did forgive me for it. He got his own back, ten years later . . .'

But as Frank Williams (Racing Cars) Ltd's business grew it became totally time-consuming. He decided that he should stay out of racing through 1967 in order to return to the fray in 1968 with a top-line car, first-rate engines and a really knowledgeable mechanic.

'Towards the end of that year's trading I was seriously looking for premises. John Batley was still helping me run the business, and eventually we found some workshop space with lock-ups and a flat over the top, quite close to Lola's works, in Bath Road, Cippenham, Slough. It was very convenient; I could live in the flat, we could store cars and parts in the garages and also prepare cars in the workshops down below . . .'

During that fallow year for Frank a friend named Chris Moore took a half-share in his small trading company in return for putting up five thousand pounds' working capital. Tragically Chris developed an inoperable brain tumour soon after, and died, Frank paying off the loan to his executors.

Meanwhile Jonathan Williams had made a name for himself driving De Sanctis F3 cars in Italy, and by 1967 he was a works Ferrari driver. Piers Courage had won numerous races in Lucas Brabhams during 1965 and through 1966 he led the works Lotus F3 team which Luke ran for Colin Chapman. He had shown so much promise that Tim Parnell took him into his BRM Formula One 'reserve team' in 1967, but he blotted his copybook in his first few GPs with a series of spins and accidents. Many observers considered Piers was in over his head, and was just not going to make it as a top-class driver.

Frank vehemently disagreed. 'I thought Piers was a super driver, and right at the end of '67 he drove a brand-new 1968 prototype F3 Brabham for me in the big Motor Show '200' meeting at Brands Hatch. The car was two-tone green. In practice Piers managed only six laps but still qualified on the front row of the grid, third fastest behind John Miles – Sir Bernard's son – in a

Piers Courage at Brands Hatch in his first drive
for Frank Williams – in the prototype Brabham BT21B
Formula Three car, 1967.

'Porridge' in the
V12 BRM – 1967.

works Lotus 41, and Mike Beckwith in the Chequered Flag Brabham with DAF automatic transmission.

'In the race heat Piers just walked away to beat everybody by ten seconds and to break the F3 lap record. That wasn't a bad start to our association. Then the heavens opened and his car drowned its electrics on the warming-up lap for the final. There was no way he could restart the engine, and we were out. Just to add insult to injury, as he walked back to the pits with the race under way, Peter Deal aquaplaned in his Brabham and smashed into the marshal's post which Piers had just reached, breaking a marshal's leg. Piers flung himself flat and the car just clipped his foot. As the ambulance was sent out it ran straight into Mike Knight's Brabham and with that the organizers stopped the race. Mike Beckwith won, we were disappointed, but Piers was persuading me to go halves with him in running a Formula Two car in the coming year's European Championship . . .'

Formula Two is Fun

When Frank Williams and Piers Courage entered Formula Two, it demanded production-based engines of no more than 1600 cc, mounted in single-seat chassis very similar to those so hard-used in Formula Three. The dominant engine was the Ford Cortina-based Cosworth FVA which, with fuel injection and massive modifications, could produce over 200 bhp. Ford's new Cosworth DFV Formula One engine was effectively two of these Cortina-based FVA blocks, mounted on a common crankcase at an included angle of ninety degrees to form a 3-litre V8. Many front-line drivers like Jimmy Clark, Jackie Stewart, Jochen Rindt and Graham Hill raced against newcomers and privateers in Formula Two, and it was in all ways a superb schoolroom class in which new talent could be groomed and tested for Grand Prix greatness.

Frank now set his personal driving ambitions aside and concentrated upon setting-up a Formula Two season for his friend Piers. 'We planned the whole thing in about fifteen minutes, we had so little clue what we were getting into. We literally sat back and figured, "Well, £2,000 for the car, £2,000 each for two FVA engines, £1,000 for a truck; add mechanics' wages, travelling expenses, we could probably cover them from start money ... umm, yes, we can afford Formula Two."'

After his BRM drives in 1967, Piers had a working relationship with the competition managers controlling the race promotion budgets at Shell and Dunlop. 'Shell came up with some money, and Piers introduced me to Dick Jeffrey, the Dunlop Racing boss, in the back of their tyre-fitting van at Brands Hatch. Dick didn't know me from Adam, but he was a man fascinated by social charisma, and with Piers' brewery family connections in mind he was intrigued by him. He gave us three thousand pounds for that first season. It was rather late in the year to order a new F2 Brabham, but luckily Rollo Fielding was having one built which he did not take up, and we took over his order. As it happened, he had ordered it in dark blue, and that became Frank Williams (Racing Cars) Ltd's new livery. We took on an ex-Winkelmann team, ex-Brabham mechanic to look after it, a New Zealander named John Muller. He was superb; a very quiet guy, independent and resourceful – a very competent race mechanic.'

While Frank set up the team, Piers was away racing in New Zealand and Australia. He had driven for BRM in this Tasman Championship series in January and February the previous year, and his hair-raising antics then had done little to make his name. Now he had returned determined to recoup his reputation, campaigning his own F2 McLaren in Saccone Gin sponsorship livery. He drove brilliantly, won one round and salvaged much of his reputation. He retained his BRM seat for 1968 and drove the new Williams Brabham BT23C in Formula Two.

The Bath Road workshops were jam-packed and busy that season as Frank's growing staff prepared and maintained customers' cars in addition to Piers' F2. They included F2 Lolas for Alastair Walker and for the wealthy Spaniards Alex Soler-Roig and Prince Jorge de Bagration. The mechanics inevitably nicknamed these patrician clients 'Solenoid' and 'B——ation'. Later Malcolm Guthrie, son of Sir Giles Guthrie, brought his Brabham to them for preparation, and a string of F3 clients joined the queue. One of them was Charles Sawyer-Hoare, whose wife Ginny was eventually to become Mrs Frank Williams.

In Formula Two Piers proved very quick. Early-season reliability was not too good, but the team slowly achieved tangible results. The Brabham was not the quickest car on all circuits, but it was by far the best all-rounder. Piers won his heat at Zandvoort, and was twice third late in the season, at Reims and Albi. The original car was sold to Roly Levis in New Zealand before Albi, and it was replaced by the prototype BT23C/1 for that race. Sheridan Thynne, finding his feet as a stock-broker at the time, accompanied the team there and recalled vividly the realization that the best was barely good enough for Frank Williams: 'There was another Brabham in practice there which we kept confusing with ours, and when Piers came in Frank asked me to stick one of his special self-adhesive racing numbers – a figure '1' – longitudinally, wrap-round style on the upper lip of the car's nose. Frank was selling these numbers for some fabulous sum at the time; I doubt if any of his customers realized that the boys at Cippenham had a set of patterns and were simply cutting them out of plain white Fablon sheet. I wrapped this number '1' around the nose lip and then Frank, to my astonishment, came round to inspect it. And he didn't just glance at it, oh no, he backed off fully fifteen feet, squatted down, closed one eye and stared at the car head-on, long and hard. Then he stood up with a look of pained disgust and said, 'No, no Sherry, it's slightly off-centre, you'll have to try again...'

On the other hand, when Piers was occupied with Formula One and Jonathan Williams had a one-off drive in the original car to win the Lottery GP at Monza, he ensured that Frank's feet stayed firmly on terra firma. Sheridan asked Jonathan Frank's reason for giving him the drive, and he dryly averred: 'Safe and cheap, Sherry, safe and cheap...'! Frank treated him to dinner.

The one-car team was well organized, and Muller's preparation was generally excellent. Frank's new secretary Norma Robb had the ability, so vital for any racing team, to book travel and hotel reservations with unerring efficiency, and ensured that Frank dealt in the right way and in good time with race organizers. The mechanics would carry the car around Europe in its truck while Piers and Frank would normally fly out to meet them at the races.

Late that summer Ron Frost arrived in England. He was prime organizer of the Tasman Championship in New Zealand and Australia, and was anxious for Piers to return after his fine showing in the private McLaren. He offered Frank and Piers six thousand pounds to make the trip in January–February 1969, Frank agreed and bought an ex-works Formula One Brabham BT24 from Ron Tauranac and ordered two brand-new 2½-litre Cosworth DFW V8 engines to power it. These were decreased-capacity Tasman Formula versions of the full 3-litre DFV Formula One engines, and could easily be modified to major-league form once again.

'They cost a fortune, something like £7,500 each, but a friend put up the money. He was Derek Mackie, an Ulsterman whose family ran a huge textile machinery works bang in the middle of Belfast's Falls Road. He lived in Switzerland and just liked racing, so he bought those two V8s for us – "924" and "925".'

In addition to his sponge-like ability to absorb languages, Frank has an extraordinary memory for numbers. He carries telephone numbers in his head and with a moment's thought can recall virtually every Cosworth engine serial his team has ever used. He reels them off by number like a dairy farmer fondly recalling his most productive Jerseys or Friesians. To him his DFV engines have assumed personalities – '924' and '925' are not mere numbers, they had character...

The Brabham had originally been powered by a Repco V8 engine, and the rear half of the chassis had to be redesigned to accept the Cosworths. Robin Herd, formerly with McLaren and then Cosworth themselves, did the re-design and John Muller rebuilt the car at Bath Road. It was the first Brabham to carry a Cosworth V8 engine, while for 1969 the works cars of Jack Brabham himself and Jacky Ickx were to use it. Now Frank Williams made the great decision:

'It was early September, I believe, and the car was going together in the workshop while I was having lunch in the flat above with Norma and the boys, when just out of the blue I suddenly thought, "We've got a Formula One car being assembled downstairs – why don't we go Formula One next year?" It came out

Pescarolo on pole position at Enna 1968 with the works Matra.
Outside him is Piers in the Brabham, attended by John Muller and Frank Williams.

purely as a throw-away comment, and our Grand Prix career started from there, literally as simply as that.

'Piers and I discussed the idea and I figured that with a little pushing I could get a current Brabham BT26. Goodyear sponsored the works Brabham team, we ran Dunlop tyres and we couldn't buy a 26 direct from Ron Tauranac because of the contractual clash. Luckily he had already released one car to David Bridges who ran his Red Rose Motors team up in Lancashire and I managed to buy it from him over the phone for £3,500.'

Robin Herd charged £500 for another chassis redesign and the car was modified in a Northampton garage by Keith Leighton – Ronnie Peterson's Formula Two mechanic – and by chassis specialist John Thompson. Now the project had to be financed: 'Piers and I talked with Dick Jeffrey before Piers went off on the Tasman tour with the BT24, and I finalized a new deal for £10,000 with the Dunlop directors while he was away. We found an extra £2,000 for the new season from Castrol, and then discovered our very first true commercial sponsor in the H. W. Ward machine tool company...

'That came about through one of our mechanics, a big jovial chap named Bob Evans – a good-hearted type with so many tall stories he became renowned in racing as 'Bullshit Bob'. The trouble was that every so often he would come out with an impossible story which was absolutely true, and this happened with Ward's.

'One morning in '69 he came in and said he'd been at a party the night before and had met a chap named John Halbert. He helped run a large machine tool company and admitted an interest in motor racing. Yes, his company would be interested in sponsoring a new Formula One team. I found Bob's story very hard to believe, but made an appointment to meet John and his principal director, Ted Williams. I was staggered when they agreed to a deal...

'So I made contact with Ted Williams, and he became a tower of strength in succeeding years. We got on very well and he adored Piers and our team. It became a big personal interest for him, he was the main owner of the business and he indulged himself. In the years to follow Ted Williams became the main factor responsible for our survival.

'Ted taught me a great deal. He wanted a commercial return from his support of our team, and that meant more than merely exposure on the car with Ward stickers. Ted explained that Ward's participation in Formula One was good for business. It gave his reps something to talk about to clients, other than the weather or the state of business. They could interest customers in the Ward racing car, it gave the company an exotic, go-ahead kind of image, good connotations. It was also a great focus of interest for his employees – how did our car do at the weekend? – and the company brought several guests along to various races to see how Piers performed. It was a good public affairs exercise, and it really opened my eyes to the potential of sponsorship...

'But our immediate concern at the end of '68 was to run a batch of Formula Two Brabhams in the Argentinian Temporada series during December, then it was down under for the Tasman Championship, and then we would be back home and into our first season of Formula One...'

Typical Piers in the early days – off course at Brands Hatch in his F2 McLaren. Later he emerged as a smooth, intelligent driver of world class.

Piers leading the Formula Two field on Cordoba's Oscar Cabalen circuit in December 1968 – Pescarolo, Rindt, de Adamich and Regazzoni in pursuit.

So This is Formula One?

Frank Williams (Racing Cars) Ltd's first Formula One season teed off slowly after a hectic winter of Formula Two and Tasman racing. First there were the four Temporada F2 races held in Argentina in December 1968. Ferrari dominated with their little Dino 166 cars, and Andrea de Adamich took the Championship title for them. Piers ran the ex-Troberg BT23C/1 which he had driven at Albi with Sheridan's stick-on nose flash, and Frank had also concluded a deal with the local YPF oil company to take out no less than four similar cars for local drivers like Juan Manuel Bordeu – Fangio's protégé of yore – Jorge Cupeiro, Carlos Pairetti and Eduardo Copello. Ron Harris did a similar deal with three Italian Tecno cars, and one of his drivers was the son of a wealthy rancher – his name was Carlos Reutemann. Sheridan today recalls that Jonathan Williams was a great fan of Reutemann's and was forever telling Frank he should give him a drive, 'but Frank didn't think he would make it . . .'

One of the Williams BT23Cs was burned out beneath Pairetti and mechanic Jon Redgrave during unofficial testing at Buenos Aires Autodrome; and while Piers' car's wing mounts collapsed in the first race there, at Cordoba he was sixth; he retired at San Juan, and then had the consolation of winning the final round back at Buenos Aires Autodrome. In that final round Reutemann did drive a Williams Brabham, financed by the newspaper *La Razon*, and he finished eighth in the first heat, before retiring in the second. It was to be eleven years before he would drive for Frank again . . .

In New Zealand and Australia the John Muller and Dewar Thomas-prepared Brabham–Cosworth BT24 proved formidable opposition for the works Lotus 49Ts driven by Jochen Rindt and Graham Hill and for Chris Amon's team of 2·4-litre V6 Ferraris. Piers excelled in New Zealand, winning the final round at Teretonga before moving on for the three concluding races in Australia.

Frank had flown home after the first two New Zealand rounds to finalize arrangements for the coming Formula One season. Finances were stretched bow-string taut with the team operating down under, £10,000-worth of Formula Two material on the high seas returning from Argentina, and Firestone in the middle of traumatic vacillation, deciding whether to press on or pull out of racing, which meant their contracted teams were looking elsewhere for supplies of tyres and money should the axe fall. Some looked towards Dunlop, who had yet to confirm their £10,000 backing for that unproven entity – the Williams Formula One team.

While he was seeking to finalize the Dunlop deal, bad news came from Australia, where Piers had reverted to his old bad habits, flying off the road and having silly incidents. Frank heard the news '. . . virtually with my hands covering my face. Here I was trying to convince Dick Jeffrey's superior at Dunlop that we would be serious contenders in Formula One, and my driver was throwing away races in Australia. Then they confirmed the deal and I had decided that if we got the money I would whizz straight out to Australia and see just what the hell was going on. So after signing the deal at Fort Dunlop I shot off to Heathrow with a friend from F3 named John Kendall and we just hopped the next plane and appeared at Sandown Park, Melbourne, unannounced,

Heading for the Casino – Piers hurtling uphill at Monte Carlo in Frank's Brabham-Cosworth BT26
before his superb second-place finish in the 1969 Monaco Grand Prix.

in the middle of practice – unshaven, bouncing across the paddock in a taxi . . . Piers was astonished. He went well in the race until a half-shaft broke.'

The South African Grand Prix started the World Championship season, but the only way the new team could compete there in March would have been to air-freight the BT24 from Australia which would have cost over £6,000 had a 3-litre engine been available to replace the Tasman 2·5. As it was, Frank held back his Formula One debut until the non-Championship Race of Champions at Brands Hatch the following weekend. The BT26, chassis number 1, was completed on the Friday before the race, and Piers gave it a brief shake-down test at Silverstone before appearing at Brands for Saturday practice. Gear linkage problems and a split fuel tank ended his race. In the wet Silverstone International Trophy race which followed, Piers had a full 9-series 1969-spec Cosworth engine behind his shoulders, and he drove a splendid race. He harried the works Brabhams much of the way before losing fourth gear; his feet were being cooked by the radiator and his wet-weather tyres began to overheat as the track dried out. He finished fifth – and the new team with their dark blue car looked distinctly promising . . .

Their first World Championship race was the Spanish Grand Prix run at Barcelona's Montjuich Park circuit on 4 May 1969, and Frank's Brabham-Cosworth ran in a total of nine GPs that season, in which Piers recorded four finishes: at Monaco, Silverstone, Monza and Watkins Glen. At Monte Carlo and in the United States Grand Prix he finished second after superb drives, and he was fifth in both the British and Italian races.

Frank: 'At Monaco, Piers chased Jacky Ickx's works Brabham as though his life depended on it, and when Ickx's car broke a rear upright he was through to finish second behind Graham Hill's winning Lotus. Second place in only our second Grand Prix was just too good to believe. This Formula One was a piece of cake . . . Piers' car ran reliably, our Dunlop tyres were excellent and he kept his head. Actually while Ickx was still running I signalled Piers 'P3 – OK'. We had to finish that race and finishing to me was all-important, even then. It was no good putting on a flashy show and lasting until the last lap, only to blow up or crash. The record books tell the people who matter who won, or who finished in the points. They don't say things like 'Graham Hill won but Piers Courage led most of the way.' It's results that matter, and I'd rather the car finished third than barged past Ickx and ran second, only for Piers to be pressured off the road and not finish at all . . .'

By Frank's reckoning the British Grand Prix was Piers' second-best race of the season: 'He ran in a group of five cars which disputed fifth place most of the way. That might not sound very impressive, but he was in there with Jo Siffert and Graham Hill in Lotus 49Bs and Chris Amon and Pedro Rodriguez in Ferraris, and every one of them had a problem. Often a driver has to work harder for a minor placing than if he is winning in a dominant car, and this was one of those occasions. Piers headed the group at the finish and took two more Championship points to add to his six from Monaco.

'At Nürburgring Piers crashed and bent the car badly. We had to cut off the damaged rear end of the chassis behind the cockpit and weld a completely new section into its place, and in five weeks we had a virtually brand-new car ready for him in the Italian Grand Prix at Monza. I slapped a limit of 15 laps on his practice there, and Piers qualified quite well through an organized slip-streaming tow from Jochen. Piers' time was equalled by Bruce McLaren but the organizers had no record of who clocked it first, and who would have prior claim to that place on the grid. We decided it by drawing straws – and Piers won!

'All season we had really been handicapped by our lack of a resident team engineer. You can't expect even the best mechanics to design out problems rather than simply correct them once they have reared their heads. We were plagued all season by a fuel pressure problem which a good engineer could have sussed out and beaten. On the credit side we had a superb engine. Sometimes one will come out of Cosworth's which just has something a little special about it. One of our converted Tasman engines, "924", was like that, it was terrific. It was really one of the quickest of that series ever built, and it always helps to be quick on the straight, especially at a place like Monza . . .

'There he drove a beautiful race in the leading bunch before our old lack-of-engineering problem reared its head again. A too small

One of Piers' finest drives: in trouble but battling grimly during the 1969 British Grand Prix at Silverstone – with reigning World Champion Graham Hill sliding the Lotus in his wake.

The 1969 Formula Two field comes screaming into La Garenne corner, amongst the wheatfields of Reims – the BT30 of Piers Courage in the lead.

non-return valve in the fuel system caused starvation, and he misfired home in fifth place for two more Championship points.

'Jackie Stewart clinched his World Championship there with the Tyrrell-entered Matra, and at a small Dunlop party afterwards he paid special tribute to Piers' clean and controlled driving in a race which had been really bitterly hard-fought at very close quarters and very high speed.'

Piers had truly established himself as a fully-fledged Grand Prix driver by this time. Ford loaned the team a third DFV engine to take with them to the Canadian and US Grands Prix. But in Canada the car just ran uncompetitively with an oversteer problem which Frank's men could not correct, and in the race one of the rubber fuel bags came unpeeled at the filler neck and petrol flooded the cockpit.

At that time the United States Grand Prix was the richest on the Championship calendar and all teams made a special effort to scoop the dollars from its prize fund. Frank's men checked and re-checked the BT26's fuel system, and Piers made a terrific practice effort which placed him fourth on the starting grid. They ran '924' – of course – for the race and 'Piers found that Ickx's works car was actually holding him up down the straight as they ran second and third after Jochen in the Lotus. Piers was actually leading Jack Brabham in the second works BT26A, and I was knocked out by the way he held him off. Jack had his chin tucked down and was looking blacker and blacker as the laps reeled by, and still he couldn't find a way past Piers. Then Ickx's engine blew, so they were dicing for second and still Piers kept his head. Both of them got a bit untidy. Piers did throw some stones at Jack by slipping a wheel into the rough out of corners, but at least he wasn't throwing them by running across the apex of the corners – it was all in the game! Jack was furious, though, and after Piers had beaten him home for second place he turned in sharply to his pit around our car and broke off one of its nose wings with his rear wheel. Still there were no hard feelings, and everybody seemed pleased for us, which was nice . . .' That race gave Jochen Rindt his long-awaited first Grand Prix victory. His number one fan was a happy man that night . . .

Piers ended the season eighth overall in the Drivers' World Championship, with sixteen points to his name. In later years such a total would have made Frank very happy . . .

During that season the team had also run Piers in nine Formula Two races, in which he finished third four times. That was about his natural position in the scheme of things, just behind Jochen Rindt and Jackie Stewart. In motor racing as in so many other spheres a talent will achieve a natural level if all other things are equal, and in Formula Two the cars were generally speaking very evenly matched.

Meanwhile at Enna, where Piers actually won the F2 Mediterranean Grand Prix in his dark blue Brabham BT30, Jacky Ickx had driven a tiny little monocoque F2 car produced by the Italian-based *Automobili de Tomaso* company. Jonathan Williams had squeezed into its very cramped cockpit during its debut race at Monza earlier in the year, and Frank was introduced to Gian' Paolo Dallara, the car's designer. Dallara had made his name with the remarkable Lamborghini Miura GT car with its incredible transverse V12 engine, and now he was working for Alejandro de Tomaso. An Argentinian-born sports car driver who had settled in Modena, de Tomaso was building an empire of motor manufacturing companies, eventually to embrace such famous names as Maserati and Innocenti. He and his wealthy American wife, Isabel Haskell, made a formidable business partnership. The badge on their own De Tomaso cars carried the Egyptian script for the Isis deity, after 'Isabel'.

At Monza during the Italian Grand Prix meeting Dallara introduced Frank to de Tomaso, who struck the Englishman as '. . . a kind of Latin Colin Chapman, bursting with ideas, and clearly very dynamic and aggressive. He proposed that he should design and provide Formula One chassis for our use in 1970, for which I would provide Piers' services as driver, Cosworth DFV engines and team organization. That seemed a great deal better than paying for absolutely everything myself and so I agreed. It looked like a good deal at the time . . .

'Ron Tauranac had offered to rebuild the BT26 for us, but how good would it be in its third season of racing? Where else could I find brand-new chassis? We saw de Tomaso's factory outside Modena and were impressed with it. He was clearly capable of

Sweet days of youth, Watkins Glen, October 1969; Jochen Rindt has just won his maiden
Formula One Grand Prix, with Piers second and delighted for them both. Within a year both
had lost their lives in Formula One accidents . . .

reacting quickly in making and modifying parts, and as an antecedent to the deal Piers drove his F2 car in the Rome Grand Prix at Vallelunga . . .'

While both Jonathan Williams and Jacky Ickx had been small enough to cram themselves into the purple-painted car's tiny cockpit without great difficulty, poor Piers was extremely cramped. Still he smashed the lap record during practice and started on pole position. In the first heat Johnny Servoz-Gavin's Matra led until Piers got by for half a lap – only to slide wide, get cramped for elbow room and wipe off a nose wing in the rough. He finished third. In heat two he was lying second before posting an early retirement with ignition failure.

'De Tomaso was impressed and the deal went through. But in retrospect he made much more out of it than I did. He spent perhaps £45,000 building us three cars as the year progressed, but I spent far more on engines, running the team and travelling. To outsiders it probably looked as if I was merely managing his team, whereas in fact I had far more at stake than he did – about two-thirds of the team's total funding . . .'

The little team was again supported by Dunlop with extra assistance from Ward, Graviner fire extinguishers, and Castrol. The faithful Brabham sat in the Modena works while Dallara studied its suspension design and adapted it to his monocoque chassis. Frank had completely wound up his trading business and the preparation of customer cars was being run-down at Bath Road. Frank Williams (Racing Cars) Ltd was to operate solely as a Formula One racing team. The Tasman BT24 had long since been sold to the Swiss privateer Silvio Moser, and the BT26 went to Team Gunston in South Africa for Pieter de Klerk to drive.

The first De Tomaso made its debut in the 1970 South African Grand Prix at Kyalami, outside Johannesburg, and Piers had a torrid race in it before bending the suspension as the brakes locked and he bounded over a kerb. The car was hopelessly overweight, by about 120 lbs, and its suspension design left much to be desired. 'But Piers' mental approach by this time was really excellent. He was a very intelligent, quick-minded person and a perceptive driver. He could describe very clearly how the car behaved, and after that race back at the hotel he sat down and talked it

through with Dallara and they emerged confident that they were aware where the major problems lay and that they knew how an improvement could be made . . .'

After his fine performances in the private Brabham during 1969, Ferrari had offered Piers a contract to drive their Formula One and sports cars in 1970, for around $80,000. Piers had refused, saying that he wanted to stay with Frank in Formula One. Frank was handling his dealing for him, and coincidentally Alfa Romeo offered a sports car contract for the long-distance World Championship races which entailed about £23,000 – some £2,000 less than the Ferrari offer for both sports and Formula One. 'I paid him only £3,000 to drive for me in Formula One, and we were both happy . . . we had achieved something in 1969 and we were going to enjoy our racing through 1970 . . .'

But at Jarama in practice for the Spanish Grand Prix, Piers crashed heavily in a modified wide-track version of the South African car. He emerged unhurt, but the car was destroyed and they were out of the Grand Prix. A second, much lighter car was being built at Modena at that moment and the following weekend the International Trophy race was being held at Silverstone. 'De Tomaso said, "We don't go to Silverstone", and we had quite a row since I considered that the car was mine, it was my team, we existed to go racing and – come what may – we were going. De Tomaso stood back, looked at me and said, "Please yourself".'

Roy Pike tested the new car to shake it down while Piers was racing his Alfa Romeo at Monza, and Jackie Stewart gave it a whirl during practice and thought it was quite good. Piers arrived on race morning and had to start from the back of the grid for the first heat in this two-part race, soaring through the field to finish third. Having managed that not inconsiderable feat, Piers was extremely put out to be told he would have to start from the back of the grid for heat two as well, rather than take what he felt was his rightful place in the outside slot on the front row. He knew Sir Max Aitken of the sponsoring *Daily Express* newspaper and made his displeasure known to him, most emphatically. Piers was a very easy-going, sunny character, but with the new-found confidence of a fully-fledged and established Grand Prix driver he was ready to rebel against clear injustice. He still had to start from the back of

Opening lap, 1970 Dutch Grand Prix – Piers on the
inside in the De Tomaso as Jochen's Lotus 72 heads
towards its maiden, but cheerless victory.

the grid, but drove a fantastic race to finish third once again. Graham McRae was driving a Formula 5000 McLaren in that race and he was full of Piers' driving: 'I was braking at two hundred yards and he went by me still flat out for what seemed like half-a-minute, then puffs of smoke as he hit the brakes, a glimpse of the side of the car and he was gone! By the time I came out of the corner there he was, a speck in the distance, attacking the next one . . .'

Piers raced the De Tomaso twice more, at Spa and Monaco, before the Dutch Grand Prix at Zandvoort on 21 June. At Monaco Frank fell foul of de Tomaso again: 'He was in the middle of deep negotiations with Ford of America at that time, who were buying his works to control Pantera production. He told me it was vitally important to get the Ford deal, Lee Iacocca of Ford was present at Monte Carlo and we had to impress him. He wanted me to start Piers with only fifteen gallons of fuel aboard so that Piers could lead the race and impress Iacocca before having to make a stop. I told de Tomaso what to do with his idea . . .'

Piers' steering rack seized during the race after running seventh, and at Spa the team were short of engines, though now they had two chassis available, including a new ultra-lightweight version. Piers retired early from the Belgian race with low oil pressure.

At Zandvoort Piers spun in practice to put one of the cars into the sand at the Tarzan Hairpin, but still qualified ninth on row four of the grid. He was embroiled in a major dice chasing the leaders in the race, and was in close contact with John Miles' Lotus, the Matras of Beltoise and Pescarolo, Peter Gethin's McLaren and Jack Brabham and John Surtees. He drove his way to the head of this bunch and pulled clear in pursuit of Regazzoni's

Ferrari – this race marking Clay's Formula One debut. Piers was sixth, in line for his first Championship point in the De Tomaso.

Then he went missing, and smoke could be seen mushrooming out of the dunes on the back-stretch. He had gone off into the fences and banks at very high speed, and was dead.

This was a crushing blow for all Piers' many friends – with Frank at their head. He had lost much more than a driver. He had lost a true and dear friend; he looked a crushed, desolate little figure white with shock – isolated and alone in the Zandvoort paddock.

'Piers' was the first real loss that ever came close to me. I worshipped him, no less. I was numbed, very, very sad indeed . . .'

De Tomaso lost interest and the team was left to complete this season which had promised so much with no spare car, no more development and, by the end of the year, no money. Brian Redman, the excellent British sports car driver, was called in to drive the surviving car at Brands Hatch and Hockenheim, after Frank missed the French race in respect for Piers' memory; and Tim Schenken, the Australian former Formula Ford and Formula Three driver, took over from the Austrian race (for full details see the complete racing record on page 161). Tim did well enough to prove himself capable of handling Formula One machinery with competence and confidence, and won himself a Brabham works seat in 1971. Frank was happy for him, but at Monza Jochen had died too . . .

Today that sole surviving De Tomaso 505 stands in a corner of the Argentine–Italian's new factory outside Modena, still with its peeling Ward machine tool and Graviner stickers, covered in dust and minus a DFV engine, the rear of its chassis just resting on the floor . . . Frank Williams does not miss it.

March, Marlboro and the Bailiffs

The team emerged from their tragic 1970 season with a massive deficit. Frank had to sell one of his four Cosworth engines to help cover his debts, 'but it never for one instant occurred to me to give up ... It just did not occur to me as an option – and never has.'

The search for a suitable chassis for the new season was the main problem, as 'the rent-a-driver' loomed on the horizon. Until the early sixties it had been normal in Grand Prix racing for enthusiastic would-be Formula One drivers to buy their own cars and enter them privately if they could not attract contracts from major teams. During the late fifties and throughout the sixties the wealthy private entrant like Rob Walker had emerged, followed by private owner-drivers like Jo Siffert and Guy Ligier – the one good enough to win Walker and later fully-fledged works team drives, and the other enthusiastic enough to establish himself as a sports and Formula One car constructor. Into the seventies the vogue grew for 'second-division' drivers who could attract personal sponsorship funds to approach established teams and buy their way into one of the vacant car seats on offer. Into 1971 Frank Williams was offering ...

Henri Pescarolo was his man. The tall, bearded Frenchman had driven well for Matra in Formula Two and Formula One, and towards the end of 1970 he had approached Frank to discuss prospects for running a Formula Two operation in the coming year. He had backing totalling around £23,000 from the French Motul oil company for a two-car team. Derek Bell – another good British driver in the Redman mould – signed on to drive the second car, and Frank bought a pair of brand-new March 712Ms from the youthful Bicester company whose designer, Robin Herd,

had pencilled the conversion work on Frank's 1969 Brabhams. Ward put up another £10,000 or so for a parallel Formula One effort, Pescarolo persuaded Motul to add a further £15,000 to the Grand Prix kitty, and an Italian journalist friend of Frank's named Giancarlo Faletti introduced him to the Politoys die-cast model company, who became very interested and provided a further £10,000 of sponsorship.

With that backing Frank was able to order a new March 711 for Henri, which appeared late in the new season, and in the interim they campaigned an ex-Chris Amon works March 701 which was later to become their second car. 'I did some deals with John Webb, head of Motor Circuit Developments, the promoters for Brands Hatch, Oulton Park, Mallory Park and Snetterton circuits to provide a car for some of his protégés. MCD paid £1,000 a time for drivers like Ray Allan, Tony Trimmer and Cyd Williams to have a go in non-Championship Formula One races with the March 701, but Cyd virtually destroyed it against a bridge abutment in practice at Oulton Park and virtually everything had to be replaced in the rebuild which followed. I sold the car finally to George Dixon, a Lincolnshire motor trader...'

The details of this season are recorded in the racing record appendix on page 161, but with both Formula One and Formula Two teams to maintain and organize, and with a staff at Bath Road of only about ten, Frank had bitten off more than he could chew. Herbie Blash, Jochen's former Team Lotus mechanic, had joined him along with Bob Evans and Kerry Adams on the Formula One team, while Tony Fox ran the F2s. Mike Young acted as general manager and held the fort while Frank was away. 'Mike was a good administrator and a good buyer, very competent and loyal. He looked after the books and generally covered for me. He stayed with me for several years into 1977, before taking a pub in Essex...

'But we were still desperately deficient in that we lacked an engineer. We were running cars as they came, straight out of the box. While other teams developed and progressed, we stood still and got left behind...'

The red-painted Williams team Motul–March Formula Two cars made a terrific impact in their first European outing after a fraught debut in a two-race February series in Bogota, Colombia. 'We took two brand-new March 712M's there for Henri and Derek to drive, and in the first race their monocoques just split apart at the front end where the front suspension picked up. After the first race there was only one thing to do and that was to take both chassis back to March at Bicester to be rebuilt and strengthened in time for the second Colombian race the following Sunday. We stripped the cars overnight in Bogota and I took the two bare monocoques with me as hand baggage on Monday morning, catching a flight from Bogota to Miami, and then the National flight to London. I was at Heathrow on the Tuesday morning and went straight to Bicester with the tubs. March set to work at once, examined and modified the lubrication system to prevent the engines throwing out their oil and starving themselves to death, and remade the front foot-box of each where the suspension picked up. They worked solidly for almost twenty-four hours, and I was back at Heathrow with the modified and reinforced chassis late on the Wednesday. By Thursday night I was back in Bogota and our lads were reassembling the cars for Henri and Derek to practice the following day. The trip was expensive – about £250 for excess baggage alone! – but we were effectively doing March's Formula Two development for them, so they covered half, and the Colombians chipped in some because I had taken a mass of parts orders with me from other teams, and they knew that if the bits didn't arrive they had little chance of staging a good race that weekend...' In fact Bell finished third on aggregate, while Pescarolo left both heats with electrical troubles.

But Henri actually won the first European F2 race of the season at Mallory Park and then led his heat and the final at Thruxton on Easter Monday before his car's engine broke. Frank was not using the most reliable engine supplier in the business, and Henri's Thruxton engine blew simply because the sump pan had not been fastened tightly, it worked loose and the oil dropped out...

'We were quite extended with the 701 and 711 Formula One cars, plus the two F2s, and I made the mistake of over-stretching our slender resources by taking on a third F2 March for the Brazilian Carlos Pace. He had shown quite well in Formula Three and was rated higher than Emerson Fittipaldi in Brazil. After our good start to the F2 season he approached me through a mutual friend because he had won some backing from the Portuguese–Brazilian bank and wanted someone reasonable to run a car for him. He brought perhaps twelve to fifteen thousand pounds with him, which was a classic mixture of the good news and the bad news. The good news was that we had found ourselves a very promising young driver, and the bad news was that the third car totally overloaded our resources...'

Pace won for the team at Imola in July, but towards the end of the season adequate preparation of the Formula Two cars was no longer possible. There was dissension within the team at the Brands Hatch round, and at Albi all three cars failed to qualify.

'We fought a bush fire operation in both Formula Two and Formula One, repairing what broke but unable to recognize or strengthen suspect items before they failed. When the March 711 arrived it took us ages to find it was nowhere near stiff enough. At Nürburgring in practice Henri came in, and we found the monocoque had actually creased in the middle over the bumps. And I was robbing Peter to pay Paul all the time. Quite a sizeable chunk of our sponsorship had gone immediately to pay off some of the 1970 debts, and I was out of my depth both technically and organizationally...'

Henri actually won Heat One of the Oulton Park Gold Cup and only had to hold his second place in Heat Two to win overall. But then the rear brakes failed, and he crashed. His best GP placings that year were a fourth in the British Grand Prix and sixth in the Austrian. In the French Grand Prix at Ricard Frank ran the rebuilt 701 for a Motul protégé named Max Jean (often referred to, wrongly, in the press as Jean Max) for a rental fee which helped

MARCH, MARLBORO AND THE BAILIFFS

ends meet, but his was really a shoe-string operation with three engines for two cars – he was that close to the ragged edge.

At the end of the World Championship season a Brazilian named Antonio Scavone organized a Formula Two Torneio series in Brazil, with an additional final race in Argentina. The existing 1600 cc Formula Two was due to expire at the end of the year, to be replaced by a new 2-litre class, and a mass of ageing F2 machinery was shipped out to São Paulo for the start of the series on 31 October, Frank Williams (Racing Cars) included...

It was a disastrous tour. Pescarolo packed up in disgust and flew home while Frank provided drives for Pace, and for Claudio Francisci, Arturo Merzario and Nestor Garcia-Veiga in his second car. The last race of the formula in Cordoba has imprinted itself vividly upon Frank's memory '... for the deaths of at least ten worn-out Cosworth FVA engines – it seemed as if they sensed their Formula was at an end, and throughout practice and the two race heats they were exploding and hurling out bits of rod, piston and valve gear, and pluming smoke all over the place. It certainly marked the end of my involvement in Formula Two, and from then on we were a Formula One team pure and simple...'

During 1971 Frank had predictably become disillusioned with running cars made by an outside supplier. His team had suffered considerable trauma and contributed much towards the cars' development, while always trailing far behind the works team cars. 'I was lucky in that we had got in on the ground floor with the Formula One Constructors' Association, which had been arranging charter travel and negotiating sensible start and prize money terms with race promoters. I really wanted to build my own cars by this time, and Politoys were interested in assisting. They made many models of racing cars and liked the idea of having one under their own name to model. They put up £40,000 for me to build and run one, but of course at Bath Road we had no proper manufacturing facility. I discussed the idea with Maurice Gomm, who ran a sheet metal business in Old Woking doing a lot of specialist work for racing people, and who had rebuilt our F2 March chassis for us late in 1971. He suggested I contact Len Bailey, a design engineer who had worked on the Ford GT40 project and later with Alan Mann on other Ford prototypes which Gomm had had a hand in

making. So Len was contracted to draw a fairly simple state-of-the-art Formula One car for us, and Gomm agreed to build the monocoque for it...'

So Frank Williams embarked on his career as a Formula One car constructor. It was inevitable. He had committed himself to a future in Grand Prix racing, and this was the only way to secure that future. But progress was slow. Gomm was perhaps overloaded with other work, and Politoys' development dragged on through 1972, by which time Frank had found new premises and a manufacturing facility in Bennett Road, Reading.

'Again it was dear old "Bullshit Bob" who found it for us. He said a friend had heard of a 5,000 square foot industrial unit coming on the market within the next few days, south of Reading. We travelled down in the fog around Christmas to have a look, had great difficulty finding it, but it was ideal. We took it next day. We actually moved out of Bath road into Bennett Road on 2 February 1972. Leaving Slough meant I also lost my flat. By that time it was virtually bare anyway, things I had accumulated during my trading days like Stereo systems had all been sold long ago to pay for F1 or F2 car parts, engine rebuilds and so on. I had had a string of fairly flashy road cars. I liked Porsches very much, but they had all been traded as DFVs had to be bought or serviced, or there were other bills to pay.

'I became a lodger living at Dave Brodie's house in Hurley. We had met years before while I was still at Pinner Road. "Brode" was a very astute young businessman running an electro-plating business nearby. He was another racer – in his case saloon cars – and he became a staunch and firm friend, and valued adviser.

'I was also seeing more socially of Ginny Sawyer-Hoare, who had left her husband. At the end of the year we set up house together in a cottage at Windsor rented from Gordon Spice, another good saloon car racer who ran a large auto accessories chain. It was the first house I had ever lived in, small but comfortable, and Ginny looked after it very nicely. I enjoyed that. I am not sure that Ginny knew what she was taking on – I never had much spare time, and I was very unreliable...'

For 1972 Frank was to continue running March cars, a 'bitsa' 721 built for a bargain price around an old 711 tub for Pescarolo, and the original 711 for Carlos Pace. At that time a brand-new 721 cost £15,000, less engine and gearbox, and in no way could Frank's team run to that...

'Motul had put in about £40,000 for that season, Politoys the same, and Ward came up with another £10–15,000. We had run way over budget in 1971, but I managed to settle most of the bills and Pace brought along about £10,000 towards his drive...'

While these sums may have seemed realistic in their day, it is worth comparing them to the Williams team's 1981 budget of around £3,500,000. Ten years previously Frank was running two cars on approximately one-thirty-fifth of that sum ... and in 1981 (as in 1971) none of his team's backing was being wasted on extravagances...

And during 1972 Henri had a long string of accidents which mangled his poor March 721 beyond belief. The agony started at Brands Hatch for the British Grand Prix, where the Politoys FX3 actually made its debut and was promptly destroyed in the opening laps. Ron Tauranac had become involved as Frank's first team engineer – if only on an honorary consultancy basis – having sold his interest in Motor Racing Developments (the Brabham company) to South London businessman Bernard Ecclestone. 'Ron was a crusty character, but I think he appreciated what we were trying to do, and I certainly respected him. He had no proper brief from us, and certainly no budget, but he made some small modifications to our cars, completed the Politoys in just six weeks after it had dragged on for so many months, and in a way worked for me for next to nothing in return...'

Poor Pescarolo, having destroyed the Politoys, went on effectively to write off the March 721 four times, and he failed to score a single World Championship point. His best finish was eighth in the first round of all at Buenos Aires. Carlos Pace, on the other hand, showed increasing promise. He was sixth in Spain to score his maiden point, then fifth in Belgium for two more. Then at Monza he announced his intention to move to the Surtees team for 1973. Frank virtually begged him to stay, to consider their gentleman's agreement for a two-year alliance. 'In retrospect I was not tough enough. I should have laid our agreement on the line. It was all part of my learning curve and I lost his services. I wasn't so

naïve as to have taken him into Formula One, half at my own expense, for just one season. He was sixteenth equal in the Championship, which doesn't sound anything fantastic, but he was equal with Carlos Reutemann, he had done a good job in what was really an obsolescent car, and he clearly had great potential...'

After his incident-packed second season with the Williams team, Henri Pescarolo slipped out of Formula One. He went on to score an historic hat-trick of victories at the Le Mans 24-hour race with the French Matra–Simca team, and was awarded the *Légion d'Honneur* for it. He drove for Frank again in the French Grand Prix but proved better suited for endurance racing: 'In practice in a Formula One car he would produce his best time quite early on, then be unable to go any quicker, however long he pounded round. He was a nice guy, quite a gentleman, but he never proved himself as quick as I had hoped he would be...'

For 1973 Pace had joined Surtees, and Howden Ganley, ex-Marlboro–BRM, joined Williams. 'Patrick Duffeler of Marlboro became a firm friend. Along with Ted Williams of Ward machine tools I owe Marlboro a debt of gratitude for helping the team survive. Patrick's reasoning was that he wanted to help one of the minor teams to develop in Formula One, and he chose us. He also had a bee in his bonnet about linking the Marlboro name with that of a prestigious luxury high-performance motor manufacturer, such as Ferrari or Lamborghini. I couldn't run to that, but my good Italian contacts suggested Piero Rivolta, of the Iso–Rivolta car company.

'So we concluded a deal with him, promising £40,000 for the season, with Marlboro providing equal support for equal space on the cars. Politoys agreed continued backing of around £10,000, and with Ted Williams' and John Halbert's unswerving support we found ourselves with promises of over £100,000 for the season. Howden was Marlboro's driver while "Nanni" Galli, the Italian ex-March driver, took the second seat with promises of £20,000 personal sponsorship from Italian sources.'

Frank's team began the new season with a pair of FX3 cars running as Iso–Marlboros, but Galli's sponsorship failed to materialize and he lost his drive. Iso meanwhile made their

Ron Tauranac flexes his muscles by the prototype Williams Politoys nose, while designer Len Bailey (in the hooped sports shirt) looks on; Brands Hatch pits, 1972. In the background on the right with the March men is Dr Harvey Postlethwaite, later to build the Hesketh cars and join Wolf-Williams for 1976.

payments anything from three to six months late, and badly fragmented payments at that. The last £5,000 was not in fact paid until well into the early summer of 1974, just before Iso collapsed in bankruptcy. Frank was desperately short of cash and it was Duffeler who bailed him out by producing an extra £15,000 from Marlboro's motor racing promotional fund. Frank never forgot: 'There was no sensible commercial reason for him to do that so far as I could see. They received very little in return from my team. So far as I am concerned, Marlboro that season proved themselves honourable people, who cared about the problems of the small team . . .'

That year saw new Formula One regulations taking effect from the Spanish Grand Prix at Barcelona in May, which demanded deformable crush-structure fuel tank protection and minimum 16-gauge skin thicknesses on the monocoque chassis outer skins. New cars had to be built, and Frank took on an ex-March design-engineer named John Clarke to do the job for him.

He was a quiet, bespectacled, rather introverted engineer who had been responsible for the 1972 March Formula Two cars, which were very good indeed. The new Iso-Marlboro IR cars were not very successful, however. 'Their oil systems were to give us terrible headaches and we blew up several engines. Ganley's car refused point-blank to run cleanly in its first three races unless he kept the electric fuel pump switched on, which was not the way it should be – a mechanical pump should take over once the engine is running. Howden was a reliable driver who plodded round and finished if the car lasted long enough. His best finish for us was sixth place in Canada that year, when the Grand Prix at Mosport Park was run in mist and rain, there were fifty-four pit stops, multiple tyre changes and most teams' lap charts blew up and everybody had different ideas about the final result . . .

'The second car was driven by all sorts of people after Galli's departure. Marlboro appointed Jacky Pretorius in South Africa and Gijs van Lennep in Holland; Graham McRae drove at Silverstone, Henri returned for the French and German GPs, and Tim Schenken drove in Canada. Van Lennep was the most successful. He was sixth for a Championship point at Zandvoort.

'At Watkins Glen Jacky Ickx drove for us. I had always rated him very highly, and he had been left high and dry by Ferrari that year, who were in deep trouble and missing several races. But he missed his plane and the first day's practice and it all went bad. He still finished seventh though, in a strange car . . .'

Towards the end of the season, in his search for engineering aid which he could persuade himself to trust, Frank called in Dallara to advise on the cars. He decided that the rear suspension geometry could be improved, advised John Clarke, and Frank insisted Clarke make the modifications. This led to a split: 'Right or wrong I decided I had had a basinful of engineers learning about Formula One at my expense, and when John objected to my calling in more experienced men over his head, like Tauranac or Dallara, we parted not on the best of terms . . .'

Duffeler continued Marlboro support through 1974 and with their backing Frank took on Arturo Merzario as lead driver. He had driven Ferrari Formula One and sports cars with some success. The second drive would go to Marlboro appointees, something which Frank did not altogether like, but agreed to so long as Marlboro would pay his starting money if they failed to qualify.

Merzario made a vivid impression on his debut for the team at Buenos Aires. He blew two engines and left both with the rev-counter lodged at a tell-tale 13,000 rpm! The built-in rev limiter would have prevented such over-revving on the throttle, so little Art with his fuse-wire figure and exhibitionist nature had been changing down as he would in a Ferrari flat-12, which revved to around 12,500 rpm in any case, and had simply punched the DFVs through the roof on the overrun into corners. Yet Frank was enthralled: 'He was a bit wild, but good for us. He gave it a go and really raced. He put his heart into his driving and gave us heart to watch him . . . He was an unusual driver in many ways. He liked to lay almost flat on his back in the car, so you could hardly see him, and the steering wheel had to be fitted perfectly straight or there'd be ructions. He couldn't stand tyre stagger – unequal tyre diameters from side-to-side which affect the balance of the car – but he was quite quick for a time . . .

'He really came good in South Africa that year, when in second day's practice only Niki Lauda's Ferrari was faster! Pace then put his Surtees on the front row alongside Niki but Art was still there on row two, lying so far back as to be almost invisible. He finished sixth, it was quite cheering. At Jarama in the Spanish Grand Prix he qualified on row four, faster than Hulme, Scheckter and Hunt, and after running seventh in the wet shot up to third as tyre changes were made. He was holding a firm fourth place when he rammed Jarier's Shadow up the tail, popped the nose wings out of adjustment and they flopped down, lifting the nose so that he understeered off at the next corner and climbed over the barrier to land in a knot of photographers. Luckily no-one was hurt but it spoiled a good run...'

Thereafter he never seemed to race so well again. His car would retire with mysterious ailments. Yet at Monza on home soil he finished fourth after an exciting and very popular charge through the field from twenty-third at the end of lap one, after burning his clutch on the start-line.

Still the team achieved little of great merit to warrant Marlboro's continued support. 'In August that year Marlboro told me they would not be sponsoring the team in 1975. Despite that, Duffeler still produced £15,000 for the new year and I found three different people – Marlboro being one – to buy us three new Cosworth engines for the year. Ward bought one, and gave another £30,000 support.'

Art Merzario was to drive again, and he was joined by Jacques Laffite, the French former race mechanic who had just won the European Formula Two Championship. He had personal sponsorship from a very tough Swiss businessman named Ambrozium, who was to pay the team £1,000 per start.

Frank had taken on a new engineer, a very dapper, always smartly-dressed and well-manicured designer named Ray Stokoe who had been working with McLaren. Tony Fox was still Chief Mechanic, and Mike Young general manager. The Williams team was one of the first in Formula One to pay its mechanics forty-five pounds a week, despite its money troubles: 'I had to pay top money because that was virtually the only thing I had to offer people to make them work for me – for sure we were not going to enjoy much in the way of glamorous success...' But he kept going because Formula One was by this time Frank's way of life; he knew no other.

'Debts were beginning to accumulate, the bills were piling up. Suppliers of basic things like steel stock, nuts and bolts, that kind of thing, were beginning to take out county court judgements against us for outstanding debts. If we couldn't pay then a bailiff would appear, and take equipment of equal value. It was nearly all small amounts, like about £33 here, or £227.75 there, but no way could we survive if we settled the instant the first invoice came in. We just didn't have the money, and we strung out credit as far as we could.

'Eventually in desperation they just had to go to the county court to settle the account, and in desperation I had to sit back and wait while they did it, just to string out a little longer credit. That was the way I had to operate, manipulating what little money we had to the team's advantage. We had to survive, I was going to stay in racing, there was no way I was going to bow out...'

The previous August, three days after the Austrian Grand Prix, Frank and Ginny had married. 'Brode fixed it up, he paid the eight pounds for the ceremony, Ginny bought herself the ring for thirty pounds. I had no money, all I had to do was get myself to the church on time. I left Bennett Road at ten minutes to two in the afternoon, arrived outside the church at one minute to, we did the deal and I was back at work at twenty past...

'Ginny had been marvellous. She had had a house which she sold, some of the money went back to her father but she had put the rest into the team over a period of time to help us survive through '73–74. I paid her back as well I could, a few hundred here, a hundred there...

'We had moved into a furnished house at Mortimer, a small village outside Reading. We lived there for three months before we could afford to pay any rent, and then it was Ginny who paid because she was the only one with a bank account. She kept a roof over our heads for eighteen months. My first ever personal bank account, 'Williams, F.' was opened in April 1975, just so that I would have a cheque book to pay the rent myself. It was £120 a month. The owner didn't approve of my failing to mow the lawn or maintain the garden, and when he did come in for an inspection he would move the cooker to see if we had swept under it...'

Ginny Williams tells how, with a baby on the way, they were eventually evicted from the Mortimer house, and how – after an interview with the country estate owner – they were selected as tenants of a beautiful but run-down old laundry-house needing renovation outside Basingstoke. They undertook to restore it, but for long months they could not afford even the simple luxury of carpeting – Frank had DFV rebuilds to pay for, and the team had to survive...

One of his most embarrassing financial problems around that time was non-payment of the team telephone bill at Bennett Road. The line was cut off, and for some time Frank Williams had to run his affairs from the coin-box down the road.

To outsiders the world of Formula One might sparkle with a glamorous sheen. To this utterly dedicated but struggling team patron the reality had become very different...

'Ted Williams of Ward was a tower of strength in those days. He had consistently supported me since 1969, and if we were in deep trouble, with the bailiffs due next day, he would lend me a few thousand, and simply write it off – just to keep us ahead. Over seven years' association he probably put up around £200,000, about half that as formal sponsorship and the other half as loan capital which he then wrote off.

'Poor Ted died in 1978, but I still see his children occasionally, and I will never forget him. He gave us the chance to survive, and the chance to build a team which would win a World Championship.'

Engineer Ray Stokoe drew a new Williams monocoque for 1975 which they called the FW04. When little Merzario arrived to drive it he complained the cockpit was too tight. Now Art had a human skeleton figure, his complaints did not ring true. The eight races he drove for the team that season have little to commend them. At Barcelona the track was patently unsafe in practice with insecurely installed temporary crash barriers lining the course. Art was one of many drivers very unsettled by the prospect of running into a collapsible barrier. This is what had killed drivers like Jochen Rindt, Roger Williamson, Peter Revson, François Cevert and Helmuth Koinigg in recent years. Art completed one slow race lap to qualify for start money, and went home. He

failed to qualify at Monaco, retired in Belgium and dropped out of the team.

'In April I had telephoned Gian' Paolo Dallara at Lamborghini for a chat. I told him I was pretty desperate. I had no money, did he have any ideas? He said there was one possibility, an Austrian-born Canadian oil man named Walter Wolf who spent a lot of money at Lamborghini, and who was talking about running a Le Mans car. He gave me a series of telephone numbers around the world where Walter Wolf might be contacted.

'I tracked him down and explained who I was and what we were trying to do. He said "Ya, I hef heard of you, und I vould luff to come und vatch a Formula Vun race." I left some tickets for the International Trophy Silverstone meeting at his London house, and he came along...'

It was a grim meeting for him to visit, for Frank Williams' team suffered agonies there as two DFVs were blown apart in two days by being hammered too hard before their oil had warmed through, and their one car entry could not start.

'In the middle of all this I was standing by the car in the paddock when this great big bloke appeared by my side wearing a leather coat and asked if I was Frank Williams. It was Wally Wolf, and he spent those two cheerless days on the pit road utterly fascinated by all that was going on around him. He paid for those broken engines to be rebuilt and supported us for the rest of that year. He came to races and enjoyed being involved, while holding markers against the team. He was no fool, he didn't just say "Here's £50,000, go out and have a good time", even though there's no way I would have done that. I would have spent it towards making the cars competitive, somehow...'

Wolf obviously recognized that intense effort on Williams' part, and appreciated it. Jacques Laffite was showing improving form. He failed to qualify at Monaco, after a practice crash and subsequent fuel problems wrecked his timetable, but there were other pluses.

'I recognized Tony Brise's immense promise and gave him his Grand Prix debut at Barcelona, where he finished seventh and won himself a seat in Graham Hill's Embassy team. But after only sixty miles' testing on a brand-new engine at Goodwood, Tony had had

Art Merzario to the fore in the 1974 South African Grand Prix at Kyalami. How could he see out?

Jacques Laffite hammering his way to second place in the 1975 German Grand Prix, the FW04 car showing off its second-hand, ex-Hesketh nose cone. This result sealed Frank's FOCA membership for 1976 and helped assure his team's immediate future.

the bearings run. We had about four engines damaged in this way one after another, and we subsequently found it was due to an oil line kinking and restricting flow under load.

'Eventually Ken Tyrrell took pity on us and allowed Tony Fox to go down to his team's works at Ockham to study their oil system and copy it inch by inch. Neither had we appreciated some of the detail modifications that the leading teams were making to their Hewland gearboxes to add reliability. Again Ken took me quietly to one side and explained how we could save ourselves some money – or at least protect ourselves against further unnecessary loss. This was all part of my personal education in Formula One. People helped us because at that time the Williams team was no threat. Times change . . .'

After the French Grand Prix the team had just one engine left, and Jacques ran alone at Silverstone, but the car failed. They went to Nürburgring for the German Grand Prix in desperate straits, and in a race dictated by those who managed to avoid puncturing their tyres on sharp stones kicked up from the verges, Jacques actually came home second behind Reutemann's victorious Brabham.

'Second place there meant a prize money pay-out of around £5,500 from the Formula One Constructors' Association and also assured our membership for 1976, with all the charter travel savings and prize money advantages that involves. To qualify for membership one had to figure among the top twenty points-scorers at the end of the season. Now we would be in, and I was a very happy man . . .'

From Germany on, Jacques' modified car proved quite reliable. If others were unlucky, he could be around at the finish to pick up points. But he always hated racing in the rain. 'In Austria we had a terrific downpour and while the stars slipped and slid and worried, Vittorio Brambilla charged round in the March and won when the organizers called the race off early. Jacques had come into the pits and said "It's impossible, I'm not going on." He'd undone his seat belts and was trying to climb out of the car while I had one hand on his helmet and was pushing him back in, shouting "No, Jacques, you've got to keep going, everybody else is – look at Brambilla!" But he wouldn't have any. He climbed out . . .'

That season saw other drivers like Ian Scheckter (Jody's elder brother), Damien Magee, François Migault, Jo Vonlanthen, Renzo Zorzi and the Italian girl Lella Lombardi renting the second car. Bernard Ecclestone recommended the Irishman, Magee, for the Swedish Grand Prix because he was interested to see how he would go in Formula One. Ecclestone covered the cost of the subsequent engine rebuild in return for Frank providing the drive. It was all part of the way modern Formula One works – showing the value of the also-ran teams, the grid-fillers . . .

More significantly, an oil trader named Richard Oaten hired that second car for his protégé Ian Ashley at Nürburgring. He paid some £7,000 for the seat, but in practice Ashley crashed heavily, missing the race and leaving his sponsor with a hefty repair bill for the car. Still Oaten was very interested and put £20,000 or so into assisting the team through the last four races of the season, without Ian Ashley.

'Then the United States GP was a disaster. Lella Lombardi was driving the second car alongside Jacques, and in practice she broke a valve spring in her engine, but didn't notice. We could hear it rippling on seven cylinders every time she went by and it eventually dropped a valve and just cut itself in half, destroying the heads, block, the whole thing. The rebuild cost over £9,000. Then, immediately before the race, Jacques mixed-up his eye-drops with a bottle of visor cleaning fluid and sprayed the wrong stuff in his eyes and nearly blinded himself. He was rushed off to hospital, Lella just couldn't fit into his car, and so we missed the race . . .'

Barking up the Wrong Tree

Walter Wolf had become increasingly committed to running his own Formula One team. It would promote his name within the international oil business and fulfil his growing personal enthusiasm and interest. As he followed the Williams team around through 1975, '. . . he began to make more noises about wanting to buy the team. He was offering sums of money I had never dreamed of, but I repeatedly put him off. I didn't relish the idea of selling control.

'Certainly we had been in deep trouble. Operating from the telephone box might sound amusing in retrospect. It makes a good story, but it wasn't half so funny at the time. But on the positive side we were assured of continued FOCA membership for '76, the car had been sorted out and was showing reasonable reliability, and Jacques himself was showing signs of developing into a very good Formula One driver, so we looked a halfway reasonable team for any promising new driver. I was pretty sure I could raise enough money to continue.

'Ward were still around, through their holding company, the Association of British Machine Tool Manufacturers, and Richard Oaten had offered support of £40,000 for the new season. I had a whisper there would be some Marlboro money available again – I could usually expect perhaps £25–30,000 from them – and with some sensible rent-a-driver deals I felt sure we could be viable.

'While I was thinking this way, two things happened. Emerson Fittipaldi walked out of Marlboro–McLaren overnight to join his brother's Copersucar team, and Pat Duffeler of Marlboro telephoned me that night in a towering rage, and said that he would never sponsor another driver, he was putting Marlboro money into teams now, would I like a hundred thousand? The light at the end of the tunnel seemed brighter already, and then I found a new engineer – Patrick Head.

'Still Walter was pressing. He offered to pay off all the team's liabilities in return for a sixty per cent interest in the team. Liabilities at that time stood at around £140,000. We kept talking, but the weeks rolled by. He was determined to find his way into Formula One and while I "ummed" and "aahed" he eventually started talking to Bubbles Horsley, who had been running Lord Hesketh's team, with James Hunt as driver and Harvey Postlethwaite as designer. Hesketh was closing down, the team had gone into liquidation, and Bubbles was trying to sell Walter all their cars and equipment for £450,000. The plan was that Walter would take over the team more or less complete, lease their premises at Lord Hesketh's Easton Neston estate near Towcester, and Harvey would continue development of their latest 308C car into the new year.

'Walter wasn't confident about the deal, and night after night he would telephone me from Bermuda for a three-hour discussion, talking through the whole project and generally asking advice from somebody with Formula One experience. I thought £450,000 was a fabulous sum of money. I'd never dreamed of such a figure in my life and it became very obvious that Walter was going to be spending a great deal to go racing properly in the coming year.

'Meanwhile, Richard Oaten's promised sponsorship hadn't come through, but the Marlboro money was just around the corner, and prospects looked pretty good . . .

'However, Wally Wolf is a very determined individual, and our lengthy telephone conversations had a cumulative effect. One night in November I went for a long walk around the lanes near The Laundry House, turning the idea over in my mind. I was very tempted by the prospect of Wally clearing off our debts, and of our team having the budget at last to do the job properly.

'By the time I walked back to the house my mind was made up. I called Wally in Bermuda and said, "Yes, you can have sixty per cent for the liabilities." He had already done the deal with Bubbles for the Hesketh cars and equipment, but now he wasn't going to lease the workshops at Easton Neston, he was going to use my works at Bennett Road, adding some of Hesketh's personnel to our own strength. This included Harvey Postlethwaite joining us as Chief Engineer, which was hard on Patrick, who had joined my team as Chief Engineer just a matter of days previously. I gave him the choice of moving on – as he would have been perfectly entitled to do – or of staying on to work under Harvey. To his credit he thought, "I can learn here", and he stayed.

'In retrospect I was very stupid to conclude that deal with Walter Wolf – not that there has ever been any animosity between us over it, because we were then and still are on very good terms. But I should have charged him much more for the team, because he immediately won full FOCA membership for two cars, which he would not have had with Hesketh. Bubbles was selling assets only, while I was allowing him to take control of an existing fully operational team and merely replace its equipment and change its name. FOCA membership instantly saved around £150,000 a year in travelling expenses outside Europe.

'So why did I do it? It seemed like an awful lot of money to have available at the time. I had never had more than perhaps £20,000 in my hand at any one time during seven seasons in Formula One. My appreciation of financial control was poor. I had no real adviser to guide me, and really lacked deep understanding of everything the deal entailed . . . It seemed a great idea at the time.'

So the almost new Hesketh 308C design formed the basis of the Wolf-Williams FW05; Marlboro money brought Jacky Ickx as star driver, with the French Formula Two find Michel Leclere in support; and Bennett Road began to burst at the seams with the influx of ex-Hesketh people and parts. But the Wolf-Williams season of '76 has passed into motor racing legend as a catastrophe. While Dr Postlethwaite's earlier Hesketh cars had carried James Hunt to victory in the Dutch Grand Prix and truly competitive performances elsewhere, the remarkably low-slung 308C was to prove itself an uncompetitive aberration. For a start an old pigeon had come home to roost, Bubbles got his own back on Frank for the Brabham-on-bricks caper, and the 308C was delivered without wheels!

The car was aerodynamically and structurally indifferent, and as it was strengthened and continuously modified during 1976, so it grew grossly overweight. Eventually it was something like 120 lbs over the minimum weight limit, so it had a second-per-lap time penalty built in. Its suspension and steering left much to be desired, primarily due to flexion, and following Hunt's complaint at the end of 1975 that the prototype car was giving him 'all kinds of funny messages', the Wolf drivers were all at sea in '76.

Jacky himself had passed his prime in Grand Prix racing, and was no longer the hungry and intensely competitive driver he had once been, while the newcomer Leclere stood no chance despite considerable effort on his part. Their best outing was Ickx's seventh and Leclere's tenth at Jarama in the Spanish Grand Prix, but they were often struggling merely to qualify. For Ickx the most ignominious failure must have come in his native Belgium, where his inexperienced team-mate made the grid, and he didn't. Mario Andretti had a one-off drive at Silverstone in April, finishing seventh and seeing enough to decide to rejoin Team Lotus . . .

'All that time we felt we were just on the brink of The Great Breakthrough. Sure we were in trouble, but competitiveness was surely just around the next corner. After the Belgian GP, Dave Brodie took Harvey and me out for lunch at the Post House Hotel near Bennett Road. Brode had the advantage of broad perspective, seeing from the outside where we lay in the scheme of things, while we were blinded by our own involvement. He simply asked if we had our heads on straight? We were astonished and demanded to know what he was talking about.

'"Well", he said, "if I were Walter Wolf I'd be bloody furious

Ill-fated combination – Frank Williams and Walter Wolf, 1976.

As Jacky Ickx struggled to qualify the FW05 for the 1976 British Grand Prix at Brands Hatch, the pit stop competition was the team's best hope. Patrick Head, standing in the background, seems to disapprove.

with you. Here I am paying all this money, all this promise and what are you giving me? Nothing. What's going on?'' We laughed it off at the time, thinking that Brode had it all wrong, Wally was OK, we were so close to cracking it, all it needed was a little more development.

'Well we were wrong, Wally wasn't OK and there was soon to be a very loud bang.

'By the end of June we were already £100,000 over budget for that stage of the season, and Walter must have been shifting in his seat. Then we took just one car to Brands Hatch for Ickx in the British Grand Prix and he couldn't qualify. He said "It has no grip, it won't turn in, it oversteers everywhere!" It was clearly undriveable and didn't make the grid. This was the last straw for Walter as he had flown over some very important guests to see his team perform in the Grand Prix – and the race was run without us . . .

'At about that time we owed many suppliers a lot of money. People were beginning to demand payment, and were looking for this Walter Wolf bloke who apparently owed it to them. That was really the end.

'In Walter's position in the oil world his word was his bond. Verbal agreement on the telephone was sufficient to settle deals worth millions, and now the team which Walter had taken over to promote his name was actually undermining it. And it wasn't his fault – it was mine – my financial management was still poor.'

Somebody's head had to roll, and his inevitably discontented and unsettled team saw Frank's go before the end of the year. Wolf attracted the team management services of Peter Warr from Team Lotus for the 1977 season, and he was to run a one-car team from Bennett Road for Jody Scheckter, who was to leave Tyrrell and sign for Walter Wolf Racing Ltd. Harvey Postlethwaite was to continue as Chief Engineer, and from mid-1976 he had concentrated upon designing a simple and practical new car for Scheckter to campaign.

'Meanwhile I had the unhappy task of informing Jacky Ickx immediately after our British Grand Prix failure that he was out of a drive. At the time we felt he hadn't really put his heart and soul into the job, but with hindsight I don't think we really appreciated that the car was virtually undriveable.'

To complete the season Art Merzario returned for the last seven GPs, but whereas the first half of the season had seen the cars qualify for nine starts and retire only once, Merzario never brought a Wolf-Williams to the finish line, and their best result was Warwick Brown's fourteenth in the second-string machine at Watkins Glen. On the credit side the close of the 1976 season saw a crisp and efficient race organization established at Bennett Road. This is the most difficult thing to achieve when going motor racing as a competitive business, and after its early-season inefficiency, Wolf-Williams at its close had emerged as a viable well-oiled team machine.

The axe still had to fall. 'Wally took me aside and told me that Peter Warr was coming in to take over the day-to-day running of the team. Wally said simply that since he had control he was going to take me out of direct responsibility for racing and make me his right-hand man. He more or less doubled my salary and outlined a scheme whereby I was to seek outside sponsorship for the team, and would be paid commission on what I attracted. I would be a team member, but I was to work from home. Peter Warr would be the new boss at Bennett Road, but I was to work direct for Walter, not Peter. I couldn't do much, other than accept. I threw myself into chasing various sponsorship deals, and found Walter asking me to do various personal things for him, like flying first-class to Frankfurt to pick up his 6.9 Mercedes, then drive it to Geneva, collect his Lamborghini, drive that to Paris ready for him to collect, then fly first-class somewhere else . . .'

If such a deal had been offered to a young Frank Williams in 1964 he would probably have thought it was fantastic, and have tucked money into his mattress to save enough for a brand-new F3 Brabham in 1965. In the winter of 1976–77 Frank's life was not at all bad, his standard of living was quite good, but he felt in some ways he had become little more than a kind of high-powered flunky.

When the team set off to Argentina for the opening round of the 1977 World Championship and Frank was left at home, he missed the race terribly. Scheckter won on reliability, achieving victory for Walter Wolf Racing on their debut with the brand-new car – but reaping the benefits of the efficient team system forged through fire the preceding year.

'Missing that race brought me up short. "My" team was racing and winning there, and I was missing it all. I wasn't a Racer any more; I was just any man, an ordinary bloke, albeit well-paid, who was never going to get anywhere nor be anyone. I did go to the Brazilian GP, and that reinforced my feeling of emptiness, of not being involved directly in racing. I just had to get back in there, and the only way to do that was to leave Wolf Racing, and start afresh.

'When I told Walter I wanted to leave he offered me an amazing deal to stay with him as his right-hand man in the oil business. It was a wonderful gesture on his part, but there was no way I could accept it. That would have taken me right away from racing, and I was a Racer.

'I had to start a new team . . . I thought Patrick Head would be willing to come along as engineer, and we were away. Williams Grand Prix Engineering had been conceived . . .'

The New Team

Entering 1977 Frank Williams cast about for the ingredients necessary to found his new team. He felt reasonably confident that Patrick Head would come with him as engineer. Now he needed a car, a driver, staff, and money . . .

Throughout his career he had made many friends and never, it would seem, a real enemy.

Friends were to play a major part in setting up the new team, and Frank's immediate strategy was to buy a sensibly-priced retired Formula One car from one of the established works teams and to operate it as a private entry during the season. It would serve to establish a Formula One workshop facility in which the first new-generation Williams cars could be built for 1978.

By leaving his original team Frank had obviously relinquished his FOCA membership and would have to qualify anew once he resumed construction of his own cars. Few doubted that he, of all people, would do just that.

During those winter months Frank was approached by Peter Mackintosh – former FOCA luminary then managing the Fittipaldi brothers' team – who was promoting a Belgian Formula Two driver named Patrick Neve.

Neve had attracted financial support from the Belgian Belle-Vue brewery company, hopefully to run a Formula One programme during the new year. This was exactly what Frank was looking for, and it was arranged that Williams Grand Prix Engineering should run a car for Neve in Belle-Vue livery.

The problem then was: what car? Frank discussed several alternatives with Patrick. The American-backed Penske team was closing its Formula One operation at that time and its cars were available, although very expensive for the period at around £20,000 each, less engine and gearbox. Used Shadow and Tyrrell chassis were also considered, but Frank opted finally for a March, as the Bicester company had an ex-works monocoque available at a reasonable price. Frank had worked closely with them before, and they were well geared to the requirements of customer racing.

Using what money was readily available from his severance arrangement with Walter Wolf, from Ted Williams and from Personal steering wheels, Frank bought March chassis '761–7' for the princely sum of £14,000, plus two very good low-mileage 1976 Cosworth DFV engines from an Italian Tyrrell private entrant named Alessandro Pesenti-Rossi; a third from Bernard Ecclestone, and a fourth – very badly blown up – as a gamble from Penske.

This last engine, 'DFV 199' as Frank's phenomenal recall for Cosworth engine numbers relates, had erupted in clouds of blue smoke and gushing oil behind John Watson's shoulders in Japan the previous October. Frank bought it as it stood, complete with mangled internals and holed block, for £1,500. Cosworth rebuilt it to standard guaranteed-output condition and sent WGPE a bill for £3,500 for their services. Frank recalls blinking when he read the bill, he was sure the block had been holed, which meant £2,200 for its replacement alone. As the months went by that bill occasionally bothered him. Even he had to doubt his luck at acquiring a race-worthy engine for only £5,000. Eventually his curiosity got the better of him, and one day on the telephone to Cosworth he asked in a roundabout way if they recalled putting a new block in '199'. Indeed they had, and it had obviously been overlooked on the bill. Many months later, with WGPE a thriving concern and Cosworth's biggest individual customer, Frank finally let on, remarking to Jack Field there that he thought he had one up on them . . . In retrospect that incident seemed to mark Frank Williams' change of fortune.

Meanwhile modest premises had been found at Unit 10, Station Road Industrial Estate, Didcot, a small town between Reading and Oxford. This property had been evaluated by Wolf-Williams when they were considering expansion, but had been rejected as too small and, for them, in the wrong place. For Frank and Patrick it looked ideal. It had been a carpet warehouse, the floor had been deeply gouged by heavy objects being dragged about, but it had good office space and room for a car bay and machine shop. There were minor delays in securing it, and while bureaucracy creaked into action, on 28 March 1977, WGPE actually set up shop at Didcot by forcing the door on Unit 10 and moving in.

The new company's embryo staff included Bob Torrie, ex-Lotus, Jon Redgrave, Alan Burroughs (universally known as 'AB'), Mike Young and Ross Brawn, ex-Wolf–Williams, while secretarial duties were covered by Allison Morris – wife of Bob Morris, a British Leyland company executive at that time, who had been a neighbour of Frank and Ginny Williams in Mortimer. Allison had worked for Frank at Bennett Road during the lean years of 1974–75, after Norma Robb had departed, covering for him – and fighting off the bailiffs.

In establishing the new concern another friend, Dave Brodie, proved a tower of strength, and became a director at the company's inception. He did not put in any money, but, more important, he put his name behind approaches Frank was making at the time. 'Brode' was a very shrewd and successful businessman with numerous interests. In Frank's words: 'If I wanted credit the money men would say "Hmm, Frank Williams, well, hasn't done very well, has he?" But Dave Brodie? Different matter then. "Aaah, Brode's a good man, confirm this overdraft, confirm this loan – *bonk, bonk* – we were in . . .'

Brode did more. He made introductions to a finance company for favourable loan facilities on buying a low-mileage Ford pantechnicon truck which was modified by Ratcliffe with a tail-lift, side access door and lowered roofline to become the new team's transporter. Financing was arranged for Patrick to buy top-quality machine tools. Ward pitched in with assistance in kind as much as cash – donating a brand-new capstan lathe and providing the services of their joinery department to make factory work-benches. Brode, typically, knew a cut-price timber supplier and recommended a jobbing spare-time carpenter who built the new team's canteen . . .

Every penny saved was another penny freed for racing, pure and simple. It was a philosophy to which the team has adhered ever since, spending lavishly on anything vital to racing, but getting by on the peripherals. Even with the multi-million pound budgets of later years theirs were not to become luxurious and opulent offices to match the top-team public image. Money was always to be spent where it mattered: in plant, men and machinery, to go racing and to be competitive.

But even before Neve's season with the private March could begin, another friend led Frank to the contact which was to assure the team's bright future – the first contact with Saudia Airlines, and the Saudis.

At that time the Saudi Arabian state airline's British advertising agency was Gordon Procter & Company. Frank had a friend there named Tony Harris who appreciated that Saudia was a fast-expanding international airline eager to project its name in the western world. He thought motor racing would be an ideal vehicle for it, and in February 1977 introduced Frank to Mohammed Al Fawzan of Saudia.

Mr Al Fawzan understood and appreciated western ways and thinking, and when Frank took him to Silverstone that March to see Patrick Neve drive in the Formula Two International, he appreciated immediately the promotional platform which the sport provided. A few days later WGPE was authorized to carry 'Fly Saudia' lettering on the rear wing of Neve's Formula One Belle-Vue March, the team receiving sponsorship of around £30,000 in return. In fact Al Fawzan had taken a flyer on his own initiative, the airline's head not knowing of the arrangement until he saw a photograph of the car with the slogan already blazoned across its wing.

Once the car had been delivered from March the Didcot crew had set about fitting it with adequate brake cooling ducts and a new air-starter system, using a pneumatic instead of the conventional electric starter motor – to save some weight. Patrick developed some other parts for the car, and it emerged some 70–80 lbs lighter. Ostensibly it used a year-old type-761 monocoque chassis, but as the old layers of paint were stripped it became apparent it had probably started life as early as 1974, wearing the orange Beta Tools livery of Vittorio Brambilla, 'The Monza Gorilla' – a man who had more accidents to his name even than Pescarolo in Frank's cars in 1972! Parts of the hard-pressed old tub had had damage cut out and repaired with new skin sections overlapping the old. It was virtually clinker-built – but it was a start...

The team's debut was to be made at Jarama for the Spanish Grand Prix on 8 May. The car was ready at last with ten days to go, and Neve tested briefly at Snetterton and then Silverstone on successive days, before the truck left for Spain with the car aboard. Neve qualified comfortably in Spain and finished twelfth.

Neve's second outing was to be on his home ground at Zolder in the Belgian Grand Prix, as Frank opted out of Monaco where the restricted field makes qualification a dicey gamble. The two Patricks went off to Zolder the week preceding official practice to test their car and set it up for the course, only for Neve to crash heavily. For a works team this would have been a logistical inconvenience. For a one-car private operation such as WGPE it was potentially disastrous.

Frank: 'It was about 11 o'clock on Friday morning when the telephone rang at Didcot and it was Patrick to tell me the car had just been destroyed. I called March immediately to see if they would have the personnel available to rebuild the monocoque over that weekend, and the truck brought the remains back to Unit 10 that evening, where Jon and the others tore everything that was usable off the twisted tub out on the forecourt, with oil and fuel dregs dribbling everywhere.

'We sent everything up to Bicester and they rebuilt the tub around its original cast-magnesium bulkheads and it was back to us, as new, by Tuesday. By that time we had assembled new suspensions for it and had a fresh engine ready. It was away to Zolder and was reassembled there by midnight on the eve of practice.'

Neve finished tenth in that, his home Grand Prix, and the 'new' Belle-Vue Saudia March competed in nine more Grands Prix that season, Neve qualifying in Sweden, at Silverstone, in Austria, Italy, the USA and Canada, but failing to make the grid in France, Germany and Holland. His best finish was seventh in the Italian race at Monza, and his lowest was eighteenth at Watkins Glen. But he retired only once from his season's eight GP starts, and that was in the final round in Canada, where his engine oil pressure warning light on the dashboard suddenly lit up, and he pulled in to save the engine – only for subsequent examination to prove that the unit was perfectly healthy and the signal had been spurious.

By that time Frank was directing operations on his own, for Patrick Head was glued to his seat in the drawing office at Didcot, designing his first Grand Prix car – the Williams FW06 – for 1978. Downstairs the much-coveted Formula One facility had begun to emerge, capable not merely of maintaining, preparing and running a Formula One car, but ultimately of constructing and seriously developing them too.

It was another fraught year, with Frank struggling to make ends meet. His sponsors had put up something in excess of £100,000 and Neve had qualified once in the top twenty on the starting grids, which earned around £800 start money. With prize money for his good race finishing record, the year's racing income reached a useful total – perhaps £15,000.

Clearly Patrick Neve hoped to be involved in Williams' plans for the coming year, but sadly for him Frank and Patrick Head had to aim higher. Neve had driven well enough and was a very pleasant young man, whose Belgian sponsors had played a vital part in WGPE's foundation. But he was not an aggressively ambitious, hungry driver of the kind who makes the grade in Formula One, and Frank had to look around. What he needed was an established, if not yet world-class name, who would be more attractive to major sponsorship and more likely to score, consistently, World Championship points. Force of circumstances led him to Alan Jones...

Formula One can be a hard life . . . Frank and Patrick
Neve in pensive mood, Österreichring 1977.

Patrick Neve and Frank Williams with the second-hand
March in the Jarama pits, Spanish Grand Prix 1977.

Nearly there – a reassuring pit signal for Alan Jones towards the end of the 1980 Spanish Grand Prix . . . and then the race lost its Championship status . . .

II · THE TEAM IN PROFILE

'In my view the real sportsman is one who regards racing not as a means to an end, but as an end in itself. It is not the easy victory, it is worthwhile results that count . . . It is not the title that makes the champion, but what he has got in him . . .'

Piero Taruffi: *The Technique of Motor Racing*, 1959.

Alan Jones, Team Driver 1978-81

The 1980 World Champion Driver was born with motor racing in his blood, on 11 November 1946, in Melbourne, Australia. His father, Stan Jones, was one of the great heroes of postwar Australian motor racing. He ran an extensive motor business, owned a farm and drove his heart out in a series of Maybach-engined specials which proved capable of taking on and beating all but the best imported exotica. Stan Jones went racing with heart and spirit and soul, racing to enjoy himself and to entertain his circle of friends. They had a good time. In a 1980 interview with Mike Doodson of *Motor* magazine, Alan recalled his late father as, 'Well, not a rough character, but a real personality. Last of the big spenders. He would go from Melbourne to Queensland (about a thousand miles) for a weekend race meeting with an entourage of about thirty people and put them up in hotels.

'Looking back it was a bit silly. I feel a bit pissed off because he sold off so much to help his ailing motor business. I still feel – perhaps I'm a bit selfish – that if he hadn't been so foolish with his money it might have helped me with my racing career . . .'

Stan Jones had won the Australian Grand Prix and the New Zealand Grand Prix, and towards the end of his lavish amateur racing career he campaigned one of the classical Maserati 250Fs, perhaps the most aesthetically beautiful of all traditional, front-engined Grand Prix cars.

Alan grew up in a family in which one went racing at weekends. It was a totally natural way of life. 'I went everywhere with him around Australia. I've never really known anything but cars and racing . . .'

He spent as little time as possible studying at Xavier College and opted out at sixteen, 'to get a driving licence; it's a funny system in Australia,' he told Ian Phillips, erstwhile Editor of *Autosport* magazine: 'In my homestate of Victoria you had to be eighteen, in New South Wales seventeen, and in South Australia sixteen. I established an address in South Australia and got my licence. This meant I could get a competition licence – and there I was in racing.'

He had found his feet in karting, and reigned as Victoria Junior Champion before aspiring to a tuned Mini 1000 which had been repossessed. Apparently it had cost £250, and Stan spent nearly £1,000 on hotting it up – rather to his horror. 'I went racing in club events with it; I thought I was the World Champion already – at the first corner I ever negotiated with the Mini, I spun. I was still sixteen when I won the Victoria Hillclimb Championship . . . it was a pretty fast car.'

The following year, 1963, he acquired an unfair advantage. 'Dad had this 2.2 Cooper in the garage. I asked him if I could take it out and clean it up and enter it for this sprint meeting at Calder. Eventually he agreed, so I became the only kid on the block with a 2.2. Wiped up everything in the Calder sprints, too . . . everyone else was in home specials, virtually . . .'

Stan had been selling up to three hundred cars a month from his Holden dealerships and was carrying a very large stock. Then came recession and a credit squeeze; business dropped away, and money was very tight in the Jones household. 'That put paid to my racing until 1969 . . .'

He came to England like so many Antipodean racers before him. He had been here before, in 1967, when he and fellow

Australian Brian McGuire toured Europe on a shoe-string, following the Grand Prix circus as spectators.

On his return home he had figured out his future: 'I still wanted to go racing and I reckoned there were two ways of going about it. I could either stay at home and with a bit of luck be Australian Champion, or else I could come to England, earn some money and then go racing.

'It sounds a typically Antipodean bullshit story – every Australian or New Zealander who ever came to England to race only had £50 – but I really only had seventy-five pounds in my pocket, my wife Bev lent me twenty-five to buy a Minivan, and Brian McGuire and I began buying and selling Minivans through *Exchange & Mart* so that we could go racing.'

They bought a spanking new Formula Ford Merlyn, and a scruffy Volkswagen pick-up to transport it. 'We went down to Brands Hatch, where the record was about fifty-six seconds. I got in it and, wow, I thought I was really flying, no trouble at all. I came in all chuffed and said: "What about that then?" "Fine," they said, "you've got down to 62 seconds".'

The chubby-faced young Australian may have been rather deflated but he was full of ambition. He didn't really fancy Formula Ford, using virtually standard Ford Cortina engines. He hankered after more power and bought a sleek Lotus 41 with a twin-cam Ford engine which he was confident he could use to learn the circuits and get to know 'the right people' and then ship back to Australia for resale at a profit, to finance a new Formula Three car. He got the Lotus running quite well, then became involved with a Formula Ford on Brands Hatch's notorious Paddock Hill Bend, and crashed mightily – destroying the car, and putting himself into hospital with a broken leg.

The enforced lay-off brought some rewards. He traded cars even more enthusiastically, and was able to buy a bent Brabham BT28 from yet another Australian racing émigré named Alan McCully. At that time Stan Jones had come to England to convalesce after suffering a stroke. He knew Ron Tauranac, the Brabham constructor, and arranged for all necessary parts to be made available to rebuild the car. After a couple of late-season 1970 Formula Three races in England Alan was invited to join the party travelling to Brazil for the Formula Three *Torneio* series that winter. He jumped at the chance, with reservations:

'My own engine was a real bitsa start-line special and Jim Hardman, who had helped me rebuild the car, warned me not to use it, so I bought a supposed Holbay screamer from Brendan McInerney. I was so far off the pace at Interlagos it was unreal. I was right at the back of the grid. The screamer was a disaster, and eventually blew up . . .'

Alan Jones was treading the path followed by so many, including Frank Williams, before him. For some it was merely an exciting hobby, an indulgence for private funds. For others like Alan it became obsessional, an end to which the means had to be generated. The majority gripped by such obsession would inevitably fall short of their ambitions. The minority with the grit, drive, determination and talent to batter their way to the top could achieve considerable fame and fortune. But there were no guarantees either way. No guarantee that one would succeed, and certainly none that one would fail.

In the last race of the *Torneio* at Porto Alegre he had to fall back on the suspect bitsa engine, and suddenly he was passing people! 'I was suddenly equal third quickest with Dave Walker in the works Gold Leaf Lotus. Peter Warr, the Lotus team manager, came up and measured the wing saying it was one thousandth of an inch too wide or something, and my father, who had already had several strokes, chased him out of our pit with his walking stick! He didn't need to check our wing. We knew so little about it, that it wasn't until we got back to London that someone told me I'd been racing the car with the front wings mounted upside down . . .'

Virtually three full seasons of Formula Three racing followed, forming the grandly titled Australian International Racing Organization for 1971 with McGuire and Alan McCully. Their Brabham BT28s were painted livid orange and ran Vegantune engines, which they were the first to use. AIRO proved to be a mistake – 'We wanted to attract a sponsor, but everyone thought we were either backed by the Australian government or were all multimillionaires.'

He won a minor race at Castle Combe, but to track-side observers it looked as though he was just another F3 hopeful, going nowhere. For 1972 Larry Sevitt of Tiran Auto promised backing for the team, which acquired three new Brabham BT38s and the former works team Formula One transporter. Alan showed better than his team-mates, but the season collapsed in animosity and recrimination and the team folded.

Off circuit, Alan Jones traded used cars to pay the bills. He had married Beverley in 1971, and there were responsibilities now.

'I was determined to make it in racing. There were plenty of times then when I was buying something with my Access card to pay off the Barclaycard bill. I'd go down to Thruxton and buy a set of slicks for the car on Sunday, not having a clue how I was going to meet the cheque on the Monday . . . But in one respect that was good, because I really appreciate what I've got now . . .'

He was back into racing at the British Grand Prix meeting in July 1972, driving a loaned GRD with a loaned engine – he just had to insure it all and pay the mechanic. It went well, and by the end of the year he could keep touch with the contemporary Formula Three stars like Roger Williamson and Tony Brise.

His new-found form impressed Mike Warner who ran GRD at Griston in Norfolk, this newish concern having been founded by ex-Lotus personnel. Suddenly the future looked bright. At the start of 1973 Warner fixed-up a GRD Formula Three drive for him and he signed a three-year contract with Scotsman Denys Dobbie's DART team, supposedly to progress year by year through Formula Three, then Formula Two and on into Formula One . . .

With a retainer being paid, plus the prospect of forty per cent of prize money and no worries apart from a few remaining bills from the previous year, Alan must have become a relatively happy man. But the team grew too big and complicated in mid-season, and politics wrecked all their good intentions. And Stan Jones died that year.

He had been living in England although crippled by a series of strokes. He died while Alan was testing the day before a Formula Three race on the club circuit at Silverstone. Mike Warner told Alan he would withdraw the car, 'But I said "No, no, for Christ's sake don't do that. That's exactly what I don't want you to do. Dad wouldn't want you to withdraw the car." '

In fact he had virtually destroyed his race chassis during a tyre test session two days earlier, and the GRD lads had hastily prepared an old 1972 tub for the race. He drove as if inspired, qualified on pole by a clear half-second – an unheard-of margin in contemporary Formula Three – and utterly dominated the race to win. 'Then when I got the laurel wreath for winning, I really broke up. It was just too much for me. I put the wreath in Dad's coffin and it went back to Australia with him for the funeral. It was a very emotional time for me . . .'

By the end of that season Alan was well in the lead of the Players Formula Three Championship, and he had merely to finish fifth or better in the last round to clinch the title. But in practice his engine blew apart and its race replacement deteriorated with every lap. He placed sixth, the round scored double points as it was the decider, and he lost the Championship.

Worse followed, as Dobbie abruptly quit racing in January 1974 and an alternative Formula Two/5000 deal which Alan had been hoping for turned to dust.

'I'd got nothing, and came close to going back home.' Tenacity is something he had never lacked, though, and he pestered everybody he could think of for a drive. One man he tried was Harry Stiller, Frank Williams' former benefactor in the early days of his Formula Three trading. The Bournemouth businessman put Alan in touch with one Mike Sullivan, who owned a Formula Atlantic March and was seeking a suitable driver. He was based in Colchester and on the telephone the equipment sounded fantastic: 'I must have broken all records from London to Colchester, but when I got there I found the transporter was an old Nestlés truck still with the Nestlés sign-writing on it, and the car was a '71 or '72 March. I thought, "Oh Christ, what have I done now? . . ."'

The car felt as dangerous as it looked during testing at Snetterton, and the men at March suggested he shouldn't drive it at all. But to continue in racing he had no alternative, and at Silverstone for the important Martini meeting he qualified on row two and won after the front-runners struck trouble.

'That made Harry Stiller sick, because he had recommended me for the drive, and his car, driven by Bev Bond, had qualified on pole.' The next race was through the trees at Oulton Park, very different from the wide open spaces at Silverstone. The ancient March felt positively evil, and for once Alan drew the line, saying he'd rather not drive.

'I knew I'd been lucky at Silverstone and had to have a competitive car. It's very difficult when you're 11,000 miles from home. You can't afford to mess about. I couldn't hop into the Datsun and go and see Auntie in Kent. I was married and I wanted to get on. That's why I was sometimes very serious. I wanted to get into Formula One, I'd got nowhere to go if I'd got a problem, so I couldn't afford to make mistakes . . .'

To help ends meet Beverley was running a boarding house for travelling Colonials in West London. It ran from 1974 to 1976 and was a means of income which gave him time for racing as well. 'We reckoned if we gave them a good breakfast and clean accommodation we could be in business. We catered for about fifteen people bed-and-breakfast and it helped to pay my rent, telephone and pocket money, and made me my own boss . . .' Still, life could not have been easy; looking back on those London days in general Alan recalls '. . . lying in bed and thinking about the £16,000 I owed. We had absolutely no chattels whatsoever, so I suppose I should have been quite proud that I had persuaded the bank manager to lend me that much. Bev helped a lot. I'm sure things would have turned out a lot different if I had been a single guy . . .'

Then Harry Stiller gave Alan a test-drive in his Atlantic March. He lowered the lap record. Regular driver Bev Bond stood down to become Team Manager and Alan took his place. The combination worked very well, won some events, lost more through mechanical failure, but led the last ten races of the year. In another team Patrick Head watched Jones go and thought he was, indeed, a very good driver . . .

At the end of that 1974 season Stiller planned to buy a new Lola T400 Formula 5000 car but the oil crisis was rumbling on and sponsorship was hard to find. Every winter had been a worrying time for the Australian driver – 'I'd never had a winter when I could relax and honestly say that I knew what I would be doing the following year. Eventually Harry phoned, out of the blue, and said, "I'm sick of buggering around. I've cancelled the F5000

deal and bought a Hesketh Formula One car. We're doing the *Daily Express* race at Silverstone."

'I couldn't believe it. From being totally messed about I was up at Hesketh's workshop, which was like a palace, being fitted into this immaculate Formula One car . . .'

He was seventh in the Hesketh at Silverstone, the race which marked Graham Hill's last drive in his own Embassy team car. At Barcelona Alan made his World Championship debut in the Hesketh, qualified well on the Spanish Grand Prix grid, but was out after only three laps having collided with Mark Donohue's Penske. Optimistically the little team journeyed to Monaco and Alan qualified for the eighteenth and last spot on the starting grid, but after lying twelfth for many laps he had a rear wheel come loose and his reliable drive was over.

At Zolder for the Belgian Grand Prix he qualified quite handsomely in mid-grid, but was rammed from behind by Jacques Laffite's Williams when braking hard to avoid a collision between Mass' McLaren and Watson's Surtees, and became the second retirement, after one race lap. In Sweden he survived the race distance to finish eleventh, but Harry Stiller abruptly closed down his Formula One team, and retired to California as a tax exile.

The instant Graham Hill got wind of Alan's availability he snapped him up to replace the injured Rolf Stommelen in his Embassy team, alongside Tony Brise. He took fifth place and two Championship points in the German Grand Prix at Nürburgring, and impressed everybody in the pit lane with his calm, methodical and friendly approach to Formula One. There was no drama, no histrionics, but Stommelen was fit again for the Austrian Grand Prix and Alan was out of Formula One.

John MacDonald gave him a Formula 5,000 drive instead, at the wheel of his RAM Racing March special, fitted with a Ford V6 engine. Alan was quickly winning in the car, and John Surtees offered a Formula One test drive with the possibility of a place in his Durex-sponsored team for 1976.

Surtees was a multiple World Motorcycle Champion, and had won the Drivers' World Championship with Ferrari in 1964. He was one of the top four Formula One drivers throughout the mid-sixties and began building his own Grand Prix cars under the

Team Surtees banner in 1970. He had retired from driving since then, but ran his team with an iron hand and almost obsessive attention to detail which some found wearing. Alan Jones was to be one of them.

'Fortunately, or I suppose I should say unfortunately, I was the quickest of whoever tested the cars and that got me the drive for 1976 . . .'

Problems started with a misunderstanding over his Team Surtees contract which was resolved at the airport with a Jumbo Jet delayed waiting to carry them to South Africa while Surtees and Jones disputed the conditions in the departure lounge . . .

'I would never have signed that contract in a million years if they weren't screaming that there was a Jumbo waiting. But you live and learn as you go along in racing. Unfortunately, when you're anxious to get your bum in a car you have a tendency to do things you wouldn't normally do and the longer you're in it you eventually realize that it's a business and it's got to be approached in a business manner . . .'

Despite his differences with John Surtees, Alan drove the TS19 cars in fourteen of the season's sixteen World Championship races, and picked up a fourth place in the last of them, at Mount Fuji, Japan, and was fifth in Belgium and at Brands Hatch. Right at the start of the year he had caused a sensation in the non-Championship Brands Hatch race, for which he qualified alongside James Hunt on row three of the grid, leading the race and finally finishing second behind the lanky McLaren star.

But after the experience of that season he felt he would rather stay out of Formula One in 1977: 'I didn't want to drive for Team Surtees, and I told John frankly that if the only way I could do Formula One was with him, then I would rather not do it. We had absolutely and utterly lost our communication with one another . . .'

He found new backing from Hong Kong millionaire enthusiast Teddy Yip, who provided a Formula 5000 car for him to drive in Australia and a USAC track-racer for the Championship Trail series, including the mighty Indianapolis 500-Miles classic – in the USA.

Stan Jones had won the Australian Grand Prix in his Maserati in 1959 and in Yip's Lola T332 Alan Jones jumped the start of the 1977 edition, won by 47 seconds, was penalized one minute for his transgression and ended up third. He crashed heavily to destroy the car at Surfers' Paradise and a replacement was flown out for Sandown Park – Yip was never backward in spending money on racing. Alan was in the lead on the fifth lap, when its engine overheated. He then started the last race of the series from pole position and lapped the second-placed car on the last corner of the race to win conclusively.

It was becoming obvious that here was a natural road-racing talent rapidly approaching maturity. But track racing in the USA was a different matter. There the banked oval tracks are generally around two miles in length with four turns at the most, all left-handers. Speeds of over 200 mph are common on the 'straightaways' and gearchanging and braking plays little part. Great road racers like Chris Amon and Pedro Rodriguez had been mystified by track racing before – Alan went the same way.

His first race in Yip's McLaren M16 track car was to be at Ontario, in California's vineyard country, but he had to wait for three days just for the wind to drop: 'I've never worn my overalls for so long and done so little. On the Saturday I did about twenty minutes of practice and the clutch went, so they whizzed the car back to the garage just as qualifying was due to start . . . I'd have to start at the back of the qualifying line. At that stage I just didn't want to sit in the bloody thing. I didn't have any feel for the car. It wasn't oversteering, it wasn't understeering . . . it just felt dead. I had no sensation of speed because there was no exhaust note' – the system being muffled by its turbo-supercharger, way back behind the driver's head – 'and you were screaming along near a brick wall – it didn't do a thing for me. I thought I was bound to start from the back of the grid and get in someone's way in the race. I wasn't happy in the car, so I pulled out.'

His Asiatic benefactor's remarkable warmth of character surfaced as Alan explained to Yip how he felt: 'He just said "No problem". Fantastic. He had flown me from Australia, paid hotels, and Christ knows what else and he was going to fly me back to Australia, and he just says "no problem" . . .'

Alan was back in Australia when the phone rang. It was Jackie Oliver of the Shadow team in England. Their number one driver Tom Pryce had just been killed in a horrifying accident in South Africa. Would Alan return to Formula One to drive for them?

'I accepted, because I thought they were a good team and they deserved to win. I reckon in Grand Prix racing there are the dead-loss teams, the ones that will never bloody win, and the ones that are always winning. I considered Shadow to be one team on the verge of a win . . .'

The Don Nichols American-inspired team had proved remarkably competitive in previous years but had suffered when they lost their major sponsor, Universal Oil Products. They had struggled on, losing their Chief Engineer Tony Southgate to Lotus, but now they were back on their feet with reasonable support and Southgate was returning: 'I knew he was coming back, it sounded as though there was a future there, so I jumped at it . . .'

Alan drove their white cars in fourteen of the seventeen rounds of that season's World Championship and after retirement in the first two, at Long Beach and Jarama, he was placed sixth for a point at Monaco, and fifth for two more in Belgium. His great day came on 14 August 1977, at Austria's Österreichring.

He had had a troubled time during practice, qualifying way back on the seventh row. But during race morning warm-up on the wet Sunday his car felt transformed. 'It's fabulous,' he told his mechanics, 'don't touch a thing . . .'

Early in the race there was little indication of what was to come. He ran tenth between Reutemann and Mass, but on lap eight he began his progress through the field, picking off Mass, Lauda and Tambay in successive laps. Three more times round, and he was ahead of Stuck. One more lap and he had taken Scheckter's scalp.

The track was slick and slippery and the rugged Australian was taking the race by the scruff of its neck, pulling off sensational overtaking manoeuvres which most others would fear to attempt. He was demonstrating his growing ability to sustain near maximum effort throughout a race distance, the talent to wear down his opposition by relentless pressure, and courage and skill.

After just sixteen laps James Hunt was leading for McLaren with Jones' Shadow sensationally in second place. With eleven laps to go Hunt's engine blew apart and Jones inherited victory, with the best race car on the track on the day, and he had made the most of it. He was almost beyond words at the end of the day, muttering, 'Unbelievable, just unbelievable' to himself, and only sorry that Dad wasn't around to see it.

And there was more to come; he was third in Italy, then fourth in both Canada and Japan to end the season with 22 World Championship points and seventh place in the competition. He was a fully-fledged Grand Prix driver now, and one in some demand as there were money problems with Shadow and he was keen to move.

Teddy Yip was having his own Formula One car built by Ron Tauranac, and Alan looked favourite to drive it, but he liked what he saw at WGPE in Didcot and accepted Frank Williams' offer instead. It brought him the 1980 World Championship title and, in the words of the mass media, international superstardom.

Such success wrought an inevitable change. He became publicly more arrogant and brash. Money had always meant much to him; some felt he made that too clear. But compared to many of his contemporaries he remained remarkably level-headed – 'sane', said the people he worked with, 'remarkably well-balanced and with his feet firmly on the ground'. But that does not deny a fiercely competitive spirit and an aggressive driving skill. He was never afraid to put his car into situations where other drivers would either have to collide with it, or back-off. A very physical driver, he was fit and strong and would sustain intense rhythmic, relentless pressure throughout a Grand Prix distance, while some of his leading competition might sustain greater pace, but only in brief bursts of pent-up energy. He would wear them down.

During the 1978 season Alan won the single-seater CanAm Championship title in the USA, driving a Jim Hall/Carl Haas-entered Lola in between his WGPE Formula One commitments. He went off to one race saying, 'I'll be taking it carefully this weekend', Patrick recalled, 'But I knew for sure that once strapped into that car he'd give it absolutely everything he's got. It's the only way he knows . . .'

As the Williams cars were developed and became successful with Alan at the wheel the criticism began. 'These cars are too easy

Alan Jones' maiden Formula One victory came in the 1977 Austrian Grand Prix at Österreichring,
where his Shadow proved dominant in viciously slippery conditions.

to drive, Jones is only where he is today because he's in the best car.'

Barbs like this understandably infuriated him. Throughout motor racing history – with the possible exception of the great Italian champion, Nuvolari, and Stirling Moss – the most successful drivers had almost always appeared in the most competitive and best-developed cars. Some of those who were decrying Jones' skill were remembering the days when they had seen him off in Formula Three – in superior equipment. And several times his Williams cars were not to be the fastest cars on the track on race day, and then his phenomenal ability as a Racer would shine through. The combative environment of the race itself always seemed to light a fire in him, right from the moment the starting lights flashed from red to green – for his start technique was outstanding, and many times he instantly made up places lost in qualification. In racing Frank Williams would signal him information only, leaving his racing mind to assess situations as they developed. There was never any question of 'Faster' or 'Slower' signals, and for the first half of a race he would never be shown the number of laps remaining – he didn't want to be reminded how far there was to go. He would give maximum effort, all the way...

Alan formed an excellent working relationship with Chief Engineer Patrick Head, and proved himself capable of painting the clear picture of the car's behaviour which was just what Patrick wanted in his relentless search for improvement. But essentially it seemed to be the act of driving in a race which gripped and fired Alan Jones: 'Once out of the car he becomes interested almost instantly in all kinds of other things. In a debriefing session you have to cram all your questions into the first ten minutes or so, when you can be sure you have Alan's total attention, and if it goes on much longer then he tends to glaze over and his thoughts are elsewhere... between races he can switch off totally, it seems. While somebody like Carlos Reutemann is ringing up and suggesting we might try the rear wing we tested three months ago, for Monaco or Zolder, we won't hear a dickey bird from Alan. But strap him into a racing car and he gives everything.'

Alan enjoyed spearheading a British team and was never averse to waving the Union Jack, particularly in the face of the French at Ricard when he beat the Ligiers and Renaults in the 1980 French Grand Prix. In Australia nobody had helped his career – it was British help which had made him a Formula One superstar.

When Carlos Reutemann became his number two driver for 1980 a protection clause was written into their contracts to give Alan priority as effective 'number one'. If both cars should be in contention, first and second within sight of the finish, Alan should finish ahead. There was hardly ever any real need to invoke the clause. For 1981 it would normally have been dropped. But Alfa Romeo made an attractive offer to the Australian, and the prospect of a second season's contractual protection as Williams 'number one' helped keep him at Didcot. In the 1981 Brazilian Grand Prix at Rio that celebrated incident occurred as Carlos ignored the 'JONES-REUT' signals brandished from the pits and led Alan home first and second. The Australian wasn't happy, but some sensed relish as he observed 'At least I know now who I've got to race against...'

His peers on the race track have perhaps understandably varied views on Jones the driver. In Brazil 1981 his chief rival, Nelson Piquet, considered: 'Alan is a great driver – probably the most determined guy in the business.' But after Nelson had sat fuming in the cockpit of his crashed Brabham for several minutes at Zolder after flying off the road, 'while the World Champion was in the vicinity', he said icily calm at Monte Carlo: 'He's totally mad. He had me off at Montreal last year, which I suppose I forgave him because of the tension surrounding the World Championship, but then he put me off at Zolder and didn't even come up to apologize. That's fine, I know where I stand, but if he does that again I'll put him off and I'll just say, "Sorry, my brakes failed"...'

Most of the drivers speak of Alan with considerable respect, though it is not surprising that it often sounds a bit grudging...

Gilles Villeneuve, Ferrari's ace: 'When you're racing close with him, you can rely on Alan not to do anything stupid. That counts for a lot...'

His predecessor as World Champion, Jody Scheckter: 'Alan's pretty quick, and he really works at it...'

Former Champion Mario Andretti – one of the most experienced and certainly the most versatile racing drivers the world has

Victory is sweet – especially over the French! Former Williams driver Jacques Laffite looks on; French Grand Prix, 1980.

ever seen: 'No question about it, he gets in there and gets the job done ...'

And the Ulsterman's view from Marlboro's driver John Watson: 'Alan's got all the team pulling in his direction. All credit to him for getting things organized to that point ...'

He is unusual for a modern Formula One driver in being a genuine car freak, poring over specifications and alternative equipment lists for the latest order, and enthusing over his 6·9 Mercedes, or Jaguar XJ12, or the off-road vehicles and motorhome. He developed quite a mouth-watering collection of Ferraris into the eighties; very conscious of their appreciating value as much as their pure motoring delight.

With success there had come the homes in Switzerland, California and Australia for the family – Beverley, and adopted son Christian. He indulged a growing interest in power boats, and watched his investments appreciate in the homes in Rancho Palos Verdes, above Los Angeles, in two apartments and a house in the Kew suburb of Melbourne and in his thousand acres of farmland – more than Dad ever owned – in Victoria

Everyone in the Williams team demands excellence; it's inbred in the principals and imbued in their staff, and Alan as their lead driver grew to expect it. Bad temper could erupt if such standards fell short, the Australian often using language he would later regret, but the storm would quickly blow itself out and few hard feelings would survive to simmer.

For much of his Formula One career he remained 'Alan the Approachable' to the Grand Prix press corps, the most accessible of the top-flight drivers. That tended to change, his team say 'almost like throwing a light switch', with one apparently trivial incident when he finished fourth in the French Grand Prix and one magazine caption described his performance as 'lack-lustre'. In fact he was the first Goodyear-tyred runner home behind the Michelin-shod Renaults and Ferraris and had driven his heart out. It was as if he realized at that moment that the worthies of the press did not and could not appreciate the effort a driver had to make to meet the demands of Formula One, and thereafter he was circumspect in his dealings with them. He explained to one

confidant, Mike Doodson: 'The truth is that I am becoming more single-minded as the pressures grow. Because of this I am shutting people out. I don't care if they don't like it. Primarily I'm in this business to win Grands Prix. If someone was prepared to pay me a retainer for talking to the press, then I'd be only too glad to take it. But I'm paid to drive a car, so I'd rather be good at that ...

'In Formula One, you must want to win very badly, you must want to beat the other guy. I don't care what the popular press or the man in the street says. And it doesn't matter what I'm doing in a car – tyre testing or racing – I have to be the quickest.'

Frank Williams understands and admires competitiveness. He recognized just how much Alan hated losing 'from the times his five-hundred dollar carbon-fibre racket has been hurled to the ground in my tennis court!' Alan admits his need to win.

'It is to feed my own ego, because I must believe that I am the quickest. When that drive stops, I'll get sick of racing ...'

His 1981 misfortunes with the virtually solid-suspended FW07C cars, which he disliked intensely, overwhelmed his enduring conviction he was still the quickest. On the eve of first practice at Monza he told Frank he wanted to retire at the end of the season, to spend more time with his family on their Australian farm. The team were appalled, their World Champion driver had agreed terms verbally for '82, was it now too late to find a top-class substitute?

Frank had been talking tentatively to Nelson Piquet and Didier Pironi, but both had re-signed for their current teams the week preceding Alan's bombshells.

Frank talked to his driver, reasoned with him, appealed to his weaknesses, 'You'll never be able to command so much money again ...' And to his eternal credit 'Jonesie', the man's racing driver, drove his hardest at Monza despite nursing a broken finger (which was his own fault for having become involved in a street brawl in London), and he hung everything on the line in Canada before utterly dominating his supposed swansong race at Las Vegas. No retiring World Champion had ever gone out on a win ... Would Alan Jones reconsider?

Clay Regazzoni, Team Driver 1979

British motor racing crowds seem to have a feel for drivers with heart. During the sixties they adopted a delightful Sicilian habit much photographed by the specialist magazines in coverage of the mighty Targa Florio sports car classic. There the locals painted slogans on walls and buildings, and on the track surface too, urging on their favourites. The graffiti read usually '*Viva Ferrari*' or '*Viva Vaccarella*' for the Sicilian champion, and '*Viva*' was rendered as the Italian abbreviation, two letters 'V', interlinked. At Silverstone before the Formula One International Trophy or Grand Prix races, '*Viva Gurney*' suddenly appeared white-washed on the track surface before the pits, and in later years, after Dan retired, the enthusiasts adopted another driver with heart – and the signs would read '*Viva Regazzoni*'.

Gianclaudio Giuseppe 'Clay' Regazzoni grew up like Frank Williams through the tough school of Formula Three racing. During the sixties he emerged as a feared competitor, an uncompromising charger who showed no fear and gave no quarter to any who stood in his way. Like so many motor racing madmen – for that is how many saw him – he was perhaps misunderstood; out of the car he was to become an open and charming gentleman.

He is Ticinese, from the Italian-speaking southern part of Switzerland, and was born on 5 September 1939, the son of a coach-builder from Lugano. His family was large, with a younger sister, an older brother and two younger brothers. At school he studied to become 'a commercialist' and qualified in arts and mechanical engineering. He later claimed his best subjects were school outings and rambles . . .

He began work in father's business at eighteen and was already an impassioned motor racing enthusiast. Stirling Moss was his hero, and when he scraped together sufficient cash to buy a car it was a frog-eye Austin-Healey Sprite which he drove in Swiss hill-climbs in 1963. These climbs make the parochial English brand look like soap-box derbys on a garden path, for while the longest British climb is less than a mile, many of the great European venues soar five miles or more into the mountains. Clay's debut was at one such classic course, at Schauinsland, where he was fourth in his class. He drove in four similar events that season, and 1964 found him hurling a 1-litre Mini-Cooper 'S' around in national hill-climbs and slalom meetings, his best result being second in a slalom at Payerne.

The leading Swiss driver in Formula Three at that time was the diminutive Silvio Moser and he encouraged Clay to go real motor racing, which meant to venture beyond the Swiss border, as circuit racing has been banned in that country since the Le Mans catastrophe of 1955. During 1965 he attended the *Schweizer Automobil Rennsportclub's* racing drivers' course at Montlhéry Autodrome outside Paris, and he qualified for his International licence.

He gathered together enough cash to invest in an Italian De Tomaso Formula Three car, but its engine failed first time out, at Imola. He was sixth at Magny-Cours, but the car was exchanged for one of Moser's Brabhams. At the close of the year, or so the story goes, he drove in a Formula Two race at Syracuse, qualified fastest but crashed on the opening lap.

In 1966 Clay continued in Formula Three as his do-or-die reputation began to grow. He won his heat in the supporting race to the Italian Grand Prix at Monza, but, in the final, Argentinian Carlos Pairetti spun in his path, the cars collided and Regazzoni's Brabham was destroyed. He was lucky to emerge with nothing worse than gashes requiring six stitches.

But his money had run out, and he felt then that his racing days were over. A telephone call changed his life. It was the Pederzani brothers, who ran the Tecno kart and racing car company in Modena. Would he like to test their new Formula Three car? It was a case of mutual appreciation at first sight, and Clay journeyed to the Argentine Temporada early in 1967 as part of Tecno's three-car team, alongside former Ferrari works driver Giancarlo Baghetti and Carlo Facetti. Clay was not to be paid for his time, but was hoping for a half-share in any prize money ...

He must have failed to impress the Pederzanis, as on his return to Europe the works Tecno F3 seat was entrusted to Jerseyman Boley Pittard, and returned to the Ticinese only after Bo's abrupt departure from the team. The new car was quick and nimble and 'Regga', as he became known, featured prominently in some of the fearfully close cut-and-thrust Formula Three racing of the day. At Hockenheim during the European Formula Three Trophy meeting Regga's reputation was emphasized as he punted off both Derek Bell of the British team and Jean-Pierre Jaussaud of the French *équipe* in the closing moments, finishing second and controversially assuring the Swiss national team of the Trophy! That October he made his British debut at Brands Hatch in the Motor Show '200' meeting where Piers Courage drove a Frank Williams (Racing Cars) entry for the first time, and in November, with a strong Novamotor-Ford engine at last behind his shoulders, Clay won at Jarama in Spain. It was his first major victory, and it put Tecno's name on the map as a serious Formula Three constructor, and won them considerable custom for 1968.

That season saw Regazzoni driving Tecnos in both Formula Two and Formula Three. He won at Monza and Vallelunga in Italy in the minor class, but the major Monaco F3 race frightened him badly and put him out of the 1-litre class for good ...

Diving left-right through the quayside chicane he lost control and spun into the new guardrail which had been installed to prevent a recurrence of the 1967 Grand Prix accident which took the life of Lorenzo Bandini. The new guardrail was not, however, properly anchored and the Tecno burrowed its way underneath while the rail somehow bowed up, cleared Clay's head, and then sprang down again in front of the roll-over bar. It was a miraculous escape by any standards.

Neither was the Formula Two Tecno particularly effective, both its handling and brakes being suspect. Third place at Crystal Palace was Clay's best European Championship result and he crashed several times. The Pederzanis seemed not to take his criticisms of the car too seriously until at the end of the year fellow-Swiss Jo Siffert joined him for the Argentinian Temporada series and confirmed all he had said.

On his return from Argentina Clay received the telephone call which every Italian-speaking driver must covet – from Mr Ferrari's right-hand man, in this case Dr Franco Gozzi, asking if he would like to drive a Formula Two works Ferrari in 1969?

The offer was a double-edged sword. The money was more than Tecno could afford – despite Ferrari never being renowned for their generosity – yet in the Temporada the Ferraris had been dominant. But back in Europe the V6s from Maranello were to be shadowy also-rans in comparison. Rumour-mongers held that the team had run 2-litre engines in Argentina, against Cosworth 1600cc opposition, and certainly in Europe the 1600cc V6s could make no impression. Perhaps the drivers were poor too?

Clay knew better. Preparation was poor in 1969 as Ferrari was attacking Formula One, Formula Two, endurance, CanAm and hill-climb competition; the Italian motor industry at large was riven with industrial unrest; and Maranello had clearly bitten off more than they could chew. Secondly the Firestone YB11 compound tyres available only to Ferrari in Argentina were now freely available to all. Thirdly the Cosworth FVA engines had been further developed, and were giving more power than ever before, while the Ferrari V6 had stood still.

Clay drove only four races in the blood-red cars and his best finish was a meagre tenth at Thruxton. After June the cars were withdrawn and he returned to Tecno. He placed fourth at Enna and crashed at Albi. Good old Regga ...

Tecno gave him another try in Formula Two in 1970, and he

Young Regazzoni in his Tecno days.

Ragged Regazzoni, slithering his Tecno around the Buenos Aires Autodrome in frantic efforts to hold off the local lad's *La Razon*-sponsored Williams-supplied Brabham – the local lad was Carlos Reutemann. Temporada 1968.

drove for Ferrari at Le Mans in their hastily-prepared 5-litre V12 long-distance cars and became embroiled in a spectacular four-car pile-up. Immediately afterwards he was asked to test a Formula One Ferrari 312B with a view to joining Jacky Ickx in the Dutch Grand Prix at Zandvoort.

That was the tragic race in which Piers Courage died. It was Clay's Formula One debut and he finished in the points. The car was very good, very fast and it became very reliable, as did Clay's driving. The old wild man image was being replaced by that of an extremely competent Formula One driver. It was his best season ever. He won the Italian Grand Prix at Monza to the thunderous cheers of the *tifosi*, chanting 'Regg-Aah-Zoooni, Regg-Aaah-Zoooni' far into the gathering September dusk long after the race had finished. He was placed third in the World Drivers' Championship and his Tecno carried him to victory in the European Formula Two Championship!

It had been a season to savour – for him.

At the season's beginning it had been expected that Clay would have to fight for his second seat in the Ferrari team with another promising tyro, Ignazio Giunti. Clay emerged ahead with his Italian GP victory and second places behind team-leader Ickx in Austria and Mexico.

He continued as a valued Ferrari team member through 1971–72, while poor Giunti lost his life in a sports car race in Buenos Aires. Clay won the non-Championship Brands Hatch Formula One race at the beginning of 1971, but Ferrari development stumbled and although Ickx won the Dutch Grand Prix that season great success eluded them. During 1972 Clay shared the winning Ferrari sports-racing car with Ickx in the Monza 1,000 Kms and in his final fling with Ferrari right at the end of that season he won the Kyalami 9-Hours 'enduro' in South Africa.

That autumn saw Mr Ferrari announcing a cut-back in Ferrari's programmes, which did not in fact materialize but which showed Regazzoni the door. The announcement that he was to leave Ferrari was made after the German Grand Prix in August and created some sensation. He was in great demand, and following an audience with BRM's imposing Mr Louis Stanley at the Italian Grand Prix, Clay's signing for the British team was made public.

He crashed one of their cars on first acquaintance, during testing at Silverstone, but made amends by clocking record laps and then qualifying his BRM on pole position for his debut race with the team, at Buenos Aires in January 1973. Clay led the race until almost one-third distance, when his tyres lost grip. After a pit stop to fit new rear tyres he eventually finished seventh, but had put new heart into BRM.

In South Africa that year he crashed heavily and was trapped, stunned, in the cockpit of his burning BRM. Mike Hailwood's Surtees had been involved in the same incident and, regardless of his own safety, 'Mike the Bike' plunged into the flames and heaved the Ticinese clear, subsequently being awarded the George Medal for his bravery.

Clay's burns kept him out of the cockpit for five weeks before he returned to finish third in the International Trophy race at Silverstone. But BRM's V12 engines became sadly unreliable and uncompetitive as the season progressed, and Clay scored only one more World Championship point with sixth place in the Austrian Grand Prix. He also tried his hand with Autodelta's works Alfa Romeo sports-racing cars during the season, but at the end of the year Louis Stanley's autocratic direction of BRM finally estranged even the easy-going and normally very considerate Regazzoni. Stanley dropped him from the team for the Canadian Grand Prix, telling him loftily, 'It is rather like a football team, you are on the reserve bench . . .'

Unsurprisingly Clay moved for 1974, returning to Ferrari as team-mate to Niki Lauda – another BRM escapee. When Ermanno Cuoghi, one of the Ferrari team's joint Chief Mechanics, described their two drivers that year as 'The experienced old man and the brilliant young boy', he was close to the truth. Lauda himself, not known for his warmth of personality, wrote of Clay: 'We were never real friends, but I valued him. He is so perfectly the type of racing driver: small, rough and stocky; moustache; likes women. He is a typical cinema champion, the kind people sometimes think of as being the real thing. He is still one of the old guard drivers . . .'

That season saw Lauda win his maiden World Championship Grand Prix and Regazzoni provide admirably consistent support. At Monaco Clay led but was crowded by Lauda and spun. A 'discussion' ensued at their hotel. Clay won at Nürburgring after Lauda's inexperience had put him out on the opening lap. Towards the end of the year Clay was in the running for the Championship, Lauda had blown his chance. Later Clay admitted: 'I can't understand why Maranello didn't want me to be World Champion. After the German Grand Prix with only four races to go . . . I was in the lead with forty-four points to Niki's thirty-eight. It would have been enough to base the team strategy for victory on me in order to put an end to the subject. At Monza I should have gone into the lead and Lauda would have covered me. Instead, both of us went all out, ruined our engines. In Canada he should have stayed close to Fittipaldi and I would have taken care of the rest, but my friend shot into the lead and then left the track. Emerson won the race, joining me at the top of the table . . .'

At Watkins Glen the deciding round saw Clay needing only three points to win – Fittipaldi needed fourth place to win, Scheckter had a chance too for Tyrrell. 'I was driving a virtually uncontrollable car. I started well and passed Fittipaldi, I only needed to stay ahead to win . . . After a few laps the Ferrari became impossible. The tyres were changed but it was the same story. The suspension was adjusted, it was improved. But it was too late. On top of this Mass in the McLaren hit my car and broke the wheel hub. End of the race. That was my blackest day, and a great disappointment, because the World Championship title would have given meaning to my whole career . . .'

Through 1975 Lauda's career reached maturity and Ferrari power and reliability brought him the World Championship, eleven years after John Surtees' last Formula One title for the team. Clay played second fiddle, scoring in six of the fourteen Championship rounds and winning again at Monza, when Niki clinched his new title and the *tifosi* just went mad with delight.

For the third consecutive season Clay ran the second Ferrari alongside Lauda in 1976, and in the first United States Grand Prix (West) at Long Beach, California he achieved the rare perfection of the ultimate motor racing performance – he qualified his car on pole position, led every race lap to win, and set fastest lap on the way. He took second places in Belgium, Holland and Italy and was fifth – for the second year running – in the Drivers' Championship.

But at thirty-seven he was an old man by modern Formula One standards (Fangio had not started racing in Europe until he was thirty-eight, but that was in a very different era), and cracks appeared in the old relationship with Ferrari.

Mr Ferrari disliked any of his drivers developing independent financial links. Clay was good-looking and promotable. He fronted for a line of sports wear and jeans. Regazzoni jeans featured the Prancing Horse of Ferrari on the backside; the Old Man was incensed. Then Clay had lost the chance of a good finish at Monaco when he clouted a barrier. A black mark from Ferrari. He pushed Lauda too hard into the first corner at Brands Hatch, their Ferraris collided and spun and chaos engulfed half the field. A blacker mark from Ferrari. After Lauda was burned in the accident at Nürburgring the team opted out of the Austrian Grand Prix, then ran a single car for Clay at Zandvoort.

The Old Man's instructions to him before that race were typical Ferrari, stoking a fire beneath the cauldron into which his drivers had for years been willing to plunge: 'Now that you are alone I do not want you to take too big a share of the responsibility. Race as you would in normal circumstances – and forget that everything depends on you . . .'

As it happened he missed second place by less than one second, but after starting his charge – the Ferrari camp implied – too late in the day. Lauda was back at Monza for the Italian Grand Prix, and Carlos Reutemann had joined the team to drive a third car. It was known that Clay was on his way out. Lauda lost his World title to James Hunt in Japan, but Ferrari retained their coveted Constructors' Championship title.

At the end of the season Mr Ferrari talked of Regazzoni at his annual press conference: 'Regazzoni is a very good friend and we wish this relationship to continue because there is no one more pleasant and correct than Regazzoni. But if you ask me for an opinion as to how Regazzoni races, I would tell you that Regazzoni races for himself – as I did . . .'

Out of Ferrari for 1977 Clay signed with Morris Nunn's one-car Tissot-Castrol Ensign team. He placed fifth in the Italian and United States (East) GPs and was sixth in Argentina – none could have done better in that car. For 1978 he moved to Don Nichols' Shadow outfit, as a driver clearly in the twilight of his career. He placed fifth in Brazil and Sweden, and signed with Frank Williams for 1979 – the season which revalued him as a driver, and brought him that memorable victory in the British Grand Prix.

Ferrari had said of Clay: 'He is a bon viveur, dancer, playboy, footballer, tennis player and, in his spare time, driver.' Clay said of himself: 'I couldn't lead a life like Lauda's, by sacrificing everything to training and preparation. I like to travel, to eat, I enjoy the cinema, golf, tennis – everything else that life can offer. I like to stay with my wife Pia and my two sons...'

And he added: 'I'm not ambitious. By that I mean I don't race to win at all costs, but that I prefer perhaps to come second or third, knowing that I've given everything possible, instead of winning badly. And I like racing. I enjoy it. If in order to go faster and to be able to give even more, I was asked to lead the life of a monk on the circuits, I would stop, because then I wouldn't enjoy it any longer. I don't think about the Championship. For me each race is a Championship, and I give my all...'

He spent a lot of time at the Didcot factory and became immensely popular with the staff there. There was a lot of humour – despite the team's on-circuit reputation. Both Patrick Head and Frank Williams can be amusing mimics. Gwen Brown, Frank's secretary: 'I thought Clay was wonderful, and one day in the office he said something to a friend he had with him, something which Frank overheard. It was a fairly flattering remark about me – Clay always made a great fuss. Later that evening I was at home and the telephone rang. It was Clay's voice. He was at a loose end in London, would I like to meet him for a meal on the town? Well of course I went all feminine and coy, and I was just wondering whether to say yes or not when the voice suddenly changed and it was Frank roaring with laughter and saying, "Ahaa, got you going that time, Gwen!" I have never forgiven him...'

But at the end of 1979 their ways had to part. Clay had done well by Saudia-Williams, and they had done well by him. His career had been revived, and it was time for the team to attract a genuine world-class driver to support Alan.

Frank: 'It had become apparent that Clay was appreciably slower than Alan in an identical car. For him to win races we needed an unusual set of circumstances, like the total domination which we had established at Silverstone. Later in the season it was very apparent the other teams were catching up. Clay was consistently about one second a lap slower than Alan, and that was too much. We needed two genuine winners in the team.

'About August I said to him that I thought I should be honest and tell him that we were looking for a new driver for the coming year. We were hoping to attract Carlos Reutemann who was unsettled at Lotus, but negotiations were going to be long and involved, and I was prepared to wait. Therefore Clay should feel free to look around...

'Naturally he was disappointed, but I'm sure he appreciated the position and our honesty. I said to him that if it didn't work out and if I should come back to him and ask him to stay on for 1980 what money would he want from us? And it was absolutely typical of Clay that he said straight away, "How much you pay me this year, I can't remember?" That was highly unusual amongst modern Formula One drivers; Clay was not a man motivated by money. If I'd said "ten grand" I'm sure he might have said, "Oh, fine, how does fifteen sound then?" He was a gentleman, we all liked him, but we had to progress...'

Clay went to Ensign for the new year, and at Long Beach smashed his legs and damaged his spinal column in an appalling accident. He was crippled, a paraplegic, but he fought it, enduring the most complex micro-surgery, and into 1981 feeling was returning, he could walk again on sticks. Still the smile was there, and the cavalier eyes, and that old spirit...

Mr Ferrari knew what he was about when he sent a cable to Clay the day after his British Grand Prix victory. It simply reminded him that Nuvolari scored his most spectacular victories when he was forty. Clay understood, but his victories were no longer to be in racing.

Carlos Reutemann, Team Driver 1980-81

All aspiring racing drivers dream of becoming World Champion. But only a tiny percentage of all those who tackle professional racing will succeed in finding their way into Formula One, and of those thirty or so men who contest each World Championship season, only one can become king.

The competition was created as recently as 1950, and when Alan Jones began his reign at the close of the 1980 season he was only the eighteenth man to wear the crown. Eight of them had been multiple Champions, with the legendary Argentinian Juan Manuel Fangio at their head, with five titles to his name during the fifties. Sir Jack Brabham and Jackie Stewart had won three times each; Alberto Ascari, Graham Hill, Jimmy Clark, Emerson Fittipaldi and Niki Lauda twice each.

It would appear to be true that the modern Championship is far more difficult to win than those of Fangio's day. There are more qualifying Grands Prix run each year and the spread of competitive cars is rather wider. But for any world-class driver the lure of that World title must be irresistible. As years go by the unsuccessful ones may grow hungrier, or may accept that it is not to be ... and then sit back on what laurels they have achieved.

When Frank Williams and Patrick Head selected Carlos Reutemann as an admirable candidate to become Jones' teammate for 1980–81, they were dealing with one of the hungriest and most experienced competitors for that Championship crown.

In the Argentina of Reutemann's youth, Juan Manuel Fangio had become almost a deity, a great international sportsman whose ability dominated the racing world – a man to emulate, if you could.

In his quest for that elusive World Championship title the tall handsome Reutemann with his piercing ice-crystal blue eyes and swarthily expressive features had been around the top teams, from Brabham through 1971–76, then Ferrari until 1978 and on to Lotus in 1979.

He had won Grands Prix for Brabham and Ferrari and had gone to Lotus at the end of a season in which their new-generation ground-effects cars had ruled the world. For 1979 their team of reigning World Champion Mario Andretti and the highly-skilled Carlos Reutemann had looked all-conquering on paper. In practice their new-series car proved a delusive flop, and Reutemann's old team, Ferrari, gave Jody Scheckter the World title while Saudia-Williams won the lion's share of races with Alan Jones and Clay Regazzoni. By the autumn of that year Frank and Carlos were talking seriously towards the new year ahead, and not for the first time the Argentinian freed himself to drive in a team whose cars would give him truly competitive edge once more ... Now that World title was again within his grasp, and at thirty-eight this could be, perhaps, his last chance...

Carlos Alberto Reutemann was born of mixed German-Italian stock in Santa Fé, Argentina, on 12 April 1942. His paternal grandfather was a Swiss-German who emigrated in the early part of the century to found a farming business in Santa Fé province. His mother had Italian origins, his grandmother coming from Castellazzo Bormida in Piedmont.

Naturally he grew up as a true Argentinian, he spoke no German but acquired some Italian from his mother, alongside Argentina's native Spanish. After an ordinary schooling he joined his elder brother on the family *estancia*, raising beef and growing cereals.

Early on he won the nickname 'Lolé'; Lolé Reutemann, 'El Lolé' or simply 'Lolé' to the countless fans who pack Buenos Aires Autodrome every year for his star appearance in his home Grand Prix. Through his early years in Europe he would seldom talk directly of his nickname's origins. Apparently it came at school, when he would be asked, 'What does your father do?' He would say 'He farms pigs.' In Spanish pigs are *Los Lechones*, and the 's' in *Los* is silent. It sounded like 'Lolechones', so 'Lolechones' he became – or more simply 'Lolé'.

Like his nickname, his interest in cars came early. He was seven or so when his father bought an ancient 1928 Model A Ford on which Carlos could teach himself to drive. Carlos explained: 'In school, when I have sixteen, seventeen years, I follow the racing of Fangio, Ascari, Farina, Castellotti and the racing in Argentina of Galvez. In the second year after I leave school I make circuit on the farm with wooden posts, driving, driving, driving...'

Fangio retired from competition in 1958 and Argentinian racing turned in upon itself apart from annual visits by a Mercedes-Benz factory saloon car team to the *Gran Premio* public road point-to-point race – more like a motor rally by modern standards. Carlos was there with his friends to watch the cars go by, the Mercedes-Benz team dominating with European drivers like Eugen Bohringer and the Swedish lady Ewy Rosqvist, and the Lancia team from Italy with Leo Cella and Carlo Facetti at the wheel.

These road races covered enormous distances, for Argentina is a truly vast country. This was the type of racing in which Fangio had cut his teeth, and in 1965 Carlos Reutemann made his debut as a racing driver.

The Fiat agent in Santa Fé was running a car and Carlos badgered him into a test drive. Three months later he received the invitation to go to Cordoba to start practising for the *Turismo* race in a Fiat saloon. There was no instant stardom, his first race ending as his car's oil pressure zeroed.

Second time out it was a different story. The venue was another public road circuit outside Cordoba, the race covering three laps of around sixty miles each – like the classical Targa Florio in Sicily. On his second lap Carlos was running second by thirteen seconds. There was a radio link with the car's owner, who told him to make his own decision: settle for second or risk all and go for the lead. To an ambitious young twenty-three-year-old that was no choice at all; he charged, and won. It was the first of his fifteen *Turismo* victories that season, the nation's extensive and enthusiastic motor sporting press was full of the newcomer's immense potential, and Lolé Reutemann had arrived.

For 1966 his sponsor acquired an Italian-made De Tomaso to give him single-seater experience. Alejandro de Tomaso was Argentinian by birth, of course, and the Santa Fé dealership people fitted a 1500 cc four-cylinder Fiat engine into the car for local Formula One racing.

With no more than 120 bhp behind his shoulders, Carlos was immediately competitive against the established single-seater 'names'. In his very first race with the car he fought his way into second place before something failed and put him out. Several more good drives followed in the De Tomaso–Fiat while he also campaigned Fiat saloons in the 1600 cc *Turismo* class championship.

He was to win that title in 1967 with seven *Turismo* class victories, and the De Tomaso was pressed into service for its second season, now with larger wheels and tyres. He scored what he considered to be a most significant success in the Paz hill-climb in Cordoba, where the event was arranged as the aggregate of two runs, the first up to the top of the hill, and the second back down again!

That season also saw the tall slim young man from Santa Fé entering *Turismo Carretera* racing behind the wheel of a grotesquely cut-down American Ford Falcon sedan stripped stark and bare, and powered by a 292-cubic-inch V8 engine delivering all of 320 bhp. This type of special, owing as much to the original production model as does a British-style stock car, occupied a very significant place in the Argentinian scheme of things at that time, and Reutemann's was a full works entry.

Since 1964 the state-owned YPF oil company had been organizing an International Formula Three race series in the heat of the

Argentinian summer, from which the series took its name, the *Temporada*. In 1968 the organizers raised the stakes and imported a representative European Formula Two field, including the Frank Williams Brabham for Piers Courage, a similar Winkelmann team car for Jochen Rindt, Tecnos for Jo Siffert and Clay Regazzoni and works Ferrari Dinos for Andrea de Adamich and Tino Brambilla. Back in the late forties similar imports had given drivers like Fangio and Froilan Gonzales an international yardstick by which to measure their talents. Now the series organizers invited fourteen pressmen to select six Argentinian drivers to represent the home side, two of them to drive Tecnos brought over by the English team patron, Ron Harris ... and others to drive Williams-imported Brabhams.

Carlos Reutemann was one of the selected six, and the final choice for the Tecno pair would be decided in a run-off at Buenos Aires Autodrome, there in the sprawling city's Parque Almirante Brown.

The car to be used was the Formula Three Brabham which local drivers Carlos Pairetti and Jorge Cupeiro – who were already provided with F2 Brabhams – had campaigned in Europe the previous year, when Pairetti had his collision with Regazzoni at Monza ...

Each driver did five laps in the morning against the clock, then the afternoon would see them running in reverse order, and reverse direction, for another five. Reutemann was third fastest in the morning but fastest overall in the afternoon. He and Carlos Marincovich were selected for the Tecno drives.

These cars were but shadowy opposition to the Brabhams in that series, but Carlos felt it was a great moment in his life as he settled into his Tecno for the first time at the Autodrome. The series was a troubled one for him, until the fourth race back at Buenos Aires when he was invited to drive the Brabham sponsored by the *La Razon* newspaper, originally brought over by Frank Williams for Eduardo Copello's use. He found the difference between Tecno and Brabham 'was like night to day', and in the first heat he battled wheel to wheel with Regazzoni's works Tecno before – inevitably – spinning off on to the grass verge. He finished eighth, which was good enough. The second heat began with one

of the Ferraris ploughing into a group of marshals and in the subsequent chaos Carlos ran fifth behind names like Rindt, Courage, Jack Oliver and Jo Siffert. The latter pair touched and spun, Lolé was third with the partisan crowd chanting his name. Next time round his engine's oil pressure zeroed and he was out.

As the fastest of the local drivers in the series there was talk of *La Razon* despatching him to Europe for the 1969 European Formula Two Championship. The paper's proprietors were prepared to pay for the Brabham car, engines and a manager but offered nothing for Reutemann's services as a professional driver. He was now married to Mimicha – and a baby was on the way. He felt strongly that his family should not be expected to support him for a season in Europe: 'I ask for the minimum money to live in England, and *La Razon* say "too much" ...'

The project was to lie fallow that year, but salvation was on the way from diminutive but energetic little Hector Staffa of the *Automovil Club Argentino*. Staffa was an arch-enthusiast with a knack for getting things done. He had been working for the ACA since 1941 when he had joined them as a sixteen-year-old office boy. From the mid fifties he pursued a private quest for the new Fangio, and for the 1969 national Formula Two season he organized a two-car team with YPF backing. Its cars were painted white; a rather suspect ex-Enzo Corti Italian BWA creation for Reutemann, and an ex-Cacho Fangio (Juan Manuel's son) Brabham BT18 for former motorcyclist Benedetto Caldarella.

There were twelve races in the series, Reutemann won ten of them and Caldarella one for the ACA team. They finished 1–2 in the national Championship. All Argentina marvelled. Most enthusiasts were not too bothered that the opposition had been slim, but Carlos ruefully admitted as much, and found that the cars' 140 bhp Fiat engines hardly made them exciting things to drive. His outings in *Turismo*, *Turismo Carretera* and SP – the Argentinian sports-prototype category – meant more to him.

January 1970 saw a new Temporada series in Buenos Aires, but this time for sports cars, Formula Two having proved too costly and of little real interest to local fans, as the Europeans had walked off with all the trophies.

There were to be two major sports car races on successive

weekends at the Autodrome and in the first Carlos was paired with Jack Oliver in a Lola T70 Coupé. They finished sixth overall and he was the best-placed Argentinian. The following weekend he did the trick again, sharing a Porsche 908 this time with the Spanish Prince Jorge de Bagration. It all made fine copy for the local press, and coincidentally Hector Staffa had been working feverishly to set up a new Formula Two team to tackle a European tour, and Reutemann's good showing settled the matter.

Staffa won backing from the ACA and YPF again, and added support from the national tourist office and from SEPAC, the Ministry of Sport. Money was no problem and Staffa, Reutemann and Caldarella were to arrive in England to put together the most lavish Formula Two team yet seen. They bought brand-new Brabham BT30 cars, eight new Cosworth FVA engines, a cavernous team transporter, and staffed a lavish London workshop with numerous imported mechanics.

The author was one of the first journalists to meet the team after their arrival in a Kensington hotel. The Embassy interpreter did a magnificent job, personable little Staffa positively bubbled, Caldarella related how he knew Europe already from his two-wheeled racing tour, and the tall, dour, impassive Reutemann in his duffle coat grinned just once, and said nothing.

It was to prove a difficult season for the ACA team. They were strangers in Europe, there was a language barrier between them and most other teams, and there was some adverse reaction to their evident wealth. Their entries were even being handled direct from Buenos Aires, and they did not mix. Aloof and apart they did not gel into the Formula Two scene, even though they might have wished to...

Their season had begun at Hockenheim, near Heidelberg in West Germany, where Carlos clipped Rindt's sliding Lotus and spun it round, sparking a multiple collision while he blared on to a good finish. In the break between heats Rindt appeared at the ACA enclosure in the paddock and indicated emphatically that Indians belonged in the jungle, not on the race track. The Argentine pressmen trailing the team set the wires to Buenos Aires alight with their copy – the fact that Carlos finished well in heat two and was placed fourth overall became submerged by the controversy.

Throughout that season Carlos proved himself a forceful and aggressive driver, but never as wild as that brief incident at Hockenheim had at first suggested. Caldarella drove poorly in comparison and family problems soon demanded his return home. Carlos had to try desperately hard to protect his team's image, and he took the responsibility very seriously. He seemed morose and withdrawn, he did not seek new friendships in Europe. The hopes of Argentina lay with him alone and when some competitors occasionally complained of his aggressive tactics, in truth he had no alternative: 'I'm driving flat,' he later explained, '... do you think it's better for me politically to be careful?'

Driving 'flat' made him the sensation of wet-weather practice for the Eifelrennen at Nürburgring, where he had spent two weeks practising in a Ford Capri. He then started at Crystal Palace on the front row beside Jackie Stewart and François Cevert. At the second Hockenheim meeting only Emerson Fittipaldi qualified faster, but in the race Tino Brambilla crushed the ACA Brabham's nose-cone. At Rouen he raced third on the heels of Rindt and Regazzoni before spinning on to the grass. Everywhere he was sideways, and very, very fast. He felt this ACA tour was a once-only opportunity – he had to make the best of every race.

But the team had made a poor choice of engine preparer and they ended the season with little to show in firm results. Nobody knew whether the sponsors would finance a return trip for the 1971 season. Back in 1948 Fangio had dominated European second-division racing on his first full tour. Staffa's chosen driver had fallen far short this time... How many appreciated how much more competitive modern racing had become?

Back home Carlos co-drove a Porsche 917 with Emerson Fittipaldi in the Buenos Aires 1,000 km. The car suffered lurid understeer in slow corners but was very fast on the back of the circuit. Unfortunately for Reutemann the slow corners were overlooked by the press stands, and his talents were criticized in his home land, virtually for the first time.

After that, any chance of a return to Europe must have seemed slim, but then came the non-Championship Formula One Argentine Grand Prix. YPF hired a car for a local driver and as the most experienced Argentinian in single-seaters Lolé was their man. The car was Jo Bonnier's ancient McLaren M7C which had been uncompetitive in the few European races for which the veteran Swede had qualified. Reutemann saw the drive purely as good experience, but still thrilled as the Cosworth V8 engine fired-up behind his shoulders, '. . . just like two Formula Two engines!' In the race he drove carefully to ensure the McLaren survived to the finish and, profiting by retirements amongst the leaders, he finished third. The public loved him . . .

The President of YPF responded by authorizing financial support for the ACA F2 team's return to Europe. Now they had a clearer idea of how to tackle the European Championship, they took on a professional agency in Britain to handle their entries and travel arrangements, found a new workshop in Slough and ordered two new Brabham BT36s from Ron Tauranac. Unfortunately the order was placed late, and the first was not available until June. Carlos Ruesch joined Reutemann as second driver, and again the vast ACA transporter was the envy of the Formula Two circus, 'with FVA engines hanging on the walls like apples on a tree . . .'

Hector Staffa and his mechanics Alberto Pilotto, Mario Quaglia and Juan Patteta concentrated upon giving Reutemann a reliable car which would survive trouble-free through race distance, and it was a new 'Lolé' who finished second to Ronnie Peterson in the 1971 European Formula Two Championship. According to one F2 reviewer that year, 'He showed polish, car control, and tremendous speed allied to a tremendously popular personality. His big day came at Albi when he beat Peterson for pole and staged a superb recovery after sustaining a puncture on lap one, finishing second behind Emerson Fittipaldi . . .' No longer were ACA a team apart: their languages were improving, they mixed socially with the rest of the F2 circus, and Reutemann himself was more relaxed and open, his now famous flashing smile much in evidence.

He won his first Formula Two race – a non-Championship event at Hockenheim – but as a realist it meant little to him for both Peterson and Emerson Fittipaldi were absent. And the season ended with the achievement of another ambition, as Motor Racing Developments entered him in a works Formula One Brabham for the end of season race at Brands Hatch. He drove intelligently and well, but the race was stopped after Jo Siffert's fatal accident.

For 1972 Bernard Ecclestone, the new owner of MRD, took him into the regular works Brabham team, alongside Graham Hill. He made a sensational World Championship race debut on home soil, qualifying on pole position for the Argentine Grand Prix in January. He was the first driver since the war to qualify so well on his *Grande Épreuve* debut. The team gambled on sticky Goodyear tyres for the race and Lolé put on a great show, harrying Jackie Stewart's Tyrrell until the tyres wore out and he had to stop and change them. His standing in Argentina soared through the roof.

He had signed for the Motul-Rondel F2 Brabham team in Europe and was third for them first time out at Mallory Park in March. On 30 March 1972, Carlos was driving his Formula One Brabham in the non-Championship Brazilian Grand Prix at São Paulo's Interlagos circuit. He was running second in the twelve-car field until Fittipaldi's leading Lotus failed, and he inherited victory – his first in Formula One.

Fortunes change shockingly fast in all sports. Just two days later Lolé lay in a Hampshire hospital in England with his left ankle shattered by an horrendous practice crash at Thruxton with the Rondel F2 Brabham.

He was back in action for the bulk of the World Championship season, but seemed understandably affected by the accident for some time. In the latter part of the season he made great progress and rarely qualified outside the fastest six or seven. But cruel luck repeatedly intervened. In motor racing a well-organized team can make its own luck, and the recently remodelled Brabham team certainly had its teething troubles.

Meanwhile Carlos' growing concentration upon Formula One reflected growing disenchantment with Formula Two. A first-corner accident in the second race heat at Salzburgring just about finished his interest in the junior class, and Ronnie Peterson took over his Rondel Brabham for the end-of-year Brazilian F2 series.

Carlos was to stay with Brabham far into 1976, although several alternative offers were to be made to him, including one from Ferrari during the winter of 1972–73. He joined their long-distance sports-prototype team that season of 1973, but remained faithful to Brabham for Formula One. Gordon Murray's latest BT42 Brabham design proved very competitive and Lolé's now calm and unflappable approach to his profession yielded a string of third and fourth places in World Championship rounds and seventh place in the competition overall. He had seemed set for victory in the Spanish Grand Prix at Barcelona, only for a drive-shaft to fail as he was reeling in Emerson Fittipaldi's ailing Lotus in the lead.

Driving Ferrari's 312PB sports-prototype cars he shared victory in the Vallelunga Six-Hours in Rome with Tim Schenken and was quite impressed with Ferrari's team organization: 'They know their job well and are very professional,' he said.

In 1974 the Brabham team became truly competitive with Lolé as their spearhead, winning three World Championship Grands Prix in Murray's latest BT44. The car was particularly good on the faster circuits, and he won his maiden *Grande Épreuve* at Kyalami, South Africa, on March 30 again, then dominated flag-to-flag in both the Austrian and United States GPs.

During mid-season his fortunes and his apparent will to win took a dive, in a manner which was to become characteristic of the thoughtful Argentinian in the late seventies. Gordon Murray rated him very highly indeed both as a man and a driver, and had a fine working relationship with him: 'Carlos liked the background to technical changes which we made to be explained to him, and he would file it away in his mind and remember it. At that time, before ground-effect cars, the driving style was generally rather tail-out and opposite-lock, sliding through the turns. But not Carlos, he was always very precise and neat and tidy – unspectacular but very fast; the fastest of all on his day. He was very quick indeed on fast circuits' – although he claimed to prefer venues 'not too fast, not too slow' – 'but he persistently suffered these psychological ups and downs.

'If everything was right on the day he would be right there, a great racing driver, but then for the next couple of races he would seem to get preoccupied with some thoughts that things weren't going to go his way, and he'd go off the boil.

'He was totally dedicated to racing – no question – I don't think he ever spent too much time thinking about anything else, but suddenly he'd look glum and say, "No way, no way today, no way for the Championsheep," and that was the end of it. He kept his reasoning to himself, but then on his day he'd click and feel good and nobody could beat him . . .'

Naturally he had felt good in the first Grand Prix of the year in Buenos Aires. His Brabham was superfast on the straights and he passed Jacky Ickx, James Hunt, Emerson Fittipaldi and Ronnie Peterson to take the lead as the packed grandstands quivered to the fans' thunderous applause. He led for mile after mile, until his car's airbox feeding the engine's fuel injection system began to disintegrate. 'The sunshine was coming across the back of the car and I could see it in the shadow in front of the pits . . .' He felt he might end his career remembering only one event, that fateful Grand Prix: 'It was my home Grand Prix, and I could imagine the explosion from the public if I'd won the race – it was close, so close, everybody was leaning over the rails waiting for the chequered flag . . .' His car's fuel system ran dry with a lap to go and he stammered to rest, seventh – not first.

He realized then the enormity of the task facing anyone intent on winning a Grand Prix on merit: 'When I lost the Argentine Grand Prix, you know with one lap to go and a twenty-second lead, and then had to go to Brazil and start again, then I realized how difficult it all was. At the exact moment I put my helmet on and strapped myself in at Interlagos I thought, "I've got to set the car up, choose tyres, do six hours of practice and try to get the car back where it was two weeks before." I then understood how difficult it was to win a Grand Prix.'

That season of 1974 also saw Lolé driving occasionally for the works Alfa Romeo sports-prototype team. He found them far less organized than Ferrari the previous year, their cars heavy and rather poorly-braked but with very powerful flat-12 engines. He shared the second-placed car at Nürburgring with Rolf Stommelen, and then had a lucky escape as he was forced to bale out of his burning Alfa at Österreichring when a tyre deflated and an exposed fuel line was ruptured by contact with the track surface.

Brabham were highly fancied for the 1975 World Championship. Carlos Reutemann and his Brazilian team-mate Carlos

National hero – 'El Lolé' with President and Señora Peron after an early Argentine Grand Prix.

Pace – ex-Williams – were armed with Murray's latest BT44B cars, and the team had attracted Martini sponsorship. Lolé was third in Argentina, where he and his team-mate dominated 1–2 for much of the distance. Pace won his home Grand Prix at Interlagos – how Reutemann must have envied him – and thereafter, until the German Grand Prix which Lolé won, the pair generally disappointed. On their day both could be brilliant, but when he felt it was not his day the Argentinian in particular could look very ordinary.

He had become the enigma of Formula One. A driver brimming with immense talent and intelligence and charm to match, but whose performances could be agonizingly inconsistent.

For 1976 Bernard Ecclestone adopted Alfa's sports-derived flat-12 engines for his Formula One team to combat Ferrari's similar and at that time dominant power unit. The cars proved desperately unreliable, and uncompetitive, and by mid-summer Reutemann was terminally disheartened. Ferrari were wooing him, and when Niki Lauda was seriously injured in his fiery Nürburgring accident and Clay Regazzoni had disgraced himself in the eyes of Mr Ferrari, it was Lolé who was signed for the Italian Grand Prix and the 1977–78 seasons, buying himself out of the balance of his Brabham contract.

Lauda recovered fantastically quickly and was violently opposed to Ferrari's intention to run three cars at Monza, for the Austrian, Regazzoni and Reutemann, but Lolé made his debut there and felt his way home ninth, while Clay was placed second and the extraordinary Lauda was fourth.

Thereafter Lauda prevailed and only two Ferraris completed the season, Reutemann sitting-out the Canadian, US and Japanese GPs. Lolé was accepted into the Ferrari fold with the usual fanfare and 'honeymoon' period, the highly politicized Italian team's style having been one of setting driver against driver. Niki Lauda reacted very badly against Reutemann as his team-mate, and was later to say some remarkably poisonous things about him in print. On Carlos' part he was thrilled to be driving for the team which had carried Fangio to one of his five World Championships, and for whom the great Gonzales had also driven.

Lolé was third in Argentina and won the next race, his third

drive for Ferrari, in Brazil. He was second in Spain and in Japan – after Lauda had won the World Championship and bowed out of the team, to be replaced by Gilles Villeneuve – and third in Monaco and Sweden. He ended the season fourth in the World Championship.

As Lauda went to Brabham, Lolé became Ferrari team leader for 1978 with Villeneuve as team-mate. Unfortunately this was the season of Andretti, Peterson and the ground-effect Lotuses, and Reutemann's four victories – in Brazil (yet again), Long Beach, the British Grand Prix at Brands Hatch and at Watkins Glen – were insufficient to challenge for the title, and he was third. Villeneuve had won his home Grand Prix in Canada, with Carlos third, but Ferrari's change from Goodyear to Michelin tyres – which on occasions were so good, on others quite indifferent – had not helped relationships within the Maranello team.

During his Brabham years Carlos and Mimicha had settled in London with their two children. He liked England: '... very nice country ... I think the people in England are very good, they respect you and are very educated.' When he moved to Ferrari, home became St Jean Cap Ferrat in the South of France, closer to the action.

The Ferrari staff say they never warmed to the enigmatic Argentinian, an excellent driver but still erratic and too introverted for them. Neither did they forgive him for start-line fumbles at Monaco and Zolder, nor accept his reasonable explanation that the flat-12 car was tricky to take off the line on Michelin rubber. Late in July it was known that Jody Scheckter would be Ferrari's new driver for 1979, but Lolé made no great fuss, only opening-up towards the end of the year with observations on Ferrari's way of racing which displeased Mr Ferrari no end. Carlos moved to Lotus with high hopes for another dominant season alongside Andretti, but after a strong start 1979 saw Lotus fortunes take a terrible tumble. Before the year was out Frank Williams was in earnest discussion with 'El Lolé', and he was to join the Didcot team for 1980–81.

There he proved a revelation. Some team members had expected to find the moody, often inconsistent driver, a superstar only on his day, that they had heard about. In fact the smiling,

Not a happy moment – one of the famous Reutemann grimaces while
the FW07B receives attention at Imola before the 1980 Italian Grand Prix.

cheerful and willing team man they discovered came as quite a surprise. He was quite badly affected by Laffite's torpedoing his car amidships while he was leading the Spanish Grand Prix, and the team were less than delighted with his lack-lustre drive at Zandvoort, but perhaps his rib injuries bothered him more than he was prepared to admit. And none could reasonably challenge his consistency as the team gelled to make 'his day' dawn more regularly than ever before, and from the 1980 Belgian Grand Prix, at Zolder on 4 May, until the 1981 Belgian race on 17 May Lolé Reutemann established a staggering world record as he drove his impeccably-prepared FW07-series cars to sixteen consecutive points-scoring finishes (in the top six) in World Championship races. During 1980 he was an amiable back-up to Alan Jones and then for 1981 took his mighty charge at that World title, which had five times been Fangio's . . .

He failed, once again his enigmatic psychology apparently convincing him that Fangio's crown was not to be his. He led the Championship until the last race at Las Vegas, where one point separated him from his nearest rival, Nelson Piquet. But he had driven dispiritedly or with uncharacteristic lapses since Hockenheim in August, and despite his usual brilliant qualifying performance to start from pole in Nevada he simply gave the World title away.

There were recriminations. He felt the team had favoured Jones, and his car's preparation had suffered. It was a charge the team resented, and one Las Vegas story, attributing his lustreless performance to chassis crossweighting imbalance, was palpably untrue.

Yet on his day, as in Brazil, or at Dijon where he nursed a blistered left-front (load-bearing) tyre for many laps and still kept pace, Reutemann's driving was wonderful. Frank Williams: 'On his day, when he felt good and things were going his way, Carlos could explore the uttermost limits of his car, producing its maximum speed, with minimum risk . . .' He was smoothly fast and fearless, relentlessly quick. Carlos Reutemann never lacked the skill to be World Champion, maybe just the character . . . and the most hardened racing drivers are so seldom the most charming people . . .

Patrick Head, The Other Half

It was in November 1975, in the lounge at London's Carlton Tower Hotel, that Patrick Head and Frank Williams first met. Frank had been searching desperately for a new team engineer at the close of his most fraught Formula One season yet. Walter Wolf was in the wings, interested in buying control of the Frank Williams (Racing Cars) team, but with promises of alternative sponsorship for 1976 there was still some prospect of Frank retaining his valued independence.

Patrick had been recommended to him as a talented and properly qualified engineer with valuable racing experience. He had done some work for Formula 5000 owner-driver Guy Edwards, and it was Guy and Ian Phillips, Editor of *Autosport* magazine, who had jointly suggested his name to Frank.

Patrick recalls his 'interview', when he thought Frank looked extremely smart and he felt rather scruffy in such plush surroundings: 'As we talked he gave not the slightest impression of being at all interested in me as an engineer – it was as though he'd talked with hundreds of engineers already and was weary of the whole thing. What he did ask was whether or not I was really committed, "Are you prepared to work twelve hours a day, seven days a week?" he asked. And I said "No I'm not, because anybody who has to do that is extremely badly organized . . ." I'm not sure that Frank thought that was the right answer, but in any case I got the job . . .' and he was to spend twelve hours a day, seven days a week working at it . . .

Patrick had barely started at Bennett Road when the Walter Wolf deal was done and Harvey Postlethwaite was brought in with the ex-Hesketh 308C design. In that short time Patrick had already drawn a new rear wing and revised the fuel system of the existing FW04 cars so that they would pick up their last few gallons of fuel. Frank was anxious to observe just what his new boy was up to. Frank explains that he had spent years footing the bills while engineers learned the ropes. In particular he was paranoid about fuel and oil systems which did not work properly, and even well into the eighties he understandably remained almost manic about checking oil levels before his cars could run.

Once the Wolf-Williams deal had been struck and Postlethwaite took over as Chief Engineer, Frank asked if Patrick would stay on under the new regime. He considered that Frank and Walter were being quite fair to him in the circumstances and agreed to stay put – through the great Wolf-Williams season of 1976 . . .

Patrick was born in 1946, only son of Colonel Michael Head who became a familiar figure to motor racing crowds during the fifties driving his own privately-entered and very successful Jaguar and Cooper-Jaguar sports-racing cars. Patrick remembers his father's racing but was still in short trousers when Colonel Head retired in 1958. His own interest grew later and was stimulated by the very different type of racing seen in Formula One and by the driving of Jimmy Clark and Graham Hill.

Patrick was studying at Wellington College at the time. James Hunt, to become World Champion Driver in 1976, was there too, as was Peter Wright – later to become a BRM and Lotus race engineering 'boffin', a gifted aerodynamicist and true originator of the modern ground-effect Grand Prix car. But Patrick knew neither of them: 'Hunt was a year behind me, and of course one never talked to anybody younger than oneself...'

He was fascinated by the technical side of motor sport and with some school friends planned a fearsome hill-climb special, using a Triumph Bonneville motor-cycle engine mated to a Norton gearbox and supercharged at about three-atmospheres pressure from compressed oxygen bottles slung alongside the engine bay.

They had calculated all the mathematics of the project and believed they would have around fifty-two seconds' boost before the bottles were exhausted, which was sufficient for the average British hill-climb distance. What they didn't think about was how to keep the engine cylinder head bolted down against 3 ata pressure, but unhampered by such practicalities they actually approached the Buckler chassis company in nearby Bracknell about building the thing. Patrick would later laugh off the idea, saying that 'Perhaps thankfully it never saw the light of day...'

He and a friend named Ian McKean also thought out an interlinked rear suspension system for cars in which the road wheels would bank into corners, like a motor-cycle. It was rather similar in fact to the Torix–Bennett system adopted for Fairthorpe cars, but the 'McKean–Head Camber-Compensating Suspension System' was patented, and they sent details to all the contemporary Formula One teams. This elicited no response, except from BRM – the team with the largest office staff – who merely replied, 'No thank you'. In 1970, quite independently, McLaren ran what was effectively one half of the system in their Indianapolis track-racing cars in America, and they won a major prize for technical innovation!

On leaving Wellington, Patrick entered the Royal Naval College at Dartmouth. He found little joy as a faceless component in a vast machine, bulling his boots and submerged into a sea of Navy blue. He bought himself out after three months, which was not easy.

From Dartmouth he found a job with the Lindsay Parkinson construction company, building the M4 Motorway into Wales. His first job with them was to paint a site convenience in their green colours. Later he became a soil-tester for them, before commencing a year's mechanical engineering studies at Birming-

ham University. He claims not to have taken it very seriously. He spent a lot of time rallying with and against fellow student Andy Dawson – 'An extraordinary character who could drink us all under the table, stay up all night and still have the stamina to show us all the way round a rally course.' Dawson later achieved international stature with the Datsun works-backed rally team, while Patrick's year at Birmingham ended in failed exams.

For ten weeks in the summer he worked at Ferguson Research, his father being an old acquaintance of Major Tony Rolt, MC, head of the company and a former Le Mans-winning works Jaguar driver, and Colditz Castle POW. 'I must have been a pain in the bum to the blokes there, son of some friend of the boss, I could imagine what they were thinking...'

Another instructive spell followed with Harry Weslake Research at Rye, who at that time in the mid-sixties were building the Eagle-Weslake V12 Formula One engines for American Dan Gurney's team. Patrick worked in the machine shop, learning much about the right and wrong ways of stocking a small engineering works, and gaining some insight into the realities of Formula One.

With this practical experience under his belt he resumed studies at Bournemouth Technical College for a year on a London University external course, before transferring to University College, London, for a final two years from which he 'emerged as a proper engineer'.

In 1970 he went to work for Lola Cars Ltd at Huntingdon, the world's largest manufacturer of competition cars. Patrick was instantly impressed by Lola boss Eric Broadley: 'He is a very bright bloke, he interviewed me for all of three minutes! Of course interviewing people for jobs is largely a waste of time – you've got to give them a go and see if they're any good. If they're not, get rid of 'em. I would recommend anybody who wants to design racing cars to work for an outfit like Lola.

'There I found myself producing bits for everything from Formula Ford and SuperVee to Indianapolis and CanAm, 2-litre sports cars, 3-litre sports cars, Formula 5000 – just about every conceivable class of competition car. Rather than having just one top suspension link to draw you would find yourself being asked to

Team strong-man – tough, outspoken Patrick Head (*left*), an outstanding
practical engineer and another fiercely competitive spirit, with Frank and
Jonathan Williams.

draw twenty, all different, and you would discover very rapidly what not to do . . .'

While Eric Broadley produced the initial design layouts for the cars and kept close control on Indianapolis and CanAm sports car projects, Patrick worked alongside John Barnard, who had started at Lola about a year before Head's arrival and was to leave three months after him. They learned a great deal together and both were to become Formula One car designers in their own right.

Lola were deeply involved in Formula SuperVee, a class catering for simple single-seater racing cars powered by German Volkswagen engines. Geoff Richardson in Huntingdon ran a small concern specializing in building and race-tuning engines, and Patrick had got to know him through Lola. 'People kept contacting us and asking about SuperVee engines and bits and pieces, and I liked fiddling with engines anyway, so I set up a SuperVee engine project, using Geoff's premises. I left Lola that June and spent three or four months producing parts and assembling two gleaming prototype engines with dry-sump oil systems, Titanium pushrods, special camshafts, etc, which performed very nicely.

'By that time it was the end of the season, and there were no immediate orders around for new engines. Then Geoff introduced me to Richard Scott and his man Mike Cane. Richard had been driving quite successfully in Formula Two and Formula Three, and Mike thought it would be interesting to build a Scott Formula Two car . . .'

By this time Patrick had invested all his modest capital in the two prototype SuperVee engines which resided in store at Geoff Richardson's Huntingdon premises, and he went to work with Cane in a damp railway arch in Battersea, where he drew a new Formula Two car which Mike would build for Richard Scott to drive.

'About five days after I had gone down there I had a call from Geoff Richardson who said, "I don't know how to tell you this, but my place has burned down and everything has burned with it . . ."'

Patrick went up to have a look, and sure enough his beautiful prototype engines had simply been reduced to shapeless lumps of melted alloy, about the size of a small coffee table, with the hardened steel internals projecting here and there from the mess. All his eggs were now in the Scott F2 car.

It emerged as a very neat and workmanlike little device which the Aberdonian drove very well when he was in the mood. Patrick had used some proprietary parts, like Brabham rear suspension uprights and Lola fronts, but the rest was very special, including a seven-inch long adaptor which was inserted between the engine and gearbox to place the mass of the power unit more amidships and achieve a better-balanced motor car.

During those days beneath the railway arch Patrick worked at a table and drawing board while Mike Cane chased suppliers on the telephone. Every single part of the car was drawn and part-numbered. This was in no way the traditional motor racing special for which the only blueprints were chalk marks on the garage floor and walls.

But then 'we cocked it up' . . .

Richard had shown great pace in initial testing at Goodwood, and for the Mallory Park early-season Formula Two meeting Mike and Patrick fitted an old airbox cowl to the engine. They did not know that the stone-guard gauze deep inside the cowl had broken up, and at Mallory some fragments fell into the throttle slide and jammed the throttle open: 'So Richard flew off and stuffed the new car first time out . . .'

Its damage was repaired and Scott was very quick at Nürburgring, then crashed again at Pau when his foot slipped off the brake pedal. The car was (hastily and poorly) rebuilt and put into store.

Meanwhile Scott had introduced Patrick to Ron Tauranac, the hugely experienced, tough, and often abrasive Australian engineer who had worked in partnership with Jack Brabham from 1961 to 1970 and had sold Motor Racing Developments Ltd to Bernard Ecclestone in the winter of 1971–72. Ron had finished his consultancy work for Frank Williams in Formula One and was about to go to Peter Agg's Trojan company in Purley to act as a consultant engineer on their racing car projects. Trojan had been responsible for putting McLaren designs into customer production for some years, but with the demise of the lucrative CanAm Championship in North America their best market had collapsed. McLaren had produced a Formula Two car of somewhat dubious merit, which Trojan had been persuaded to put into series production for a market which did not materialize. To salvage something from the wreck, Tauranac was called in to develop the F2 design for Formula 5000 racing, using American 5-litre V8 engines, and Patrick went along to help him with that programme.

He was also involved with London taximan Ron Grant, who was an enthusiastic Lola Formula SuperVee driver, in building FSV engines. Then for 1974 Peter Agg commissioned Tauranac to develop a Trojan Formula One car to promote the company name and that of Agg's Suzuki import franchise. Tim Schenken drove the car and Patrick travelled with the team to three or four Grand Prix races; his early introduction to what was to become his business.

When the Trojan money ran out it was back to building FSV engines with Ron Grant, and then the Scott was resurrected briefly to run in Formula Atlantic races – at that time a club single-seater class in Britain – using 'a dreadful old-nail engine which Geoff Richardson literally cobbled up from old discarded pieces lying around in his workshop.' But despite its dubious parentage that engine was fantastically quick, so quick that Harry Stiller bought it to put into the car which was being driven for him at that time by an Australian ex-Formula Three driver, whose name was Alan Jones. He led virtually everything in Atlantic that year and Patrick was quite impressed. Guy Edwards then appeared upon the scene, inviting Patrick to help run his Formula 5000 car. And there was Alan Jones again, doing well in a V6 Ford-engined March . . .

It was at this stage, at the end of 1975, that Patrick began his brief tenure as Chief Engineer for Frank Williams (Racing Cars) in Reading, for after ten days or so his post became that of assistant engineer, working under Harvey Postlethwaite at what was now Walter Wolf Racing. Their cars were to be known as Wolf-Williams FW05s, developed from Harvey's Hesketh 308C design – and that memorably traumatic season began, with Patrick involved but insulated from the front-line flak. He admits that he would not have missed the experience of 1976 for a fortune: 'Harvey was in the firing line, not me, and I learned a lot about what not to do in Formula One. We all made a welter of huge errors that year, which compressed several normal seasons' experience into one intensive period. I know that experience saved me from repeating some of those errors in later years.

'But it's not really profitable to dwell too much upon that season. There have been many bad Formula One cars and the '05 was just one of them. It was just a bad, bad car, and it is best forgotten . . .'

One major lesson he learned was to reject the temptation to make 'a quick bodge' in the vague hope that it might improve the car. Occasionally such a stab in the dark might indeed work well, but once it had been built into the car, whatever else might be done would only compound a bodge, and bodges are heavy. If one of the subsequent expedients does not work out, then the engineering team will not know whether the latest expedient itself is at fault, or whether blame lies in the expedient to which it is bolted. Into the eighties the Williams design ethic was broadly, 'Try to do things once properly, rather than four or five times quickly, and badly.' Combined with Frank Williams' 'Excellence is not quite good enough', this formed a formidably demanding but almost peerless philosophy.

Once set free to design his own cars his own way, Patrick admitted to spending more time thinking about what he wanted to do or to produce – thinking whether it was necessary or not and, if so, then exploring the very best method of production – before ever setting out on serious design drawing.

He has a healthy regard for his drivers' highly-tuned skills and competitive instincts, but believes it to be a myth that drivers develop racing cars: 'Drivers would probably love to enlarge upon the idea that they can come into the pits and say "I am slower than driver X because I can feel the chassis undergoing 10/64ths of an inch torsional deflection through Paddock Bend, what we should do to correct it is . . ." etc, etc . . . but I know of none who can do that. What does pay dividends is when your driver can paint for you – the engineer – a very clear picture of how the car feels while he is driving it in certain situations, and of its behaviour. Then it's up to you to go away, reason out what is happening, and to decide a course of action which hopefully will improve matters and make the car quicker. Most good drivers will just sit there in the car, probably with steam coming out of their ears, and say, "*What* have you done to make the —— car go quicker!" Racing is their job. Engineering is yours.'

After the axe fell at Bennett Road and Frank Williams was effectively, as he puts it, 'given the sideways elbow', Patrick worked on towards 1977, looking forward to developing the latest Postlethwaite-designed Wolf WR-series car with such a highly competitive world-class driver as Jody Scheckter. Frank was keeping him informed of progress towards establishing Williams Grand Prix Engineering, and in the middle of a test session at Kyalami in South Africa Frank finally telephoned Patrick from England to say that sponsorship had been finalized, WGPE was in existence, would he like to join?

Patrick's future wife, Kate, tipped the scales of his judgement in favour of joining the new team, and so he left Bennett Road to follow his future. Peter Warr contended that he was committing motor racing suicide. That may have seemed a reasonable judgement at the time. Events proved there's life after death . . .

Running the show: Jeff Hazell, Frank Williams, Charlie Crichton-Stuart and Patrick Head watch practice progress on the team's Heuer electronic timing equipment.

III · TOWARDS THE WORLD CHAMPIONSHIP

'You cannot define talent, all you can do is build the
greenhouse and see if it grows . . .'
William P. Steven: *Time*, 1963.

A fish-eye view of the Williams pits – British GP, 1978.

Finding their Feet

While Patrick Neve and the reliable Belle-Vue Saudia March completed their 1977 season, Patrick Head was working in his drawing office at Didcot, designing his first complete Formula One car for the coming season. With rare exceptions every new Grand Prix car design draws deeply upon the most effective features of its recent predecessors. Patrick conceived his first car: '... virtually as an extension of the thinking which had been applied to the Wolf WR – very light, simple and strong, with as good an aerodynamic shape as we could achieve. We couldn't afford wind tunnel time, and so what became the Williams FW06 was designed by rule of thumb...'

By August 1977, as Patrick embarked upon the new car project, WGPE's staff was about ten strong. A former Loughborough College graduate named Neil Oatley joined Patrick in the drawing office. He had been involved in dynamometer installation designs and was used to working with the high degree of care and precision which Patrick was to demand, not only of his staff but also of himself. More skilled craftsmen were taken on, with experience honed at nearby establishments like the Atomic Energy and Research facilities at Aldermaston, Harwell and Culham.

That season of 1977 had seen Lotus herald the age of the ground-effect car with their Type 78 design, and the following winter found most teams fudging together Lotus look-alikes for the coming season. Patrick was unable to investigate the theory behind such cars in the wind tunnel, and therefore opted for a traditional design. In retrospect he explained why: 'I'm fairly conservative by nature, and the 78 had failed so often that it didn't really look so dominant to me as I suppose it really deserved.

Frankly I did not understand how the Lotus worked, and so I opted to build a light, straightforward and rugged conventional car.

'I did understand what made front and rear wings work effectively, offering good uninterrupted airflow both in front and behind them, and when the '06 appeared it offered the highest lift/drag ratio of any conventional car that I know about. It had quite a wide front track and a far-forward front wing with a lot of room behind it. I drew a front suspension system with the coil-springs and dampers tucked away out of the airstream within the monocoque, and anti-roll bar arrangements very similar to the contemporary Ferrari.

'At the back I used a cast magnesium oil tank-cum-gearbox spacer-cum all sorts of other functions, which was nothing new – Lotus had introduced the idea on their 78, but poor Frank became paranoid about it. It was going to pick up the rear suspension, the anti-roll bar, form the outer casing for the air-starter motor and it would have the clutch mechanism built into it as well. Obviously it was going to be quite an expensive item, and Frank was rightly suspicious of expensive oil tanks which in his experience often didn't work. Over the years he had had any number designed for him which made very expensive engines go BANG, I think he wasn't really too confident that I really knew what I was doing. He knew that I was taking a great big bite, but was I capable of chewing it?...'

Then Alan Jones appeared upon the scene. Frank and Patrick had been discussing a suitable driver for their projected one-car operation in 1978. Their pre-requisites were a good reliable driver who spoke English, could communicate well, who was preferably based in England to be readily available when required for testing, and who would not make a habit of crashing his cars.

Frank spoke with Gunnar Nilsson, the fast-rising Swede who had been Andretti's team-mate at Team Lotus; with Jochen Mass, the German driver who had performed reliably with McLaren; and, very ambitiously, with Ronnie Peterson, the great Swedish ace who had become the standard-setter of his time but who was just emerging from a poor season with the uncompetitive six-wheeled Tyrrells. Then, as Frank recalls, 'Quite simply, Alan Jones was the one who became available. It wasn't me being bloody clever and recognizing his intrinsic greatness – oh no – just circumstances pushed him in our direction . . .'

Nilsson signed for the new Arrows team but tragically developed terminal cancer. Mass opted for the German ATS team, and Peterson rejoined Lotus in Nilsson's place. Alan Jones, meanwhile, had won the Austrian Grand Prix for Don Nichols' Shadow team at about the time that Patrick was putting the first lines of FW06 on to paper at Didcot, and he completed the season with twenty-two Championship points to his name, but little money, which was important to him.

So it was a rather disgruntled Australian who was looking for an alternative seat for 1978. Both WGPE principals rated him quite highly, and if they could emerge from 1978 with twenty-two Championship points they would be highly delighted . . .

Alan visited Unit 10. There was not a lot to inspect but he struck up an immediate rapport with Patrick, and Frank was able to offer a one-season retainer of £40,000. Alan possibly figured that if he only received two-thirds of that figure, he would be no worse off than with Shadow the previous year.

Above all there was an unmistakable impression of energy about the activities at Didcot. Alan said, 'I think we've got the makings of something good here, I'm prepared to give it a go . . .' The effectiveness of his efforts were to amaze and delight Frank Williams, while his team's inability to provide a reliable car must have caused bitter frustration . . .

In December the prototype FW06 was complete and ready for the Saudia–Williams team press presentation at the factory. Al

Fawzan's board had been intrigued by the airline's exposure on the wing of the Belle-Vue March, and Saudia's then Director-General, Sheikh Kamal Sindhi, was flown in by helicopter, landing on the recreation ground behind Unit 10 to inspect car and team. The Sheikh's son Adel was to become an avid motor racing fan, while the Sheikh himself was shortly to become his nation's Deputy Minister of Aviation.

As the rotor-wash of the Sheikh's approaching helicopter battered the football pitches behind Unit 10, Frank strode out to meet his VIP guest. The journalists present could sense the nervous tension in him, the accomplished front-man, about to do his stuff with his always-genuine charm and courtesy. Suddenly, mindful perhaps of his often rocky road towards that crucial day, he abruptly turned, flashed one of his famous dazzling smiles and quipped simply, 'Don't let me down lads!' From that moment the British motor racing press were right behind the latest Williams venture . . .

He was heavily involved with sponsor-hunting as Patrick took the new car to Buenos Aires for Alan Jones to make his debut in the first round of the new year's World Championship. The engine misfired in practice and Patrick attempted to cure the problem overnight. Frank would have fitted the spare immediately, had he been present – it was part of Patrick's racing education. Alan qualified a lowly fourteenth, and retired when the overheated fuel system vapour-locked, starving the engine.

Frank joined the team for the trip to Brazil, and what occurred there in Grand Prix practice at Rio's Jacarepagua Autodrome was electrifying . . .

There were early problems as a wheel nut worked loose and a stub-axle sheared. The rebuilt car understeered more than was comfortable, but on the second day of practice on standard Goodyear tyres – without the softer, stickier and faster 'qualifiers' then being provided to the leading teams – he was suddenly eighth fastest.

Frank recalls: 'Suddenly Derrick Williams of Goodyear was in front of our pit shouting up at me with his Wolverhampton accent, "'ere Frank, you're eighth fastest without trying, queek, fit this set of qualifying tyres!" I was almost speechless . . . What?

December 1977: Saudia's
Sheikh Kamal Sindhi and his
board visit Didcot to inspect
the prototype FW06 and meet
the team.

Brazil 1978, and suddenly Alan Jones is among the quick boys . . .

Qualifying tyres? For my car? For my team? In our second race with the new car? . . .

'It was a completely new world to me. I had difficulty coping with the sudden enormity of it. Alan was among the quick boys . . . for years I had become accustomed just to hanging in there hoping to qualify, and now we were showing real signs of becoming truly competitive once again . . .'

In the race a wheel bearing problem allowed one front wheel disc to scuff continuously against its brake pads, that tyre over-heated and began to burn out and Alan found himself handi-capped with worsening understeer as the car tried to plough straight-on in corners. He stopped three times to change tyres, but his emergent class was evident as he showed no sign of giving up nor easing off and clocked second-fastest race lap, just 0.18 second slower than Reutemann's best in the victorious Ferrari . . . and quicker than all other Goodyear runners.

At Kyalami in practice for the South African race Alan crashed the brand-new FW06/2 spare car and was handicapped by a poor engine in attempting to qualify 'No 1'. He started eighteenth on the grid, had a head cold but put his head down and began a tigerish drive.

In the Saudia–Williams pit Frank could not believe his lap chart: 'Alan began simply ripping through the field, passing car after car. He was twelfth ending lap five and fought his way through the pack to seventh as the race progressed. It was fantasti-cally exciting. It really stirred me and I remember calling to Patrick, "You know, even if we don't finish, this will be my best race, if it doesn't come round next lap I'll still be happy."

'It was like one of Piers' drives. It took me some time to appreciate fully that Alan really was that quick. It was as if I had been in prison for ten or twenty years of a thirty-year sentence and somebody had suddenly come up with the key and set me free. My initial reaction was, "Bloody hell, I'm not sure I can cope with this, help! Please let me back inside . . ."'

Towards the end of that race Alan had to submit to his illness and sit back, he just didn't have the fight left to tackle John Watson there ahead of him. He finished fourth, and Saudia–Williams had won their first three World Championship points.

At Long Beach Patrick recalls: 'It was a typical Alan race for us that year, qualifying eighth, as so often with the '06s, then running far above that level in the race. He always out-raced his practice performance, we were always doing better than we dreamed possible; he was assisted by one or two cars dropping out, but the rest he just plain passed.

'He pulled himself up on to Carlos Reutemann's tail in the leading Ferrari and said he felt he had the measure of him, running second and poised to take the lead – when the nose wing collapsed. In fact he couldn't see its tips drooping from his position in the cockpit and didn't realize he had a problem, but then his engine started misfiring as well and that was it: he dropped back, and finished seventh. It was heartbreaking . . .'

To finish first, you must first finish. With the time and money and skill to invest infinite care and patience in the preparation of a Grand Prix car, it should be possible to operate in Formula One like a NASA space-shot, to sift out the variables until mechanical failure will not occur. But in contesting more than a dozen Grand Prix races each year, time is always at a premium, few teams have the money and even fewer the men. There is a background story to be found behind every race failure, and that of Alan's nose wing at Long Beach is quite typical – and all the more frustrating in that it could have been avoided:

'When I first set out to design the '06 nose wing I couldn't understand the difference between the shapes required for the underside of full-width nose sections' – in which the nose body-work of the car extends in front of the wheels on either side – 'and those required for a separate full-width wing mounted on a narrow nose section. So I made the upper surface of the wing to the shape we knew would work on conventional full-width wings, while the underside would be the shape normally required for a full-width nose section.

'We had drawn the full-width wing and narrow nose for the March the previous year, drawn them freehand – none of our sections came from the standard NASA book on the subject. The March wing was made from light-gauge aluminium sheet and we produced a nose mounting for the March to carry it. This mounting had its supports spaced about fourteen inches apart, and there were ribs equally spaced within the wing to pick them up.

'On the '06 prototype for the new funny-shaped front wing, the mounts were spaced only ten inches apart, flanking the oil cooler which we recessed into the nose. We were about to go off to Ricard for the first test session when I realized it would be foolish to go without some form of baseline. So I took the full-width front wing off the March, and had some ten-inch-wide mounts made up to adapt it to '06. This meant that the mounts were no longer directly underneath the internal ribs in that wing, but inboard of them, bearing directly upon the unsupported skin.

'During testing at Ricard that wing actually proved far more effective than the new '06 wing, and so – because of course we were trying to do far too much, in too short a time, with too few people – we made one more March-type wing before leaving for Argentina, and took it out there along with the original wide-ribbed wing as a spare.

'There were no problems. We made several March-like wings for the new car with properly-spaced internal ribs, and I really rather forgot about the original wide-ribbed wing. At Long Beach "Sod's Law" struck when we were running second and Alan was poised to challenge for the lead . . .

'That law holds totally in motor racing. If it can apply in any way at all, it will. We fitted the wide-ribbed wing unthinkingly at Long Beach, and its unsupported bottom skin simply collapsed beneath the load.

'The instant Alan appeared in the pit straight with the wing bent in the middle I knew exactly what had happened, and why. I had a lot of chastening experiences that year, and that was one of them . . .'

Back home when Cosworth Engineering stripped Alan's mis-firing race engine they could find no obvious problem, although the ignition unit fell under suspicion as there appeared to be an intermittent contact in its circuitry. But later events were to suggest more strongly that this had been a recurrence of the Argentinian fuel vaporization problem.

At Monaco Alan again showed promisingly until billowing smoke trailed from his car and it was soon to retire, out of oil, a stud having come adrift from the oil tank. Frank knew the engine was desperately at risk as he went by the pits lap after lap trailing smoke, '. . . but the Saudis were with us for the first time, and I would rather have Alan running up there for thirty laps of the most popular road race in the world than pull him out after only five laps to save the engine . . .' In 1970, when Alejandro de Tomaso wanted to impress would-be clients, Frank had been on the other side of the fence; times change.

In fact Prince Mohammed bin Fahad bin Abdul Aziz al Saud – whose enthusiasm for the team was to motivate the growing Saudi consortium which came to sponsor it – had flown from Riyadh to Paris with several members of his family to watch the race. On arrival in the capital the Prince had decided that Monte Carlo would be too crowded and opted to watch the Grand Prix from the comfort of his Parisian suite. But his young cousin Prince Mohammed bin Nawaf travelled down with some friends including Mansour Ojjeh, whose father owned *Techniques d'Avant Garde* (TAG) – an advanced technology concern with broad aviation interests.

Mansour was to become one of the team's most ardent supporters, flying worldwide to watch them race, then jetting back to his business desk in Paris. He fitted in very well with the team; a likeable, unspoiled heir to enormous but discreet wealth. TAG were to acquire an increasing share of the Saudi consortium's sponsorship as time passed, the team becoming in 1981 TAG–Williams rather than Saudia–Williams, largely through Mansour Ojjeh's immense enthusiasm. At Monaco that day in 1978 Charlie Crichton-Stuart was liaising between the team and its Saudi guests, and at the end of the year he would join WGPE full-time in that capacity.

The season swept on, the team out of the hunt in Belgium and Spain but back in the thick of things in Sweden where Alan became embroiled in a fierce battle for third place behind the controversial Brabham 'Fan Cars'. His main adversary was Riccardo Patrese in the Arrows, who was blocking off the white-and-green '06 all round the Anderstorp course. At last Alan muscled his way by, only to be rammed smartly up the tail at the next corner and go sailing off on to the sandy verge. He rejoined,

'The Law' strikes at Long Beach . . . With Jones poised to challenge for the lead,
the FW06's nose wing is already drooping, and soon the engine will begin to misfire.

furious, and tigered round only to hurtle into the pit lane two laps later. The right-front wheel bearing had seized and the car was retired.

By this time Alan was regularly winning Goodyear qualifying rubber in practice, for he was the best of 'the rest', outside the star teams who used them of right. Frank: 'We were always willing to test and did enormous test mileages for Goodyear. Patrick had adopted a very professional approach to a sensible test programme. At Long Beach we did some testing at Willow Springs and bought an ex-VDS Team, CanAm transporter over there which subsequently became our test-car truck in Europe. Jeff Hazell, our new Team Manager, handled that purchase...'

The Wolverhampton tyre men found Alan Jones and the Saudia–Williams team an unlikely boon. Lotus were working hard to perfect their new Type 79 ground-effect chassis. Brabham was running Alfa Romeo engines which were too unreliable for consistent testing. James Hunt didn't like testing in any case, so that made McLaren of little use. Then Jones became competitive, and WGPE were more than happy to test – as at Ricard pre-French Grand Prix, 'when Alan ground round for hours, about 460 miles virtually non-stop except for tyre-changes, occasionally going for a pee or taking a cup of coffee.'

Patrick recalls the irony of those interminable test sessions: 'The car would run round and round, round and round, trouble free, mile after mile, and nothing ever went wrong. Then Alan would battle his way into a good position in a race, and the car would let him down...'

Alan still finished fifth for two more points in France, where he got deeply involved in a dice with Watson and Gilles Villeneuve, whose Ferrari was a lap behind after tyre changes. Reutemann, in the other Ferrari, had changed even more tyres but was very quick in between stops and was caught up behind the dice involving the Williams. Tomaini of Ferrari was most put out, and every time Alan went steaming past the pits with the Ferraris behind him, many laps in arrears, Tomaini would leap up and down beside the pits rail screaming 'Jooones – Gedoudadaway!' – much to Frank's amusement...

By this stage of the season the Lotus 79s driven by Mario Andretti and Ronnie Peterson were totally dominant, but at Brands Hatch for the British Grand Prix Alan qualified sixth on the grid and slotted into an instant fourth place in the race behind the Lotus pair and Scheckter's latest ground-effects Wolf.

Frank: 'He was unhappy with a little oversteer on the warm-up lap, but by this time Patrick had excellent "feel" for his car, he could analyse Alan's problem and after a small adjustment on the grid it was perfect. Alan is never one to boast but he said after the race that it should have been a piece of cake, he had the measure of Jody and felt sure there was another half-second or so he could take off him...'

Since both Lotuses struck trouble and Scheckter was leading with Jones second this should have given Williams the lead, but a driveshaft abruptly broke and Alan was out. Again the failure stemmed from an organizational shortcoming: 'It was a driveshaft from the first batch made by a new supplier. It had been through the proper procedures but it was actually formed from the end of a rolled bar and there was an inclusion – a fault – in the material. Although our drawing demanded crack tests at various stages during manufacture they hadn't been done, because time was short and the supplier "thought it didn't really matter..." After that experience every item made, and every process applied, was pursued to aircraft standards, with release notes at every stage, to minimize the uncertainties. We were slowly creating the system which would give us reliability...'

Patrick left the next race, at Hockenheim in Germany, to Neil Oatley's growing experience, and again Alan looked set to win in what was probably the '06 car's best performance. From sixth on the grid Alan took third on the road behind the Lotus twins after disposing of Niki Lauda's Brabham on the entry to one of the fast Hockenheim circuit's chicanes. Lauda retired soon after, when his engine failed, and as he walked into the pits he told Frank '(expletive deleted) Frank, your car's quick! I was just turning into the chicane flat out and Alan came past me on the outside as if I was standing still...'

Certainly it had become apparent that Alan Jones was no man to monkey about, especially early in the race if he was on the charge. He was very much the aggressively determined 'nut-brown

Charlie Crichton-Stuart of WGPE with Mansour Ojjeh of Techniques d'Avant Garde (TAG),
who soon became the team's major sponsor.

Australian', straight out of the Sir Jack Brabham mould – and 'Black Jack' had been three times World Champion.

But on lap twenty-nine of the scheduled forty-five Alan rushed into the pits with a misfire. It was clearly fuel vaporization again, for iced water poured over the high-pressure fuel pump cured the trouble, but only temporarily, and he was out after proving the '06 car the best of the rest, after the Lotuses.

Patrick: 'There were oil pipes running through the crushable structure beneath the fuel tank to connect the oil cooler up front to the engine, which was also bolted against the back of the monocoque tub – where the fuel lay – without any insulation because we didn't appreciate that we needed it. So the fuel heated up and where it was at low pressure around the pick-up point to the mechanical pump it boiled, the engine drew vapour and misfired. We insulated the system properly after Hockenheim and were not seriously troubled again . . .'

At this stage in the season Frank was enjoying his new-found status and had come to terms with it, and he and his team were geared to win and hungry for real success. Just six months earlier they had been geared merely to continued survival and Frank was struggling hard just to pay the bills. At Hockenheim Peterson's Lotus had retired and although Andretti's sister car won, it was on its last legs near the finish. If Alan had been there to press him hard it could easily have been Williams' second success in consecutive races . . . 'If'.

Frank was in Riyadh as the Austrian race was run and Goodyear persuaded Patrick to run different-pattern wet-weather tyres front and rear in the rain-swept race. This was a set-up which the team had not tested – 'An amazing decision' according to Frank, whose greater experience would never have allowed it to be accepted – and Alan spun off, out of the Grand Prix.

Worse followed at Zandvoort where the left-front stub axle broke and FW06/2 lost a wheel and crashed at high speed into the chicken-wire catch fences. Alan was trapped in his cockpit amidst a bundle of netting, unable to escape. 'It was bloody frightening, I'll tell you. I couldn't get out, couldn't do anything. I reckon it was at least half-a-minute before any marshals got to the car . . .' The unspoken fear of fire is ever present.

The team had adopted new front wheel bearings to eliminate their season-long problems and had tested them successfully for 115 miles at Silverstone the preceding week. Now apparently the new bearings had exacerbated stub axle loadings and one had failed under the strain. This was an agonizing experience for Patrick, especially when Alan asked him if the wheels were going to stay on the second car, before he took it out to resume practice: 'It's immensely difficult for any designer to answer that type of question, but I considered they would. He simply nodded, then drove as hard as ever, just putting any doubts completely out of his mind . . .'

In the race the Morse throttle cable parted – an unbelievable failure, and almost unprecedented, as these cables are immensely strong and this particular one was in only its second race. They normally did six before being retired, and they never failed in normal circumstances. Sod's Law repeated . . .

Then the Italian Grand Prix at Monza was ruined by the multiple accident which claimed Ronnie Peterson's life. Alan had qualified sixth on Goodyear 'specials' but just 0.21 second less would have placed him fourth, on the second row. He was very quiet as he stepped from the car after that fastest lap. He padded past Frank and sat on the pit counter. Frank asked him how it had gone: 'He just looked up with his eyes cold and said "I had a BIIIG moment on the grass at about a hundred and forty at the second Lesmo Corner; I thought I was into the barrier for a moment there . . ."

'It was obvious he had been right out on the absolute limit, where any normal human being would have been over the limit and crashed. He sat on the pit counter for about two minutes without talking to anybody. He had just, just, managed to get it back under control, hold it and get himself out of trouble. We have seen him like that a couple of times since, after pushing really hard . . .'

The restarted race was shortened as the evening drew on, different tyres were selected since temperatures had dropped, fuel was pumped out to lighten the cars for the shorter distance and Alan ran fifth until a tyre began to deflate and had to be changed. Early in the season Goodyear had rejected a batch of suspect nylon-seal tyre valves. Just like the case of the nose wing at Long Beach, Sod's Law had struck: one had remained in the tyre company's system, and it found its way on to Alan's race car.

At Watkin's Glen for the United States Grand Prix (East) all Alan's season-long promise in the '06 cars was rewarded with second place behind Reutemann's victorious Ferrari. It had been an impressive drive, a terrific performance, but it is not a race that Patrick Head enjoys recalling.

It was early in the first practice session there that a batch of cars all came rumbling into the pit-lane at once, the track fell quiet, and it became obvious there had been a major accident. Patrick: 'It's never a very nice experience, sitting in the pits when that happens. You are immediately looking for your bloke, and you have two things instantly in your mind – "My God, I hope he's all right." and "My God, I hope he hasn't badly damaged the car . . ." If I'm honest, I'm not sure which order they come in.

'That day Alan did not appear, and he was obviously the one who had gone off, and once it was clear that he had had a shunt I felt pretty certain that something had broken. Eventually he was brought back to the pits by the marshals, and he climbed over the barrier, looked around for me and tossed me something, which I caught . . .

'I looked at it, feeling as sick as a dog, a really horrible feeling. It was the right-front through-bolt which holds the wheel on. Its hub-nut was still attached, and it was clear from the broken end that this was not a fatigue failure – not something exceptional which would only happen with one individual bolt. It was instead a ductile failure in which the three-quarter-inch-thick bolt had simply been overloaded and had sheared off. It just wasn't strong enough and that meant that none of our spare bolts would be strong enough either . . .'

By that time Frank was at his side, asking if it would be all right to send Alan out in the spare car. He was ready to go, even though he had just survived a shockingly high-speed accident, for the car had been slinging downhill through a very fast left-hander when the wheel broke away and the car had instantly hurled itself into the barrier at 125 mph or more. The whole right-side of the monocoque had been destroyed. Alan had said little to Patrick on

his return – the mute action of tossing that through-bolt to him had been enough.

'I told Frank we could not run the second car until we had done something about these through-bolts. We moved everything from the pits back to the garage and drew out from the spares containers every through-bolt we could find. I studied their histories and sorted out four brand-new front through-bolts, all zero-mileage.

'Practice had ended and I explained to Frank that there was no way we could possibly run again until we had done something to make these bolts stronger. Long faces . . . I had to explain that it was an engineering problem, it was *my* problem, and we would just have to sort it out.

'Charlie Crichton-Stuart was there, and I asked him if he could locate any heat treatment centre in the area which might be open that night. If we could heat-treat our new spare bolts and so improve their tensile state we could run again. If not we would have to pack up, go home and miss the race.

'Charlie went roaring off into Watkins Glen township and returned with a copy of the local trade classified telephone directory. We found an outfit called Elmira Heat Treat which worked non-stop, and drove there to have the bolts treated overnight.

'We explained to the chap there what we wanted, and he refused point-blank to help. Owing to the American product liability laws he wouldn't touch a thing on any racing car. Charlie turned on all his British gentleman's charm, and asked him for the name of the company President. He called him on the phone and at about eleven o'clock at night literally charmed him out of his nice warm comfortable home to come out to the works and help us sort out this problem . . .

'It's like Hades in a heat treatment plant, roasting hot, dusty and dirty, and I simply felt sick to my gut, knowing that next day I was going to be responsible for us missing the United States Grand Prix.

'Eventually the President arrived and Charlie went to work on him. He didn't want anything to do with these nasty racing cars either, but Charlie persuaded him that once we had left Elmira Heat Treat with our through-bolts the Williams team would never have heard of them, we never even knew of their existence, and that as far as we were concerned we were English, and the only law in the world was English law under which product liability did not exist in the American sense...

'Much against his better judgement, as he kept telling us, he eventually allowed his guys to have a look at our through-bolts, they took the broken one and cut it up. It was high-quality nickel-chrome molybdenum steel from the British Steel Corporation; heat-treated to a condition known as 55–60 ton tensile. It could easily be taken up to 85 or 95 ton tensile without being made brittle, but US metal specifications are different to British standards, so they had to identify the nearest American equivalent first before choosing which heat-treatment process would be applicable.

'They sectioned the broken bolt for analysis and photographed it through a microscope at 800- and 1500-times magnification, and found that the material was full of all kinds of rubbish which would hardly be permitted in the lowest grade wrought iron under American standards. That put British steel-making squarely in its place.

'After all types of comparative tensile tests on various steel samples they chose the type of treatment to apply, and by this time it was about two in the morning and three or four of their people were working with us. At last the new bolts went into the oven for about ninety minutes. They hadn't quite tempered down to the expected level when they were brought out, so they put them back in for another twenty minutes or so.

'All this time the company President was standing beside us wringing his hands and looking sick. This problem had fallen into his lap from a clear sky and he had just been charmed off his feet by Charlie. I don't think he knew anything about racing, he had just been talked into helping this very courteous and persuasive British gent – and his very scruffy and morose engineer...

'Eventually – at about seven in the morning – we had four front through-bolts heat-treated to 80 ton tensile, we took them to the circuit and they were fitted. Alan ran tests with full tanks and empty, got the car balanced and set out for a time.

'He was extraordinarily matter-of-fact about the whole affair. He never asked what had happened. He merely assumed that, since the cars had been taken out of circulation for a while, something had been done. And on his first flying lap he was fastest overall to that point, and he finished up third quickest on the grid behind Andretti and Reutemann.'

Such speed of reaction seems unique to motor racing and should demonstrate its value to industrial thought in general. After that epic 'fix' Patrick simply sat in the pits with his head in his hands at the start of the Grand Prix and did not see a lap of it. He did not see Andretti's Lotus hit trouble and the two Ferraris take the lead with Alan hard on their heels. Nor did he see Villeneuve's Ferrari break its engine and Alan inherit the second place in which he finished, to earn six more World Championship points. In some measure it was vindication for Patrick, and for his team. It was certainly a measure of Jones, the man.

In Canada there was disappointment as Alan started fifth on the grid after running out of fuel in practice – Frank's 'drop-off', he admitted – and after making his usual fantastic start he trailed Jean-Pierre Jarier's leading Lotus for seventeen laps. But the '06 was oversteering, its tail wagging in corners, and he began to fall back. There was no obvious problem to be seen or heard from the pits, until a dark smear grew around a tyre – it was deflating. The pit crew made a double-quick change and Alan staged a tigerish come-back drive, smashing the lap record several times, only to finish ninth.

WGPE ended its FW06 season ninth equal with Arrows in the Formula One Constructors' Championship, and Alan Jones was eleventh equal (with eleven points) alongside Riccardo Patrese in the Drivers' Championship. The Didcot team was becoming case-hardened into an efficient and competitive organization. They had learned rapidly, from their mistakes.

Piers Courage sliding Frank's Brabham BT26 down towards the sea
on his way to second place in the 1969 Monaco GP.

Arturo Merzario at Monaco, 1974 – the Iso-Marlboro on the approach to the Old Station Hairpin.

Competitive at last – Alan Jones in
the FW06 running second in the
British GP, Brands Hatch 1978.

The first victory – Clay Regazzoni
celebrates at Silverstone after the
1979 British GP.

Worthless victory? Political disputes after the event cost Alan Jones
these nine valuable World Championship points. Spanish GP, Jarama 1980.

The World Championship won – Alan Jones,
Canadian GP, Montreal 1980.

Waiting in the wings – Williams v. Brabham,
Osterreichring 1981.

LEFT The Scourge of France – Alan Jones, Frank Williams and Carlos Reutemann at Ricard-Castellet for the 1980 French GP.

RIGHT Moments that Alan Jones would be glad to forget: unable to avoid Villeneuve's spinning Ferrari, he collides with it and plunges into the fencing. Watson cruises safely past in the McLaren on his way to victory. As Alan trots to safety, the damaged Ferrari limps away.

The Williams team at Silverstone for the 1981 British GP.
Left to right: Patrick Head, Frank Williams, Carlos Reutemann, Alan Jones.

Frank makes a point to Carlos during practice.

World Championship leader from April to October, Carlos Reutemann in the FW07C.

Vindication – Winners at Last

Plans for the new year had been laid as early as July '78 when Frank Williams and Dave Brodie had gone to see Alan Jones in his home in Ealing, West London, to discuss terms for the coming season. He was offered quite handsome money to stay with the team, and by the time of the Austrian Grand Prix had accepted. The team thus had one less variable, one less problem to contend with as the winter approached, and Frank and Patrick – who became a full partner in the company – committed themselves to running a two-car team.

Provided they could operate both cars efficiently this would improve the team's chances of success. Two cars provide better exposure for their sponsors than just one, and a two-car entry also made it easier to raise the money required to support a Didcot staff growing from around eighteen at the turn of the year to forty-five or fifty by its close. An additional major factor was FOCA's preference for two-car teams, and after completing their successful 1978 season WGPE had qualified for full membership for one car. To gain membership for the second, Frank did a deal with Bernard Ecclestone to buy John Surtees' two memberships, which he was surrendering as his Formula One team closed down. There were precedents for this type of commercial arrangement: Max Mosley had sold March's membership to Gunther Schmid of the ATS Wheel Company in 1976, and (of course) Walter Wolf had acquired Frank's original membership. Now Frank returned one of the Surtees qualifications to FOCA, enabling them to embrace twenty-one guaranteed entries for every World Championship Grand Prix.

Now a second Williams driver was required. Frank: 'We wanted a good reliable number two who would always be around at the finish; one who would not give us problems by crashing his cars; one who would be quite quick and above all happy to support Alan. We considered Hans Stuck, Jochen Mass and Clay Regazzoni.

'Prince Mohammed did not give his full approval for the additional budget required until November '78, by which time the annual driver market was ready to close.' Mass had been the number one choice, but he had grown understandably restless with the delay and joined Arrows. Patrick considered that Stuck, at well over six feet, was too tall and would have required a longer car to accommodate him. This would have destroyed the commonality between cars and would have multiplied the engineering problems disproportionately. Stuck proved he could sit in Alan's '06 by raising his knees higher than normal. They discussed terms and the German went away to sleep on it, only to say 'No thank you' next morning – a decision he probably grew to regret as it was effectively the end of his Formula One career . . .

So then the drive was offered to Regazzoni, the veteran Ticinese who had had indifferent seasons with Ensign and Shadow in 1977–78 after being dismissed by Ferrari.

Frank: 'I liked Clay's experience. In good equipment he had proved he was quick, for Ferrari he had been little slower than Niki Lauda and at Long Beach for instance he had won hands down. He told us that he was not happy at Shadow – we seemed to have become a haven for their former drivers – and that he would love to join our team. Naturally Alan's acceptance was very important, and he was very happy, he liked Clay and they got on well together . . .'

Patrick was to arm these men with his first ground-effect car, the Williams FW07, which was to win itself a place beside the most successful Grand Prix designs of all time.

He had realized very early on in the career of the FW06 '. . . that aerodynamics were the biggest single factor affecting the performance of a Grand Prix car, and that the rest of the machine was there simply to carry those aerodynamic loads and ensure that the rest of the thing was held securely in place.

'Lotus had introduced us to a completely new era of Grand Prix car design with their Types 78 and 79, and I was aware that they did much of their wind tunnel testing at Imperial College in London, using quarter-scale models. Their tunnel incorporated a moving ground surface beneath the model being tested, and I appreciated why that was important since racing cars do not fly through the air, but roll along a road surface on their wheels.

'So I found the telephone number of Imperial College, asked who headed their Department of Aeronautics and was put in touch with Dr John Harvey. We met, and he explained that Lotus used their tunnel, he did some consultancy work for Arrows, and there was room for one other team. We wanted to be that other team, so he showed me how it all worked and explained that they simply made the tunnel available for a certain period during which the client was on his own to run it and to test his models, and collect his data . . .

'Having seen the Lotus 79 dominate that season we had a clear idea what we wanted to do. We didn't copy the 79 line-for-line, but it was undeniably the major influence on the design of '07, as it was on most other Formula One cars being built for 1979.

'We made a crude wooden model of what we wanted to test, put it in the wind tunnel and found it was unbelievably good. Then we tried a model of FW06 and found it was unbelievably bad! We ran several more tests with models of differing types – including one rather like the Lotus 80 which was being built at that time, with very long ground-effect undersurfaces extending right back beneath the driveshafts at the rear and up to a flip-up spoiler on the tail. That indicated the most prodigious downforces, but I shied away from using it because we were very new to this area, and I wanted something fairly straightforward . . .'

His conservatism proved very wise as the Lotus 80 turned out to be an expensively unmanageable flop during 1979. Its huge aerodynamic ground-effect was unstable, and the car would 'porpoise' at speed, pitching front-to-rear and forcing Lotus to fall back on their old Type 79s, which by that time had been left far behind by other teams' developments. In Formula One such a fall from the heights by a team dominant in the previous season is quite common. Few can maintain the effort to stay on top in both technological and organizational terms for more than one season at a time. This dual challenge was about to be accepted by WGPE.

Meanwhile Patrick designed '. . . something rather like the Lotus 79, but I tried to optimize that type of layout.' He and Neil Oatley were deep into the project and about this time Frank Dernie joined the team from Hesketh where he had designed the Formula One cars which Bubbles Horsley had been running for rent-a-drivers in 1977, and where he had worked subsequently on the Hesketh motor-cycle project.

Patrick '. . . felt it was important to have a wide-based engineering team and had talked to Frank Dernie about joining us at least six months previously. He had qualified at Imperial College and had gone to Hesketh via the David Brown group, where he worked in marine gearbox design and vibration analysis. By January '79 when he joined we were probably fifty per cent into the '07 design, and manufacture of the first car was beginning, very slowly . . .'

Patrick was still suffering the after-effects of the Watkins Glen trauma: 'Those through-bolt failures had made me extremely conservative in design. As Chief Engineer I felt that it was my prime responsibility to see that things didn't fall off or come apart, and I took that very heavily for the next few months. It was one of the major factors which made me rather slow in completing FW07. I purposely wanted to take a long time over it to ensure that every calculation was double-checked and confirmed, to be certain that everything was sound and strong enough . . .

'What also slowed the introduction of '07 was that we set out with a staff that was still tiny and were attempting to compete against fully-established two-car teams like Tyrrell, who had probably fifty people . . . Our manpower shortage definitely conditioned the rate at which we could make things . . .'

He also believed that after finishing second and then running second in the last two races of 1978 the '06 cars could remain competitive into the first Grands Prix of 1979. He was wrong. He had underestimated the development pace of most other teams, and the non-ground-effect '06 cars had been left far behind as the new season's World Championship commenced in Argentina.

Jones and Regazzoni finished ninth and tenth there, and in Brazil Clay finished fifteenth and last, while Alan retired. It was even worse in South Africa, where Clay finished ninth, but Alan suffered a rear suspension failure at around 150 mph in the very fast kink before the pits, and was lucky to emerge unscathed from a hair-raising spin.

Sponsorship money was still in short supply come the US GP (West) at Long Beach, where '07 made its debut appearance but was not used. Ground-effects are not what is demanded by the Californian street circuit, and Alan stormed home third for his first Championship points of the new year, and Clay lost a consistent seventh place with mechanical failure.

For much of its time at Long Beach FW07/1 lay shrouded by dust sheets in the Williams team's corner of the Formula One garage. Morris Nunn, the always financially beleaguered but very likeable head of the Ensign team, was as keen as any to see it and had been saying repeatedly, 'C'mon, show us yer car.' Early one morning Chief Mechanic Ian Anderson walked in to find a shape moving about beneath the sheet and a foot protruding. Like any self-respecting Chief Mechanic he grabbed it and yanked, and Mo emerged, red-faced and protesting! His curiosity had got the better of him. That time it was amusing . . .

By the end of April, money had been freed and the team had two '07s available for their drivers in the Spanish Grand Prix at Jarama. They qualified thirteenth and fourteenth on the grid and both retired from the race, which was nothing very impressive, but in pre-race warm-up Alan had shown Andretti's Lotus a clean pair of heels under a full tank. Mario was convinced the new '07

must have been running light: 'I couldn't stay near him' – but Frank knew the tank was full. In the race Alan set second fastest lap after Villeneuve's Ferrari, which was using qualifying tyres to regain ground after a pit stop. The Williams men began to appreciate the FW07's enormous potential.

It was to become probably the best of the so-called 'ground-effects' cars then in racing. The box-like pods slung either side of its slender chassis backbone carried carefully shaped 'underwing' panels. Just as airflow over an aircraft's wings make it fly, so airflow beneath the Williams' underwings drew it down against the roadway. This aerodynamic effect loaded its tyres to increase their cornering grip and traction under power and braking. On either side the pods were closed off by vertical panels. Below them extended spring-loaded rigid 'skirts', which slithered along the road surface on bottom edges protected from wear by ceramic skids. These skirts acted as aerodynamic fences to divide the airflow beneath the car from that around it. At around 180 mph the Williams could generate a staggering 4–5,000 lbs downforce in addition to its normal static weight of 1,300 lbs. But should a skirt stick up and not seal against the road surface, then air would spill in beneath the pod side and instantly reduce that suction effect by a factor of four.

That could mean the difference between a driver committing himself safely to a curve at 160 mph, and sliding wildly off into the barriers at a 'mere' 145 mph, or less . . . Skirts were vital to the car's performance and to driver safety, but they were vulnerable.

In practice for the Belgian Grand Prix at Zolder on 13 May, Patrick Depailler spun his Ligier and in avoiding it Alan spun too and damaged his car's skirts on a kerb. While the two Ligiers of Depailler and Laffite dominated qualifying, Alan was third fastest with the skirts still broken. 'The car is fabulous,' he said. 'If the skirts had been working properly I guarantee you I would have gone a second quicker.' From such a man, not given to exaggeration and certainly not to praise, such words were highly significant. Clay went out of the Grand Prix after a collision on the opening lap, but Alan ran second, splitting the Ligiers. By lap twenty-four he led.

It was the first time since Piers had briefly led the 1969 Italian

Grand Prix in Frank's Brabham that a Williams car had led a Grand Prix; the first time ever for a car bearing Frank's own name.

The spell lasted until lap forty, when Jones went missing. On the back of the circuit he had pulled on to the grass verge and abandoned the white-and-green Saudia car when its engine cut abruptly, having suffered a complex electrical failure.

Monaco was approached with as much optimism as any realist can muster in Formula One, and Alan had virtually promised himself pole position there, or at least a front-row start, for over-taking is extremely difficult around the Monte Carlo streets if one is trapped further down the grid.

Patrick recalls how it went wrong: 'We had an engine in Alan's car which had been test-run on the brake at about 3 a.m. and its fuel metering unit had been set up accordingly for maximum power. Of course that's a lovely time – all cold and damp – engines love it, but in the heat at Monaco that engine simply would not run properly throughout the first practice session, which handicapped Alan badly.

'After a few laps at the start of the second period he came in to have the engine leaned-off' – a fuel mixture adjustment – 'when we found that an exhaust bracket had cracked and he was delayed while it was wired up, sitting strapped into the car with me listening to him effing and blinding. He went out of the pits as if it had been a pit stop in the middle of a race, and halfway round that lap – wallop – he was into the barriers. It was the first time I had ever seen him do anything even remotely silly...'

Alan had to start ninth on the grid and climbed to third behind the two Ferraris of Scheckter and Villeneuve by lap twenty-two. He was pressing them hard until his white car fell away abruptly and on lap forty-three hurtled into the pit lane. He had clipped the guardrail at the Tabac Corner, and the steering and front suspension were bent.

He was out, but Clay had been running fifth after starting sixteenth on the grid, and was making further progress. On lap fifty he jinked around Jochen Mass' Arrows into the right-hander at Ste Dévote and took third place on the climb towards the Casino. Four laps later Villeneuve was side-lined and Clay held second place to the finish, for his and '07's first six Championship points of that remarkably promising season.

Frank considers '... we were lucky at Monaco in many ways, but on the debit side Alan would not have finished in any case, even if he hadn't hit the guardrail, because his gearbox had no oil in it. We were still struggling to perfect our preparation and racing systems, we were still building an effective race team. But what was more to the point was the presence at Monaco of Sheikh Kamal Sindhi, Director-General of Saudia, who was delighted to see Clay finish so well – it really showed that although we still had some problems we were making progress...'

One characteristic of Formula One racing which seems to elude the public at large is the unrelenting calendar pressure applied to every team. At the height of the European season there are normally just fourteen days between Grands Prix, which hardly leaves time for normal beings to sit back and take stock of recent events, regardless of pursuing complex technical development and testing. In 1979 there was a much longer gap, however, between Monaco and the French Grand Prix, for the Swedish race had been cancelled and this allowed breathing space for major development by several teams – most notably Renault and Saudia–Williams.

Regazzoni's car was taken direct from Monte Carlo to the French Grand Prix course at Dijon-Prenois for three days' testing, and it simply murdered the existing lap record. After further development the team arrived feeling uncharacteristically self-confident for the French race. Frank: 'We were very soon put in our place by Renault, who had been very fast indeed in private testing, and had kept it quiet. It was their first serious race with their latest twin-turbocharged cars and they slaughtered the rest of us with times in the 67.1s and 67.4s while everybody else – except Villeneuve – couldn't get below 68s, until Alan did a 67.99, only for the stewards to cancel his entire session because, they said, he had gone too fast through the scene of an accident. On the Saturday Alan lost more time when his brakes locked on and he came in with them virtually on fire – the heat was enormous and the discs, calipers, the whole lot were just scrap ...'

To add accidental insult to injury, Clay's car crushed one of Alan's nose wings in the pit lane and finally, while warming up in

In the 1979 Belgian Grand Prix Jones led for fourteen laps in the new FW07 – the first time a Williams-entered F1 car had led since 1969 – but an electrical failure ended his hopes on lap 40.

Monaco 1979 – Clay Regazzoni on his way to second place and the FW07's first six Championship points.

the pits Alan's engine suddenly coughed into silence after a dull thump, and a lazy wisp of smoke spiralled from the intake trumpets. It had dropped a valve and broken internally. This was possibly the legacy of the money shortfall earlier in the season, when some of the team's engines had lain in store since they could not afford to take delivery of them. That period of storage had seen them lying with some valve springs inevitably under load, now one had broken within minutes of the engine being started, and the valve had dropped.

And there was more. While he was running, Alan had drifted wide on to a verge and had been unable to bring the car back on to the track before slamming end-on into a kerb. The shock against the right-front wheel had bottomed the suspension and kinked the top skin of the monocoque chassis. It was later partially reskinned back home.

The Renaults won their maiden *Grande Epreuve* on their home soil, split by Villeneuve's Ferrari – and all on French Michelin tyres. Alan was fourth, the first Goodyear runner, and Clay sixth, unable to do anything about the relative giant teams ahead of them.

Frank thought this was possibly the start of a new age, in which the industrial giants like Renault, Alfa Romeo and Fiat – operating through Ferrari – with their vast engineering resources would kill the established specialist teams such as his own – and then what would the future hold?

'But then we went testing at Silverstone, and it really came home to me just how good Patrick's '07 car was becoming . . .'

There in the Goodyear pre-Grand Prix tyre tests, Niki Lauda's Brabham ran a slightly softer set of tyres than Alan's and clocked 1:13.6 against the Williams driver's 14.0 or 14.1 on a poorish engine. 'Then Patrick and Frank Dernie did some wind tunnel work and came up with an undertray faring to fit beneath the engine. We went back to Silverstone and I could not believe my watch as Alan went out and on his second lap did a 14.6, then 14.0, 13.6, 13.2 and in. When he got down to 13.6 I thought, "This can't be right, I'd better just check these watches", but there was no mistake, and with the underfaring he was suddenly down to 12.6! Although we didn't realize it immediately the improve-

ment was assisted by his running a very strong engine, but by the end of that day Alan was slamming in 12.6s and 12.8s as he liked [against an existing record of 1:18!] . . . and just blowing everybody's mind!

'As I was handling the watches that fantastic feeling swept over me again, just like the previous year in Brazil, or at Brands when Alan was suddenly fourth fastest . . .

'I just could not believe that after all those years of mentally straining and wrestling, thrashing about trying to make things come good, sometimes thinking here we are, this is it – and BANG – it would all blow apart and we would be back at square one straining and struggling once again, and here Alan was going record-breaking in almost unprecedented style . . .'

In official qualifying for the British Grand Prix Alan clocked a barely believable 1:11.8, averaging 144.55 mph! Alan Jones and a Williams car were both on pole position for the first time in their respective careers, and Clay qualified fourth fastest in the other '07 behind Jabouille's Renault and Piquet's Brabham. The Renaults had been tipped to dominate with their turbo power on the open expanse of Silverstone, but British chassis power had overcome French CV.

The Williams twins ran 1–3 early in the race, split by Jabouille's Renault until its tyres burned and he headed for the pits on lap seventeen. For twenty-two more laps Jones and Regazzoni ran 1–2 when suddenly it was the Australian's turn to dive into the pits. For a fleeting moment the team-mates were side-by-side, one in the pit-lane, the other leading on the race track, and then Alan was stationary, bitterly disappointed – for the neck of his Cosworth engine's water pump had cracked, and dribbled all the coolant away.

Clay Regazzoni, popular Clay, blared round untouchable, lap after lap to win the British Grand Prix. Renault had won their first, on home soil, only days previously, and it was fitting that this most British of teams and most British of team principals should now emulate that success.

On the podium Clay excelled, pointedly putting down the traditional bottle of Champagne which was pressed upon him and sipping orange juice instead, in deference to his Saudi sponsors'

Silverstone 1979 – for Jones the thrill of pole position
turned to disappointing retirement, but Regazzoni roared
on to score Williams' first Grand Prix win.

abstinence. Frank felt happy, satisfied for himself and the team, but desperately sorry for Alan, whose success this should have been. He felt almost embarrassed it had taken his team so long as the congratulations and praise showered around his ears. His secretary, Gwen Brown, saw him walking along the pit-lane after Clay had won – a small, dapper figure, looking almost stunned by what his team had at last achieved. 'Congratulations Frank,' she said, and kissed him on the cheek. He grinned briefly, and for the moment couldn't answer.

'In fact,' he recalls 'that was a glorious day for us and for our sponsors, because purely by good fortune it was the first race that Prince Mohammed actually attended. It was a lovely summer's day, Alan had dominated practice, and the press and TV had given us marvellous exposure. I had hired a helicopter for the Prince, and he arrived over Silverstone to find the scene set, you know, one hundred and five fixed-wing aircraft already on the ground there, parked alongside thirty-five helicopters, a vast 105,000 crowd – and he was put down into all this atmosphere; it must have been very, very impressive.

'I had driven out from the paddock to pick him up in Alan's Mercedes 6.9 and as he stepped from the helicopter the Red Arrows RAF aerobatic team arrived overhead to begin their display. He was fascinated by them . . .

'When I drove him and his entourage into the paddock there was a great scrum of photographers gathering round. I thought that this was going to be bad news, but he seemed not to object, and he sat in a car, met the drivers, really became involved . . .

'Normally he would have left immediately after the race, but he seemed intrigued by everybody's reaction. Clay was immensely popular with the crowd, and people were flooding over the safety banks and massing around the pits cheering for him. The Prince spent a couple of hours with Clay in the motorhome, and then he actually insisted on walking back to the helicopter with me, through all the crowds. He didn't want to be driven.

'When we got to it he took off immediately, no delay, and he was whisked back to London. He was immensely proud, and for him it had been a perfect day. I could not have wished for better, if only Alan's car had not failed him . . .'

That first victory was both moving and momentous, but it was merely one battle in a wider war and now the team were hungry for more success. It came in the German Grand Prix at Hockenheim where Alan won at last and Clay was second in support, after the powerful Renault had taken pole position, and a Ferrari set fastest lap.

In Austria Alan won again and Clay was fifth. Renault took pole and fastest lap honours. While the cars were on the grid, a rival team manager was found measuring up the spare FW07 in the deserted paddock! In Holland Alan won his third in a row, a momentous hat-trick for the driver, and four in a row for the team, but yet again Renault took pole, and Ferrari fastest lap. The British team raced well, and some were saying that Alan was no qualifier but a great and natural racer. There was an element of truth in that opinion.

There in Holland Clay was sidelined before the first corner when his left-front wheel was ripped off against Arnoux's Renault.

At Monza for the Italian Grand Prix, engine power ruled the day: Alan qualified fourth, behind the two Renaults and Scheckter's Ferrari, while Clay – who celebrated his fortieth birthday during practice – was sixth quickest a row behind. He was to set fastest race lap and finish third behind the Ferrari team, but Alan struck trouble.

His start was uncharacteristically slow, and after five laps he pulled into the pits for the battery and ignition 'spark box' to be changed. Despite an insuperable handicap thereafter he tigered his way back into the race. Alan Jones had repeatedly proved himself one of the great self-motivators in Grand Prix driving, and this was a classic instance. But his team-mate was travelling even faster in his late-race efforts to catch the works Ferraris. Clay would have loved to have beaten Ferrari on their home soil but it was not to be, and at the chequered flag his car was stammering along, almost out of fuel. It ran dry on his slowing-down lap, and Alan stopped to pick up Clay, only for his own car to run dry in sympathy. It was a close-run thing.

By this stage of the season Scheckter was assured of the Drivers' World Championship, with 51 points to Villeneuve's 38, Laffite's

36 in the Ligier and Alan's 34, with just two rounds remaining to be run. Clay was fifth in the table with 27 points. In the Constructors' Cup, Ferrari led with 95 points, but Saudia–Williams lay second with 62, one point clear of Ligier.

The Canadian and United States (East) Grands Prix completed the season. Alan and Clay finished first and second at Montreal, where the Australian almost achieved the perfect performance. He had pole position and fastest race lap also to his credit – but he had not led throughout, having followed Villeneuve's Ferrari for thirty laps early on, conserving his brakes and gearbox and watching to see how the race would develop. The Williams and Ferrari banged wheels as Jones made his move and took the lead which he was not to lose.

At Watkins Glen, Alan again qualified on pole while Clay was fifth, and again Villeneuve led away with Jones on his tail. The start was wet, the track dried and tyre changes had to be made. On lap thirty-six Alan relinquished the race lead to make his stop, but the right-rear wheel hung up briefly. The other three were off and replaced before Wayne Eckersley managed to slide his fresh right-rear on to its locating drive-pegs, and before he could tighten the hub-nut fully Jones had been signalled away. In half a lap that wheel broke loose, and Alan found himself slithering out of the race in a three-wheeled Formula One car. Clay, in his final drive for the team, had already lost seventh place by sliding in the wet after his tyre change and ramming the right-rear wheel of Piquet's Brabham, to retire with damaged steering.

So Alan Jones ended the season third in the Drivers' Championship table, with forty points to Villeneuve's forty-seven in second place and Scheckter's fifty-one at the top of the tree. Yet while Scheckter had won three Grands Prix that year, and Villeneuve just two, Alan had four to his name. WGPE's early disappointments with the FW06 cars and the late development to full competitiveness of the superb '07 had cost them the World Championship . . .

On the Title Trail

Into 1980 Leyland Vehicles joined the Saudi consortium as co-sponsors of WGPE's race team, in which Alan Jones was joined by Carlos Reutemann. Williams now had two truly world-class talents – in proven cars. During the winter of 1979–80 Patrick, Frank Dernie and Neil Oatley had been working to update their existing '07 design in its end-of-season form. Patrick and Frank knew that the opposition would have made great strides during those short closed-season months: 'We reckoned we would need a car that was two seconds a lap quicker in order to win. We thought that was necessary, because for sure the existing cars would only be good for the third or fourth row of the grid in the first race of the new year at Buenos Aires...'

From 3 to 7 December 1979, Goodyear organized a tyre testing programme at the Argentinian autodrome, for they had introduced a vital change in their operation, in that Formula One tyres were no longer to be made at their Wolverhampton plant, close to the action in Britain, but at their home base in Akron, Ohio – America's 'tyre-town'. Frank, Jeff Hazell, Neil Oatley, Alan Jones and four mechanics made the trip with one car and three engines. This type of expense-no-object testing was becoming typical of the effort demanded to stay near the top in Formula One. The trip cost around £39,300 (shared with Goodyear) and the results seemed promising.

For the Grand Prix itself on 13 January 1980, the team returned in force with the new FW07B stiffened-monocoque cars with their much modified aerodynamics, reaching towards the Lotus 80-type form. But practice in the Parque Almirante Brown quickly revealed major problems. The FW07B spec which had seemed so promising during winter testing at Ricard-Castellet in France proved unstable there. Alan Jones: 'For sure it had more down-force, it was much quicker than the 1979 car through the slow sections, but I couldn't get it balanced through the fast bits...'

There was no question of the race engineers standing on their pride. They had a Grand Prix to win, if possible, and the spare standard '07 which had been left in Buenos Aires since those December tyre tests was race-prepared for Alan, while Reutemann's new car was stripped of what B-spec components were instantly removable.

Despite such dramas Alan qualified on pole, from the Ligiers of Laffite and his new team-mate Didier Pironi. He took an immediate race lead, while Carlos qualified tenth, and ran fourth early in this, his home race.

It was to prove a dramatic race, as a newly resurfaced part of the track broke up in the South American summer heat, to form an unpredictably slippery patch of 'marbles' which caught several drivers out, including the leader. He spun twice, but his car had already scooped up a plastic bag in a side radiator duct which sent oil and water temperatures soaring. He tried to reach out and grab it, almost losing his arm to the airstream in the attempt. It was impossible. On lap seventeen he tore into the WGPE pit, where his crew plucked the bag clear and topped up the car's water system from the pressurized quick-fill canister thought-fully provided. Alan was away again after being stationary for just seven seconds.

He rejoined, fourth and charging. He picked off Villeneuve, Piquet and Laffite. By lap thirty he was leading again, with twenty-three to go. His car's water and oil temperatures remained dangerously high, but he found he could hold off Piquet in second place by hammering hard for a lap, then feather-footing his way round for a few more while temperatures stabilized, then hammering hard again. He broke Piquet's heart. The young Brazilian would be closing for lap after lap, then mysteriously, easily, the white-and-green Williams would blare away from him again. Right at the end there was an evil glow from the amber oil pressure warning light of Alan's car. It was a very relieved Australian who finally took the chequered flag, for his sixth Grand Prix victory.

Back in England some immensely relieved and delighted Leyland Vehicles executives saw their very brave decision to back the team immediately vindicated, as TV coverage of the race showed the white car with 'Leyland' lettering on its flanks blaring round, lap after lap, in first place.

Meanwhile Carlos had a rather disappointing race on his home ground after a hectic early battle with Piquet and Laffite. On lap eleven he charged off on to the grass after a bold attempt to wrest third place from Piquet, and had to call at the pits, where grass was shovelled out of the radiator ducts. He rejoined, but survived just two laps before his engine cooked itself to destruction. It was his first retirement in an Argentine Grand Prix, an ignominious start to his Williams career.

In Brazil the frost-damaged Interlagos circuit upset the FW07 cars, whose aerodynamic skirts were being forced so high into their housings by the bumps that the guides would jam and refuse to spring down again. Robbed suddenly of their downforce, the cars proved frighteningly unpredictable for both drivers. Interlagos' long curves still created enormous 'G'-loadings for ground-effect cars, and the drivers experienced new problems as their neck muscles suffered under the strain of supporting those heavily helmeted heads. A local masseur came to the rescue.

Carlos had qualified fourth and was keen to win again at Interlagos, while Alan could not improve on tenth. But Lolé's car broke a drive-shaft joint on the startline and he was out immediately. Alan plugged away manfully during the race, and finished third to maintain his World Championship lead by four points from René Arnoux, whose Renault won.

Obviously the Renaults would operate well in the South African Grand Prix at Kyalami, where their turbocharged engines would not suffer from the altitude-rarefied air, unlike the atmospheric-induction-engined brigade. After troubled practice periods Carlos again out-qualified Alan Jones, but the Australian made one of his customary blistering starts and was third behind the Renaults for the first seven laps until Laffite's Ligier went by under braking at the end of the main straight. Carlos lay fifth in Alan's wake, but the Australian's gearbox was losing oil through a broken cooler union. After thirty-four laps he was out. Reutemann's left-front tyre was showing the distinctive darker streak caused by growing heat blisters, and a stop to replace it dropped him back to sixth place at the finish – his first World Championship points for Williams. Arnoux won, to take the lead in the Drivers' Championship, and with two wins to one, Renault displaced WGPE at the top of the Constructors' competition.

Alan had been suffering more than damaged pride at losing his lead. Testing in bad weather at Silverstone and then a damp hotel bed in South Africa seemed to have contributed to a dose of pleurisy, and at Long Beach for the United States Grand Prix (West) on his adopted home ground he was stricken by shooting pains in his chest, and was coughing so badly that he could not sleep. Dr Rafael Grajales, the 'circus' physician introduced to Formula One by Fittipaldi, dosed him with pills enabling him to drive, but with Alan fifth and Carlos seventh on the grid, it did not look very promising.

The race was Nelson Piquet's and Brabham's – the perfect racing performance, starting from pole, leading all the way to win, and setting fastest lap. Alan chased Depailler's Alfa Romeo in the early stages: 'His Alfa was unexpectedly quick, 10 mph faster than my car in practice along the fastest part, and it had more acceleration out of slow corners. But I was definitely quicker round the left-hander that leads up to Shoreline Drive hairpin, and it was there that I was able to overtake him . . .'

Some of the art of Grand Prix driving emerged as he recalled: 'It required a bit of deception . . . I hung back for three or four laps, staying there without indicating that I was about to overtake. Then I got a really good run at him coming out of the left-hander, pulled out on his left side under braking and managed to swing round the outside of him.'

Disaster followed as he attempted to lap the other Alfa Romeo: 'Bruno Giacomelli knew I was following him. I could see his head moving around inside the cockpit . . . so he must have spotted me in his mirrors. I'd been there for three laps and it was time for me to make a move . . . The best passing place is under braking into the Queen's Hairpin. I nosed inside him there to let him know I was coming through . . . and he turned across in front of my car, we bashed wheels and my left-side steering arm came off worse . . .'

He was out, joining Carlos, who had been side-lined by another drive-shaft joint breaking. Incredibly, he too had fallen foul of Giacomelli, in his case on the fourth lap, when the young Italian was running fifth at the head of a queue, and spun under braking for the hairpin leading on to Shoreline Drive, where Jones had passed Depailler. In a desperate attempt to recover, Giacomelli had selected reverse and backed away from the right-side barrier, collecting Carlos as he dived for the narrowing gap behind the Italian car. Scheckter was trapped behind the stalled Williams in his Ferrari, and was struck by three cars in train. Reutemann restarted on the onboard air-bottle, selected first in fury, popped the clutch and that constant velocity joint sheared . . .

Alan had fallen to third in the Championship behind Arnoux and Piquet, while Renault and Brabham now shared the Constructors' Cup lead ahead of Williams.

When the European season opened on 4 May with the Belgian Grand Prix, the team had further modified B-spec cars available and they worked well, although qualifying problems meant Alan actually set his pole position time in the spare car, which Carlos used also to win fourth place on the grid. This was some measure of how the team had weathered its bad patch from Brazil through Long Beach, and its strength in depth was about to show. In the race Pironi's Ligier led from flag to flag while Alan had to drive for a finish, preserving a blistering left-front tyre as their practice alarums had prevented full-tank testing and a too-soft tyre spec had been chosen. Still his six points put him back into second place in the Championship chase, nineteen points to Arnoux's

twenty-one. Carlos ran fourth much of the way and inherited third place for a team 2–3. Williams were elevated to the head of the Constructors' competition table, with twenty-five points to Ligier's twenty-three and Renault's twenty-one.

Meanwhile, trouble had long been brewing between the English-dominated Formula One Constructors' Association (FOCA) and the French-dominated governing body of the sport, the *Fédération Internationale du Sport Automobile* (FISA) under its autocratic and FOCA-phobic new President, Jean-Marie Balestre. At Zolder Balestre had decreed that a driver briefing would be mandatory, threatening $2,000 fines for non-attendance. The race regulations made no mention of any such meeting, so Alan Jones was one of several leading drivers to stay away . . . and be fined.

At Monaco, Pironi ran away with the race early on with Alan and Carlos on the Ligier's tail in their FW07Bs. Lolé had out-qualified Jones by 0.6 second for second place on the grid behind Pironi (only seven-hundredths of a second faster) but the Australian powered past him up the hill towards the Casino on the opening lap, having reasoned that since the cars would be sluggish under full tanks first gear was the one to use rather than second out of Ste Dévote corner at the foot of the rise. As the race developed, Alan sensed that he had the measure of Pironi, but on lap twenty-four there came a horrible vibration from the rear of his car, accompanied by grinding noises, and as the car began to steer itself it was obvious the differential had failed.

This was a body blow for the Australian's hopes, but for the team Reutemann was now poised in exactly the position he had been recruited to adopt: ready to step forward and maintain Williams pressure upon the Ligier. The gap was three seconds, and Pironi seemed able to maintain it, although he was actually troubled with the transmission jumping out of third gear. On lap fifty-five he entered the Casino Square marginally too fast, third gear disengaged at that moment, and Pironi became merely a passenger as his car hurled itself into the guardrails. Lolé inherited command to cruise home to his first Saudia–Leyland Williams team victory.

Their lead in the Constructors' Cup had grown to five points, with thirty-four against Ligier's twenty-nine and now Brabham's twenty-two. Nelson Piquet of Brabham had stolen the Drivers' Championship lead with twenty-two points from Arnoux's twenty-one, and Alan Jones' nineteen...

On his return to England, Alan found a missive awaiting him from the Belgian Grand Prix organizers, demanding payment of his $2,000 fine. There had been another of Balestre's briefings at Monte Carlo, from which several drivers absented themselves. Now there were rumours that the dissenting drivers would be banned from the following Spanish Grand Prix, unless they paid up.

The conflict brewing between FOCA and FISA was coming to a head, and it erupted at Jarama, the Spanish circuit north of Madrid. Bernard Ecclestone had produced in FOCA an organization capable of guaranteeing full twenty-four-car grids for World Championship Formula One races world-wide. The cost to race promoters had inflated, but they were presented with a ready-made and guaranteed race package.

Meanwhile the International governing body, recently re-modelled from the old CSI as FISA, had lost both influence and power – diluted by its weak and often demonstrably incompetent executive. Balestre considered that FOCA was taking too much upon itself in the development and running of what was, after all, FISA's World Championship competition. When he had assumed the FISA Presidency in October 1978, the fur had begun to fly. At Monza in 1979 some measure of agreement had been reached, which achieved a degree of harmony for a brief period, until at Rio a FISA meeting had been convened, after which Balestre announced that aerodynamic skirts would be banned from 1 January 1981. This move was seen by most FOCA constructors as a device to cripple the Cosworth engine users, whose chassis power consistently compensated – and more – for the British engine's disadvantage in sheer power output against the turbocharged Renaults, 12-cylinder Ferraris and Alfa Romeos.

FOCA quite reasonably wanted a major say in such vital technical matters as the use of skirts and the setting of minimum weight limits. Balestre, however, had not followed established procedures in making his statements, and several team principals had

actually ordered their drivers not to attend his imposed briefings, the Association indicating it would pay their fines. FISA duly enforced those fines, they remained unpaid, and Balestre rescinded the culprits' competition licences...

The scene had been set for a trial of strength in Spain. FOCA threatened not to race at all unless the fines were dropped. The *Real Automovil Club de España*, anxious for their race to proceed, offered to deposit a sum equal to the outstanding fines with FISA, but Balestre demanded the drivers should pay, in full. RACE responded by dispensing with FISA's representation at their Grand Prix meeting and ran it supposedly under the direct auspices of the *Fédération Internationale de l'Automobile* (FIA), which is the governing federation of automobile clubs. FOCA announced, rather rashly, that the race would go ahead and would count 'for the official 1980 Formula One World Championship', which was a status not theirs to give. It was reasoned that since this was no longer a FISA race, FISA licences were not required.

At this point the major manufacturer teams of Renault, Ferrari and Alfa Romeo opted out. They had too much to lose through possible bans in other forms of motor sport, outside Formula One. Under this great black cloud the Jarama race was run with Laffite on pole for Ligier, from Alan, Pironi and Carlos. For the first time the swarthy Argentinian out-dragged his team-mate from the start, and No. 28 led No. 27, but already Alan knew he was in trouble, again...

'My engine had shown signs of overheating on the warm-up lap, and I stole an extra lap by coming into the pits for a chat with Frank, and we almost decided then to switch to the spare car. You can imagine how I felt, going to the start with a dodgy engine...'

On lap thirteen he missed a gear, and as his car ran wide in that corner Laffite, Piquet and Pironi rushed by in their pursuit of Reutemann. Laffite closed on the leading Williams until, on lap thirty-six, both came upon the slow Spanish driver Emilio de Villota, whose private 1979 Williams FW07 was running last, after a pit stop. Carlos passed him on the right, the startled Spaniard veered left, and there was Laffite, committed to passing him on that side. The Ligier's right-front wheel was crushed back and it hurtled straight on across the following left-hand turn into which Reutemann was just locking over. The Ligier torpedoed the Williams amidships and both cars flailed into the catch-fences. Carlos was badly bruised and winded, understandably shocked by this lightning stroke from a clear blue sky, and with his ribs more damaged than perhaps he would want his team to know.

Piquet inherited the lead from Pironi and Jones, who was worrying his way round with water temperatures of 135 degrees instead of the usual 100. To save thermal load he was changing-up at 10,200 rpm instead of his usual 10,800. Piquet's transmission failed. It was Pironi leading Jones. Alan drove as he had in Argentina, charging hard, then sitting back while temperatures stabilized, and then charging again. Suddenly the Ligier lost its right-front wheel. 'Jeez, I said to myself, this has got to be my lucky day ... When you think the engine could have quit at any moment, or the gearshift could have let me down again, you'll understand how happy I was to see the chequered flag ...'

There was a four-week interval between the Spanish and French races, and at one stage it looked quite likely that only Ferrari, Renault and Alfa Romeo would be running at Ricard-Castellet, as the FOCA–FISA dispute rumbled on. The Spanish Grand Prix was to be deleted from the Championship by FISA, and the nine points both Alan and the team believed they had scored there would be void. There were strong feelings in Britain that the French-dominated governing body of the sport was attempting to ensure French success in the World Championship by manipulating the rules. Hard things were said, and agreement for the FOCA teams to run at Ricard only came six days before the race, and the circus arrived as normal. By this time there was a healthy disrespect at Didcot for almost everything French, and Alan Jones especially was boiling 'to put one across the Frogs on their own patch ...' What followed was the most satisfyingly hard-won victory of that whole season ...

Frank Williams: 'At Ricard we weren't favourites by any means. We had to work all weekend to become at least as fast as the Ligiers ... Saturday speed trap times showed they were 15 kph quicker than us. We were beavering away with Carlos on the Friday and Saturday, sorting tyres, while Alan sorted out the chassis. Carlos did something like 150 miles on full tanks on Saturday morning to prove the tyres, because Ricard is notoriously abrasive. Even in the middle of qualifying he went through his two sets of softer tyres and then filled his tanks again, just because we were worried about choosing the right race tyres and the cars' balance on them.

'He tested almost to the point of boredom: B tyres or C tyres, Bs on the left-side, Cs on the right-side, full tanks, try everything; get after it! Alan had sorted the chassis, both he and Carlos liked a virtually identical set-up, which simplified matters enormously for the team, and we made another fine adjustment on the grid. I thought, "Well, with a bit of luck we'll come out of this with a third and fourth," expecting the Ligiers just to ease away. But in the race Alan fought like hell and simply outdrove them, and they burned through their front tyres ...'

Alan's car was super fast down the long *Mistral* straight, and he conserved his relatively soft Goodyear tyres while Laffite and Pironi progressively lost front-end grip. Alan simply muscled past Pironi for second place, and on lap thirty-five out-braked Laffite into a chicane, and the race was over.

Patrick Head: 'Alan is a very strong, physically rugged driver. People think I'm heavily built, but they haven't seen anything until they've looked at Alan's fore-arms. He's strong and fit, and whereas some drivers might exhaust themselves by stringing together say ten or a dozen laps at near maximum effort, Alan can maintain that level throughout a race. He'll just take a Grand Prix by the neck and throttle it to death. He simply grinds down the opposition until they can't hold him off any more ...'

While Alan won, Carlos was caught behind Arnoux's Renault, which would power away along the straights and then block him through the tighter turns, since the Williams' engine proved down on power. They finished fifth and sixth, the Frenchman having gnawed his lower lip until it bled while holding off 'El Lolé'.

Even without his nine points from Spain, Alan Jones now led the Championship table with twenty-eight points to Piquet's twenty-five and Arnoux's twenty-three. And Williams maintained their Constructors' Cup lead, by forty-four points to Ligier's thirty-nine and Brabham's twenty-five.

The British Grand Prix was run at Brands Hatch, and was the

With the damaged cars of Laffite and Reutemann in the background, Alan Jones
nurses the overheating FW07B to victory in the 1980 Spanish Grand Prix.

race Alan most wanted to win: 'It had been an ambition of mine since I arrived from Australia to begin my professional career in 1971 . . .'

Pironi and Laffite qualified on the front row of the grid, with Jones and Carlos on row two. It was Ligier-versus-Williams with a vengeance. After race-morning warm-up Alan was disturbed: '. . . my car was understeering too much . . . so the team went into a big huddle in the motorhome to decide what to do . . . as it happened Carlos had his sister car set up rather differently from mine and wasn't complaining about any understeer, so we copied some of the settings from his car. I managed to steal a second warm-up lap immediately before the race, and the car was much better balanced . . .'

The Ligier team were hell-bent on avenging their defeat on native soil, and Pironi got away in the lead while Alan's initial charge was shouldered off on to the grass at the entry to the first corner and Laffite set about keeping him back in third place. But the Ligier wheels gave trouble. Pironi had a tyre deflate and stopped to change it, then Laffite developed similar problems but pressed on until his tyre collapsed and he flew off the road.

Jones: 'I knew that I was in the lead for sure when I came into Clearways, the last corner before the pits, and saw the fans on their feet, waving programmes, beer cans, anything they could find. They were cheering all round the circuit too. It's an extraordinary feeling to know that so many people are on your side. I know Carlos gets that sort of support from his home fans, but it's much less common with the less demonstrative British.'

He had had to hold off Piquet's Brabham, was wary of the patchily slippery track, and when another car tossed up a broken-off section of Tyrrell bodywork it slammed back into the FW07B's nose. Still the car ran reliably to win . . . 'My victory lap was something I shall remember all my life. I had time to wave to all those wonderful fans and marshals. Somewhere in the crowd I even spotted flags waved by a couple of the guys who work in the factory . . .'

Carlos had perhaps been over-careful with his tyres early on. He inherited third place behind Piquet on lap thirty-one, and made his effort to challenge for second place too late – setting his fastest lap on the seventy-fifth of the scheduled seventy-six. But Alan was now six points clear of Piquet and the team eighteen points ahead of Ligier. Their systems were operating very well indeed. Their last retirement had been Alan's at Monaco, three races back, and the race team had stabilized into a totally committed group of highly skilled and extremely capable men.

Two very fast circuits followed in the Championship calendar, with the German Grand Prix at Hockenheim and the Austrian at Österreichring. These were venues where the turbocharged Renaults should return to form, and so it proved, although in Germany Alan qualified on pole ahead of Jabouille and Arnoux in the yellow French cars and Carlos' second Williams. The Argentinian experienced immense pre-race drama as his car caught fire due to a loose fuel union. But he made the race, in which Jabouille out-gunned Jones from the start and led until lap twenty-six, when valve-gear failure side-lined the Renault. The white No. 27 was leading a Grand Prix once again, until lap forty when Alan blared into the pits with the left-front tyre punctured. Both wheels were changed to provide a balanced set, and after losing nineteen seconds he rejoined in third place, behind Reutemann and Laffite. The Ligier won, with the Saudia–Leyland cars second and third. Alan's Championship lead was still growing – he was now seven points ahead of Piquet. The Williams marque enjoyed a nineteen-point lead over Ligier.

The fast open curves of the Styrian mountain circuit in Austria provided a Renault benefit, as Arnoux and Jabouille qualified 1–2 on the grid ahead of the Williams twins. Jabouille won at last, after his team-mate's left-front tyre had overheated, he had stopped to replace all four, and finished ninth. Jones was second and Reutemann third, again . . . Laffite was fourth and Piquet fifth.

Thus there were eleven points between Alan and Nelson as the teams trucked their cars home – few people at that stage suspecting that Brabham and Piquet were about to emerge from the next race forward as the most potent single threat to Williams' Championship hopes. After his victory there the previous year, which had completed his wonderful hat-trick, Alan Jones must have been looking towards Zandvoort, and the Dutch Grand Prix, with some relish . . . the great battle was about to begin.

Grinding down the
opposition – a great day for
Alan Jones and the Williams
team as the French
favourites, Ligier, are
beaten on their home
ground at Ricard-Castellet.

The Championship Lost and Won

Alan Jones was disgusted with himself. He knew he'd blown his chance of winning the Dutch Grand Prix. He had started this race at Zandvoort as favourite for the 1980 World Championship. He held an eleven-point lead over his nearest rival, Nelson Piquet. Now he had probably given him nine points on a plate . . .

Just ninety seconds earlier he had made a superb race start. He had catapulted his white-and-green Williams car from fourth place on the grid up alongside René Arnoux's turbocharged Renault. Through the long right-handed Tarzan Hairpin he had charged around outside the French car to take the lead, and back behind the sand-dune circuit's paddock and away into that dauntingly fast swerving backstretch he drew away.

Completing that first lap Jones led handsomely down into the Tarzan loop. Accelerating hard behind the paddock he slung his way left, then right through the lazy S-bend there, then ran hard over the brow and down into the braking area for the wicked left-hander by the Dutch circuit's control tower. This turn, the *Hugenholtzbocht*, is edged at its exit with sloping red-flecked white concrete kerbstones, and Alan had crashed heavily there in practice.

Jones had ripped out a spectacular hundred-yard lead but now a momentary lapse would throw it all away. He took a long look in his rear-view mirrors, braced high from the car's resin cockpit coaming; searching perhaps a tenth of a second too long.

That was enough to commit his car too deep into the *Hugenholtz-bocht*. He went hurtling in so fast that not even the Williams' road-holding could prevent it sliding wide past the left-side apex, across the road and up high on to that sloping outside kerb.

In a flurry of dust the car's right-side wheels rode over the kerb and the concrete slabs punched the skirt hard into the top of its housing. Jones could not wrench the car back on to the roadway for fear of spinning broadside across the track, but before he could gently ease it down the kerbstones ended – and there was a drop of perhaps five or six inches to the grass verge. It was enough.

At around 110 mph the car hurtled off the final kerbstone and, set free, the leading edge of the right-side skirt sprang down. Instantly it jammed deep into the yielding soil and the car's forward flight simply smashed it.

Immediately Jones knew he was in trouble. When the front tyres broke adhesion into the next turn and the car's nose slid wide, he knew he would have to stop at his pit.

His pit crew did him proud, putting him back into the race after losing just three laps, but that still left him eleventh and resoundingly last at the finish, despite an heroically aggressive come-back drive. The skirt replacement was a fiddly job.

Patrick Head later likened the Williams crew's feverish three-lap repair to changing a complete engine in around twenty minutes. The tough Australian driver's reaction to his own error had been typical as he drove his heart out to compensate, but the team was less happy with Reutemann, who did no more than soldier reliably into fourth place without showing the fire, skill and pace expected of him. Perhaps the lingering effects of his rib injury bothered him more than he was willing to say, but his performance that day was a lack-lustre effort. Nelson Piquet had won for Brabham and was now only two points adrift in the Championship chase.

Jones leads the Dutch Grand Prix at Zandvoort, before a momentary
lapse costs him nine precious Championship points.

Promoting its sponsors, drooping its skirts, Alan Jones' FW07B is prepared for practice, Jarama 1980.

Next day at Didcot, however, Frank remarked thoughtfully to Patrick Head that although the Dutch race had been a black day for the team they still led the World Championship chase, and on current form they could still win it. They were still on top, and must not lose sight of that . . .

There were three rounds remaining. The Italian GP was to be held at Imola on 14 September, followed by the Canadian GP on 28 September, and the US GP on 5 October. At Imola, Jones was under intense pressure and found it difficult to respond. His practice periods were punctuated by engine failures and spins, and Reutemann qualified faster for the team with a sensational ten-tenths effort. Frank Williams felt that his Argentinian driver could dominate the race, but after making the best initial start his car suffered a transmission fault which handicapped him throughout the race, although he still finished third.

Meanwhile Nelson Piquet's Brabham again performed superbly early on and he established a lead which Jones, fighting grimly against his own tensions and some distaste for the circuit's ludicrously tight chicane corner, could not diminish. Towards the end both the Brabham and Jones' Williams – in a doughty second place – were in brake trouble, but they still finished first and second.

Piquet's nine points took him ahead of Jones in the Championship table, by just one solitary point . . .

Minutes after the race finish the Brabham sponsors' helicopter chattered into the air above the *Autodromo Dino Ferrari*, carrying Brabham boss Ecclestone and Williams towards Bologna, where a jet waited to fly them to London. As they swept northward over the hazy Emilian plain Frank felt strangely content:

'Throughout my life I'd been the underdog, used to coming from behind. I am an habitual worrier – I always worry, but I reacted better to the situation after Imola than I had to that after Zandvoort, when we still led the Championship. I said to myself "Well, Nelson's a point ahead, but there's now one less round to go – with maximum effort in America we can still pull it off."

'Patrick and I think very similarly. We both felt that the situation was tense, but it wasn't yet beyond the team's capabilities. It is terribly easy to psych yourself out in racing. We decided instinctively that we were going to cross the Atlantic for these last two races utterly intent on enjoying our racing. We might get blown off by the Brabham, but we hoped it would be a good race nonetheless. If Nelson won the Championship, OK, we had been beaten, but at least we had gone down honourably . . .'

World Championship titles are not delivered within one's reach on an annual basis, and back at Didcot no expense was spared to ensure that the team's drivers had the very best equipment available for Canada. When they set off for Montreal's *Île de Notre Dame* circuit the team travelled with four cars, eight engines, $5\frac{1}{2}$ metric tonnes of spares and twenty-six people . . .

In practice on the island circuit there, out in the St Laurence Seaway, Nelson Piquet stunned the Williams team in practice by suddenly – miraculously – running a whole 1.5 seconds faster, after having trailed Jones and Reutemann for a day and a half. Miracles like that simply do not happen by chance in motor racing, and they subsequently discovered that Brabham had fitted a specially tuned 'screamer' engine. On race morning the final session in which the race cars are tested reflected the true situation. Both Williams machines were 0.3 to 0.4 seconds faster than the Brabham. Piquet's team could not afford to run the highly-tweaked special engine in a two-hundred-mile Grand Prix.

The atmosphere was tense as the cars hesitated on the starting grid. The green light flared, Piquet took off from pole position and Jones made his customary superb start from his second grid position, staggered back to the Brazilian's left. They speared side-by-side into the first very fast right-hand curve. For their cars it was flat out – just – if the driver had chosen the right line. Jones, in the centre of the track, was on that line; Piquet, on the inside where he had just moved to pinch-out Pironi's charging Ligier, was not . . .

Into the curve Jones could not see the Brabham's nose from the corner of his eye. He reasoned that he was more than three-quarters of a car's length ahead and drove determinedly for the right-hand apex. Piquet, equally set upon winning this sprint for the first corner, refused to back off. The Williams' right-side rear wheel met the left side of the Brabham's body and as Jones bounced clear and tore away into the next left-hander to lead the race, the Brazilian began to spin.

His Brabham's nose crumpled against the right-side retaining wall and bounced it back into the road. The pack began to dodge, and amid a flurried confusion of shredded bodywork and scattering fragments eight cars were disabled. The red flags went out immediately to stop the race for the surviving cars. After a decent interval to repair, refuel and wheel out spare cars, the Grand Prix was restarted, with Piquet this time in his practice car – still fitted with that specially potent, but fragile, Cosworth engine.

Sure enough, he stole the race lead and stormed away while Alan ran patiently second in his wake. Pironi was third.

The Williams men had anticipated a long and hard race on this gruelling course. It is hard on brakes and gearboxes, and it fatigues drivers quickly. Alan Jones was immensely rugged and fit, with deep reserves of strength. He would not tire, but would the wiry little Brazilian ahead of him? In their pre-race discussions Frank, Patrick and the Williams drivers had appreciated that the first thirty laps or so under full tanks would be very hard on tyres. It was agreed that if Piquet should make a break then Alan would merely try to keep him in sight, rather than in touch. The plan was to conserve tyres, brakes and gearbox until the last third of the seventy-laps distance, when Alan could mount his attack – if he was in a position to.

That was a major question as Piquet lapped imperiously fast and dominated the race – until lap 24, when abruptly, without warning, that special engine simply burst apart. Jones whistled by to inherit the lead, but then Pironi was charging hard on his tail.

In the pits Frank was sitting on a folding chair beside the guardrail, his face a mask of concentration as he entered car numbers and times upon his lap chart. Someone stopped by to bawl above the wail of passing cars, 'Pironi's been penalized one minute for jumping the start!'...

Frank was galvanized. He turned to his team manager Jeff Hazell and asked him immediately to tackle the Clerk of the Course for written confirmation: 'I wasn't about to signal Alan "Pironi, plus-60 secs" if it wasn't so, but I did not want him to think he had to fight off the Ligier if it wasn't necessary...'

Hazell soon returned with news that the Clerk of the Course could not confirm the penalty in writing but that Gerard Ducarouge of the Ligier team had been informed. Once the penalty notice had been served, so to speak, it cannot be withdrawn. Frank was happy and the signal went out. Alan Jones gently rolled off his pace without disturbing his habitual automaton rhythm. Carlos Reutemann closed into team formation on his tail and Pironi went on to take the lead on the road, only for his time penalty to place him officially third.

With two laps to run, Jones' actual race lead was 35 seconds over Pironi. Two laps between Alan Jones, the Williams team and their World Championship. Eric Bhat of the glossy *Grand Prix International* magazine was watching, and he reported: 'Patrick Head turned his broad back to the track. His face was impassive, yet the very action indicated that he couldn't bear to watch.

'For the penultimate time Didier Pironi drove past the Williams pit, Frank Williams conscientiously wrote the number 25 at the top of the penultimate column, and waited to write the number 27 when Jones passed ... the Williams followed the Ligier 25 seconds later. The Australian driver had just one more lap to do before victory and the World Championship was his.

'It would soon all be over. Nelson Piquet, watching from the side of the track, was resigned to second place in the series. Alan Jones, in the cockpit, worked away at the wheel. Patrick Head crossed the pit lane to rejoin Frank Williams, whose face was already beginning to crack into a broad smile. "Get out the flag, wave it high," said Frank to the mechanics.

'The Union Jack fluttered above the Armco in front of the Williams pit, celebrating their win, their one-two, and the World Championship title. "Thank you for your help," said Frank to his mechanics. Jones took his foot off the accelerator, relishing the slowing down lap as one of the most enjoyable laps of his career. Not surprisingly he was utterly satisfied. He'd achieved what he had set out to do – win the World Championship. After the previous weeks of tension, his satisfaction and relief were immense.

'On his way to the rostrum, Frank Williams made a small diversion via the Brabham pit, where he took Gordon Murray's hand. The Brabham designer's face was impassive with dis-

Williams *v* Brabham on Montreal's *Île de Notre Dame* circuit. One of many confrontations, this one sealed the 1980 World Championship.

appointment, but it broke into a smile. "Congratulations Frank," said Gordon. Anything more was unnecessary. Straightforward appreciation from loser to winner was almost homage in itself . . .'

On the rostrum Alan admitted that his new World Championship title had yet to sink in. His voice was tense with uncharacteristic emotion as he told the watching TV audience in Australia how he hoped they would be proud of him, and then it was a scrum of excited pressmen before the brief peace of a shower.

Great emotion has no place in the Williams team. Obviously they were happy to have achieved their aim, but not self-satisfied, for there was to be another Grand Prix race in just seven days' time. *Techniques d'Avant Garde*, their leading Saudi Arabian aviation sponsors, held a discreet reception that evening in a Montreal hotel, then it was early to bed. The Monday morning saw the Williams organization back at work, perhaps more relaxed and smiling than twenty-four hours before, but concentrating hard on an early team breakfast to plan the job-list for the following Sunday's race at Watkins Glen in upper New York state.

Formula One team principals are, almost by definition, obsessed with the present and the future. Yesterday has little place in their thinking, and of none is this more true than Frank Williams. That Monday morning he had already set victory in the World Championship, the achievement of one intense ambition, behind him: 'After winning the Canadian GP first and second and clinching the Championship titles, we felt sure everybody else was waiting for us to fall off the wire at Watkins Glen. We were desperately determined that would not happen, absolutely steely about it. People would be saying, "That's it, they've won their Championship, now watch them go downhill." We just were not going to let that happen . . .

'I have always enjoyed the North American races which mark the end of the Formula One season. They have a kind of end-of-term atmosphere about them which I suppose as an ex-minor public schoolboy I found very attractive. Well, as it happened, Alan and Carlos finished first and second again – for the second time in a week – and it was probably the best whole-team performance of the season. It set the seal on our World Championship title . . . it was very satisfying, very satisfying indeed . . .'

Perhaps that night he could allow himself just a few brief moments' reflection on the long years he had been struggling to reach this pitch. If ever anyone had risen to World Champion level in any sport through sheer single-minded commitment, and will to survive, it was Frank Williams. Now his team's target was simply to stay on top, to secure a future which just four short years before would have been impossible to predict.

Championship Defended, Title Lost

The 1981 season began in uproar with Formula One racing's now notorious 'winter of discontent'. The French-dominated governing body of the sport, the *Fédération Internationale du Sport Automobile*, or 'FISA', had gained new strength under its forceful new President Jean-Marie Balestre in 1979–80. He reacted aggressively to years in which, as he saw it, political power in this major league of motor racing had been snatched from the official governing body by the Formula One Constructors' Association. He objected to FOCA's influence in rule-making and detested that organization's control of the financial dealings between the teams – operating as a group – and race organizers, TV companies for coverage rights and so on. The battle lines had been drawn for a dispute in which Balestre fought to regain the balance of Formula One power from FOCA. The battleground he chose concerned the use of sliding skirts to increase download and so enhance cornering speeds.

The war flared and died spasmodically through 1980, the Zolder driver-briefing fines and the demotion of the Spanish GP from Championship status being symptoms of a disease which was to do considerable harm to the image of Grand Prix racing. In Spain the major manufacturer teams of Ferrari (representing Fiat), Alfa Romeo and Renault had sided with FISA and withdrawn from the outlawed Grand Prix, leaving the specialist proprietary-engined FOCA loyalists to stage a superb motor race on their own. It was not a simple allegiance to FISA which led the major industry teams to defect. FISA is merely the motor sport governing delegate body of the *Fédération Internationale de l'Automobile* ('FIA') which handles the whole vast range of government–motor industry regulation and acceptance dealings world-wide. This meant that the major industry teams dare not estrange FISA because of the wider implications upon their dealings with the FIA, while of those major manufacturers Fiat, Alfa Romeo and Renault had deep interests in other forms of motor sport outside Formula One – activities in which FISA could make life very difficult.

Then there were deeper motives. Mr Ferrari in particular was deeply opposed to aerodynamic aids evolved by the British team engineers which his own multi-million-pound facility proved painfully incapable of matching. Early in 1980 his reigning World Champion Jody Scheckter acted in his capacity as President of the recently revived Grand Prix Drivers' Association to present a document signed by many drivers expressing their concern at the increase in cornering speeds and hence G-loads being engendered by the use of such effective aerodynamic aids. But whereas many of Scheckter's signatories contended that the document was intended as 'an expression of our concern, to make our feelings publicly known', Scheckter presented it as a concerted vote 'to ban skirts'. The GPDA faction was split, for those drivers handling good ground-effect skirted cars were happy with their advantage, while those drivers whose teams were stumbling in the aerodynamic wilderness saw a skirt ban working to their immediate advantage.

In fairness it must be recorded that Ferrari's sliding skirts never worked properly. They would jam, and ground-effect download would be lost abruptly in the middle of a high-speed corner. To drivers Scheckter and Villeneuve they must have felt horribly unstable. Perhaps the belief was genuinely that since their ground-effect sliding-skirted cars felt so dangerous then all such cars must be dangerous, but this simply was not so.

As the winter of 1980–81 approached the FISA–FOCA confrontation hotted up, with the question of a sliding skirt ban to the fore. Mr Ferrari began talking of his own team plus Alfa and Renault as the *Grande Costruttori*, dismissing the British proprietary engine teams – plus Ligier from France – as mere *Assemblatori*, kit-builders, despite the fact they had run his red cars ragged . . . For Balestre, too, the British were mere *Garagistes*.

The theory was that Ferrari's forthcoming turbocharged Formula One engine for 1981, plus Alfa Romeo's promised unit plus Renault's established turbo, would have such a power advantage over the British Cosworth V8s that any diminution in British chassis power would clear the field. Without sliding skirts to seal their ground-effect undersections, the British teams would be struggling, for the turbo brigade would have horsepower to spare to pull massive conventional nose and tail wings through the air, wings whose downloads the panting Cosworth cars could not hope to carry – for their massive drag would absorb horsepower which could not be spared.

As the dispute hotted up, the FOCA faithful propounded their own World Federation of Motor Sport to run an International Formula One race series without FISA sanction, but the circuit promoters involved suffered understandably cold feet as their other race promotions would be refused FISA sanction in reprisal.

During all this turmoil the teams continued testing, the *Grande Costruttori* without sliding skirts, the *Assemblatori* mainly with their skirts in place. It became clear that FISA had the power but lacked the cars, FOCA had the cars but lacked the power to convert race circuit promoters world-wide to its cause. Equally clearly a compromise would have to be achieved, and the winter feuding had on balance given FOCA a position of greater strength from which to compromise. A string of top-level meetings between team principals on both sides and FISA resulted in a complex accord christened the Concorde Agreement. FOCA gave ground on sliding skirts, accepting their ban, and Ferrari and

Renault, whose turbo cars were grossly overweight, forced through an increase in the Formula One minimum weight limit from 575 kg to 585 kg – again closing the gap of competitiveness with the British-style cars. FOCA retained control of Formula One finances, distribution of pit passes and so on . . . It was thought that peace had returned.

Meanwhile, during those winter months, WGPE had run one FW07B car for Alan Jones in his home Australian GP at Calder Raceway, which he won handsomely in the presence of Giacomelli's Alfa Romeo, while on December 4 the whole world of Formula One had been dealt a crippling blow by Goodyear's abrupt withdrawal of tyre supplies. This left Michelin, contracted to Ferrari and Renault, and Pirelli – tentatively about to feel their way in with the new Toleman turbo-Hart-engined team. Frank Williams: 'That was a stunning blow. Leo Mehl just telephoned and said, "Frank, I've got something I must read out to you", and it was Goodyear's press release announcing their withdrawal. We had had no warning whatsoever, I had to go cap in hand to Michelin, along with the other former Goodyear runners, and Pierre Dupasquier there was very frank, and not particularly encouraging. He had to honour his existing team contracts and could promise no more than four sets of tyres per driver to all other interested teams. It seemed then that Michelin could manipulate the new World Championship as they saw fit. Their contracted teams would get the hot tyres, and the others would get the concrete tyres. I walked out on to the street and was very depressed, more depressed than I can remember . . .'

The FOCA circus ran their Michelin tyres at Kyalami in the South African GP of 7 February 1981 – the traditional season-openers in Argentina and Brazil having been set back while the war raged. Still the Modena and Heathrow meetings which spawned the Concorde Agreement were yet to take place, and in South Africa FOCA flexed its muscles by proving itself capable of fielding a nineteen-car grid and running quite a sensible race, even if it lacked the pizzazz of a full Grand Prix, with Ferrari, Alfa and Renault all absent . . .

Naturally the cars ran with sliding skirts, and after a frightening practice spin in which he was almost strangled by the catch-

Team-mates or rivals – Carlos Reutemann and Alan Jones 'made up' after the Brazilian difference of opinion . . .

In Brazil this signal was shown to remind Reutemann of his agreement when leading Jones in the closing laps. Here in Argentina the Reutemann fan club in the main stands waved 'REUT-JONES' banners, and Frank responded with this signal . . . It was all good clean fun.

fencing, Carlos Reutemann qualified his FW07B on pole position. The race started wet and dried, Carlos opted for slick dry-weather tyres at the last moment and when Nelson Piquet's Brabham stopped to change from wets to dries after 26 laps in the lead, Carlos moved rapidly forward and led from lap 30 to the 78th and last, winning as he pleased. Alan was worried by tyre wear in dry practice, started the race on wets from third place on the grid, but missed second gear and was engulfed by the pack. He rushed up to third place, changed to dry tyres on lap 17, then spun and damaged his rear wing, which was changed, but he retired after 63 laps because skirt damage had sent the handling awry.

FOCA 'hoped' that Kyalami would be counted towards the World Championship, but FISA decreed otherwise, the new agreement banned sliding skirts, a six-centimetre ground clearance gap and the new 585 kg minimum weight limit were also agreed upon, so the lightest cars (like Williams and Brabham) had to carry bolted-on ballast weights to comply.

Now Long Beach opened the official Championship on 15 March, and hectic weeks of development and new car construction at Didcot produced the unskirted 'clearance car' FW07C design, chassis 11 and 12 built to the spirit of the new laws. Dave Neal and his men in the factory had worked themselves into the ground to prepare the cars, Frank had warned his labour force in one of their regular canteen meetings that the face of Formula One had changed, the major manufacturer FISA teams had been testing all winter unskirted, and it was going to be an uphill battle to defend 'our' World Championship title. Imagine the elation of that Monday morning as AFN radio and BBC news bulletins announced another TAG-Williams team 1–2 victory – Jones first, Reutemann second, first and second fastest race laps (both set on lap 31) and only Patrese's Arrows surprisingly faster than the Williams twins in practice . . .

Already shadows were appearing. Colin Chapman's latest Lotus 88 was considered to be driving a coach and horses through the new regulations, with its movable-body aerodynamic envelope suspended independently of the monocoque chassis nacelle, and was banned during practice amidst much acrimony. Gordon Murray of Brabham had looked carefully at the letter rather than

the spirit of the new regulations and devised a soft air-spring suspension system in which aerodynamic download crushed the car down closer to the roadway at speed, whereupon fixed mini-skirt sections beneath the car regenerated virtual sliding-skirt era ground-effect values. As the car slowed on its return to the pits the soft air-springs recovered and the car rose to its legal clearance height of six centimetres, ready for the scrutineers to re-measure it. The system refused to operate properly at Long Beach and was removed for the race; in Brazil two weeks later the Ecclestone team operated their car straight from the pit garage to keep it away from prying eyes, and Nelson Piquet qualified on pole. The Lotus 88 ban was confirmed, Frank Williams gave notice to Bernard Ecclestone that if the lowering-suspension Brabham BT49C ran its flexing skirt system in the Argentine he would be forced to protest it . . . The Williams new lowering system was set aside . . .

Out on circuit the Rio course was soaked by heavy drizzle throughout the race, Reutemann and Jones led throughout the 63 laps in their FW07Cs from second and third grid places and achieved the team's sixth consecutive Formula One race victory, and their fourth 1–2 in those six events. 'I rate that as a greater team achievement,' Frank observes, 'than Watkins Glen the previous year, because team 1–2s in the wet, with all the variables it introduces, are very, very rare . . .'

Still there was another problem. Late in 1980 Alan had been offered a fat contract by Alfa Romeo, and had been tempted. Frank had retained his services by being able to offer a second season's protection clause in his Williams team contract. If Alan was second to Carlos near the end of a GP, Carlos should allow him to go by to take maximum points. Carlos agreed, because in 1980 the clause had only once come close to being enacted. Here in Brazil the 'JONES–REUT' signal went out to the Argentinian and he ignored it, drawing away to win from Jones, who was struggling. Both cars ran variable-rate springs at that meeting, Carlos's being a prototype set and Alan's from a production batch. It was subsequently found that many of the production-batch springs were faulty, and at Rio the Australian's car's handling was suspect. He was sick with himself after the finish for having allowed Carlos to draw away, resting on the safety valve of their

Carlos Reutemann made a determined effort to win the World Championship during 1981, and here at
Imola in the San Marino GP his Williams FW07C leads team-mate Alan Jones's similar car.

contract agreement – now he knew how the Argentinian felt he would not let it happen again. It was going to be dog-eat-dog if necessary. Frank and Patrick were disappointed that Reutemann should have ignored his agreement, and he was paid second-place money instead of first – 'The only sanction a Grand Prix driver will understand is one which hits his pocket . . . we're not about to pull him out of his own Grand Prix – the next event in the calendar – because that would be cutting off our nose to spite our face . . .'

Buenos Aires Autodrome saw the new lowering-suspension BT49Cs in balance at last; Piquet was untouchable, and drove past Jones's FW07C on the first lap as though it was touring. The Brazilian won handsomely, Hector Rebaque in the second Brabham drove past Reutemann to take second place before his car's electrics failed, and Carlos finished second, while Alan was fourth.

Yet again the Lotus 88 was banned amid great drama and fuss, Balestre being present in person to orchestrate litigation, while few FOCA teams seemed willing to protest the flexible skirts being employed by Brabham. Frank and Patrick felt differently, but their protests were simply ignored by Argentine officialdom, no explanation given, no discussion allowed . . .

It came down to an argument about the term 'rigid' when applied to skirt materials. How 'rigid' is 'rigid'? The Forth Bridge flexes, an aircraft wing bends, rigidity is indefinable without massive literal complication in the framing of the law. Soon all teams were to run what to the man in the street would constitute 'flexible' if not 'floppy' skirt materials, and every team would run lowering suspensions to comply with the six-centimetre ground clearance regulation at the point of measurement in the pit lane, while dropping the car to a ground-effective ride height at speed out on circuit.

No major Formula One team can allow another 'to make a monkey out of us', and in Brazilian practice Patrick had experimented with a lowering suspension system on Alan's car which did not work well enough, and at Imola for the San Marino GP which opened the European season all teams ran some form of lowering device. But Chief Scrutineer Cadringher, who worked normally on the Tornado aircraft project for AerItalia, declared the flexible skirt unacceptable. Only Brabham, Fittipaldi and Talbot-Ligier (now running Matra V12 engines again) ran lowering suspensions in the race and Piquet won again, although out-qualified by Villeneuve's powerful new Ferrari 126C turbo and by Reutemann.

The Argentinian had established over a period of years an enigmatic reputation. On his day, when things were going well and he felt happy, he could dominate a race. If he felt fate was against him, or felt unfairly treated, he could look mediocre, and there were degrees of unhappiness-cum-determination in between. Frank: 'We have found we have to hold his hand and look after him for him to give his best, and his best is terrific! When he is happy and driving well he is totally remorseless, he will explore the uttermost limits of his car and produce maximum speed with zero risk. He consistently qualified ahead of Alan, but Alan is a much more determined and combative character and often raced better, certainly when things were against him. Carlos also seemed to take too long to recognize a race situation before waking up and making his big effort, while Alan would just bludgeon the opposition into submission by driving flat-out from the flag . . .'

At Imola Carlos was hampered by Michelin wet tyres revolving on their rims and sending the wheels out of balance; he finished third in a race many felt he could have won had he adapted more quickly to his car's minor problem. Alan threw his chances by punting his team-mate and having to stop to replace a dinged nose wing and change to slick tyres. He changed three times and finished twelfth, two laps behind.

The Belgian GP at Zolder saw the Formula One season reach its nadir. In practice a young Osella team mechanic stepped in front of Carlos's Williams in the pit lane, was tossed into the air and died from head injuries sustained as he landed. Carlos was distraught – characteristically he is one of the most careful drivers in the pit lane. In a shambles at the race start an Arrows mechanic was pinned between his team cars; in practice scrutineers had complained that the 6 cm ground clearance rule was impossible to police and FISA had accepted driver-operated jacking suspension systems which effectively robbed Brabham of their lead in this

Alan Jones led the Belgian GP in terrific style before crashing when his car 'jumped out of gear' The value to the team of having two top drivers was amply demonstrated as Carlos Reutemann swept on to victory.

area with their painstakingly balanced automatic system. Gordon Murray was incensed, as was his lead driver Nelson Piquet when Alan Jones reputedly bundled him into the catch-fencing on the eleventh race lap.

It was Carlos who took pole position, but Didier Pironi's Ferrari which led until lap 12, when the charging Jones took over until lap 20 when he crashed heavily and allowed his team-mate to inherit first place and victory. Alan explained that his car had jumped out of gear; his crew were not so sure. He scalded his leg quite badly as the car's radiator burst on impact. His team-mate went on to win.

Carlos Reutemann was running away with the World Championship lead, he had finished in the points in sixteen consecutive GPs – an all-time record, and a massive tribute to the Didcot team's preparation of his cars and his mechanical sympathy for them . . .

At Monaco Carlos's luck ran out. He rammed Mansell's Lotus at the Old Station Hairpin and had to change the nose cone and front wing. Out on circuit he found other drivers moving over for him – all assuming he was the race leader! He tore back through the field, only for second gear to fail – it was the wrong specification, having slipped unseen through inspection. 'That was down to the team,' Frank recalls, '. . . we let him down.'

Meanwhile Alan had bulldozed his way through the field from fifth place to close rapidly on Piquet's Brabham. After the Belgian incident the excited Brazilian had threatened mayhem if Jones should crowd him again. An expectant hush settled on knowledgeable observers as the cars closed, then abruptly Piquet had psyched himself into the barriers and Alan was by, towards a certain victory.

Then the misfire began. It worsened. He hammered into the pits for a fuel top-up. It made no difference. Villeneuve's Ferrari barked by to win, Alan's FW07C limped across the line, second in the race and now second to his team-mate in the Drivers' Championship.

In the Spanish GP at Jarama Alan led the race for 13 laps, pulling away until he locked up the front brakes and went careering off the road. He restarted sixteenth and finished seventh, after losing second gear later in the race. Carlos qualified third, just

behind Jones and Laffite (with the powerful Ligier on pole). He lay second for a lap, then watched in shocked surprise as Villeneuve just drove round him at the end of the main straight ending lap two. He sat behind the Ferrari, unable to find a way past until gearbox trouble began. Third gear was jumping out. The Argentinian retained his World Championship lead, with fourth place, and 37 points to Jones' 24 and Piquet's 22.

Despite the British teams' initial misgivings, Michelin had played scrupulously fair. Frank: 'Michelin treated us superbly well. If their top uncontracted teams wanted an extra set of tyres they would supply them, and a fresh set in qualifying was instantly worth a quicker time in their first lap or two. Their product was superb, quality control magnificent, and they had a fantastic system. If we wanted to re-use the front tyres we'd run the day before, for example, their chap would go to a stack of five hundred used covers, study his list and pick them out from under . . .

'But they would not give us a contract, and after Monaco Goodyear approached us. They were interested in supplying us and Brabham. It seemed the reaction amongst their divisions to their sudden pull-out had not been too good, and for sure they were disturbed at the prospect of Michelin dominating US races at Long Beach and Las Vegas, and in Canada, and perhaps in Detroit too in 1982. If Goodyear weren't competing in Detroit – the heartland of the American motor industry – who would they be? Just another tyre company, just like any other . . . Formula One gives them stature.'

The Goodyear deal was done with healthy retainers attached, and the Williams and Brabham cars ran American rubber again at Dijon for the French GP. Piquet's Brabham dominated until rain interrupted the race, Michelin had the greater stock of wet-weather rubber for the restart, and Renault grabbed their chance and won with Alain Prost driving. The FW07Cs carried modified sidepods developed from research in the team's new rolling-road, quarter-scale wind-tunnel at Didcot to prevent a porpoising effect in early season. The new section proved slower in practice, and the modification coinciding with the tyre change knocked Williams off the pace. They qualified on rows four and five, Reutemann ahead of Jones. Alan tangled with Andretti's Alfa on lap one and was out of the running, finishing 17th and last; Reutemann's car developed a misfire and he nursed it throughout the major part of the race with a blistered left-front tyre – the load-bearing one – and he nursed it, Jim Clark fashion, for many miles.

At Silverstone the cars were still slow, but by the end of the meeting development engineer Frank Dernie knew what was at fault. Alan was taken off early on by Villeneuve's spinning Ferrari, Carlos was unhappy and drove a lack-lustre race to inherit second place. Still he led the Drivers' Championship, with 43 points to Piquet's 26; Alan's efforts to defend his title were flagging, he was third with 24. The team dominated the Constructors' Cup competition which they had led from the first round in Long Beach, 67 points to Brabham's 31!

The German GP followed at Hockenheim, where the FW07Cs appeared aerodynamically revised and truly competitive. In 1980 Alan had had trouble handling the turbo Renaults; in 1981 his Williams had the advantage, despite the Renaults qualifying 1–2 on the grid, and Alan cut out Prost after 21 of the 45 laps and drew away – only for the mysterious misfire to return. He made a late pit stop and finished eleventh, and lapped; robbed of another victory, as at Monaco. Carlos meanwhile had been forced to drive the spare car and ran strongly third before his brand-new John Judd-prepared engine – which are normally excellent – broke a valve spring and put him out. Nelson Piquet won for Brabham, and at a stroke Carlos's points lead was slashed from 17 to 8. It was the turning-point in the season...

Dernie took a test car away quietly to investigate the mysterious misfire. It seemed only to occur on the team's most powerful engines in the heat of a race, never in qualifying. The precise cause was never isolated, but a change in fuel system from that which had basically worked so well since 1979 seemed to side-step the problem.

The new generation of lowering-suspension cars which raced in Austria had as little suspension movement as a mere quarter-inch at the front and only three-quarters at the rear in order to maintain a constant under-skirt gap and thereby maintain consistent ground-effect downloads. Should the car be allowed to bounce, the skirt gap would open, the download would be reduced and the

driver scared half to death! Now teams chose the lesser evil, the cars felt rock hard, hammered their drivers to pulp over bumps and tortured man and machinery equally – and all to satisfy a 6 cm ground clearance rule measured in the pit lane...

Alan drove courageously with an ill-handling car, suffering from a broken coil-spring cap at the rear which compromised its handling. He still finished fourth, while Carlos was fifth, cautiously leaving run-off space round the fast corners of the Styrian course and threatening nobody.

At Zandvoort the Dutch GP again proved something of a Williams Waterloo, for Reutemann sat behind Laffite's Talbot-Ligier for 17 long laps, having been out-qualified by the Renaults, Piquet and Jones, and then launched an extraordinary effort to pass the French car on the inside (over the kerb!) at Tarzan Hairpin, ramming its right-front corner and putting both out of the race. Laffite said later, 'It was desperate points to lose for both of us,' and he could not believe that such an experienced driver should have attempted such a move.

Prost won for Renault, Piquet was second, and Jones, who had led for half a lap, was third after the team's gamble on tyres failed as the car's left rear wore out. Reutemann seemed rattled by Championship pressure; now he and Piquet were level on 45 points each, Laffite third with 34, having won in Austria, and Jones not yet beaten on 31.

But Alan was increasingly unhappy with these unlikable cars, yearning for the sun and freedom of his Australian farm. He travelled out to Milan for the Italian GP on 13 September with Charlie Crichton-Stuart. Frank saw Charlie first in the team's hotel on that Thursday night, the eve of first practice. 'Alan's got something to tell you,' warned Charlie. 'He's thinking about retirement...' Frank was chilled. He and Alan had already agreed terms verbally for 1981, it was late in the year, other top drivers were no longer available. Alan walked in. 'We've gotta talk,' he said to Williams, and explained what Frank felt were not carefully considered reasons for retirement. 'That in truth didn't bother me so much as the immediate problem. Alan had got himself into a fight after carving up a couple of West Indians in London traffic, he'd broken his little finger and had it bandaged to the fourth finger of his gear-change hand.' Frank made it plain what he thought of professional personalities becoming involved in a street brawl, and left the subject of retirement to simmer...

Arnoux took pole for Renault, Carlos was second fastest, then Prost, Laffite and Jones. Carlos elected to race without a nose wing on his car, while Alan ran bewinged and drove a superb race, climbing through the field to finish second behind Prost. On the grid a softer left rear tyre had been fitted to Alan's car to match the other three, Carlos retaining three softer 'C' compound tyres and a hard 'B' on the high-stressed left rear. It rained in mid-race and the disenchanted Argentinian drove in as lack-lustre a manner as only he can – relative to his immense skill – when he is unhappy. He lost several seconds avoiding John Watson's amazingly lurid McLaren accident, but in the rainy patch at the Parabolica corner Alan passed him so rapidly that the Australian thought his team-mate was in trouble... Even so, he still managed to finish third, as Piquet's Brabham blew up on the very last lap. Now Reutemann led the Championship with 49 points to Piquet's 46; Jones and Prost were tied on 37; Laffite had 34. Williams led the Constructors' Cup with 86 points to Brabham's 57. Brabham would have to finish 1–2 in both Canada and Las Vegas to deny Didcot of the double...

Montreal was shrouded in low cloud and driving rain for the Canadian GP. Goodyear's wet tyres were manifestly incapable of pumping the water necessary to prevent aquaplaning in the race, and although Piquet qualified on pole with Reutemann and Jones behind him, it was Carlos who led into the first corner and 'just seemed to stop'. Jones tore away into an heroic if short-lived lead, while Carlos drove on carefully to finish a pointless twelfth. Alan lost his lead, dropped back, spun, stopped, rejoined, stopped again and gave up. Laffite won, Piquet – on Goodyears too – was fifth. Carlos held the Drivers' Championship lead with 49 points to Piquet's 48, only Laffite could steal the title from them, should he win in Vegas, and Jones' hopes had gone.

Careful preparation preceded the trip to the Caesar's Palace car-park circuit, serious teams testing at the similarly tight and confined Croix-en-Ternois course in northern France. Carlos carefully prepared himself for the race, arriving a week early to examine the sinuous new circuit. With just a one-point cushion after leading the Championship all season, he could afford no errors – and Piquet on recent form would have his measure.

Team and drivers operated slickly, Carlos qualifying on pole, Alan next up, but in race morning warm-up the Argentinian was complaining of ill-handling, the car's corner weights were measured and found spot-on. On the warming-up laps he was still disturbed, while Jones in his broadly similar car was happy. Amid great tension the cars lined up on the grid, with Reutemann on pole position, then the lights were red, flashing green and Alan rocketed into the lead he held throughout to win convincingly in what was supposedly his last-ever Formula One appearance. Carlos' Championship hopes virtually died on the line; Piquet nipped him out in the early half of the race and drew away. Reutemann missed a gear past the pits but continued with no visible ill-effects but no more sign of attacking his World Championship challenger.

Towards the end the multi-cornered anti-clockwise circuit sapped the muscular strength of most drivers, fighting to keep their heads upright against G-forces. Alan didn't bother, allowing his head to loll against the cockpit coaming. Piquet was in a terrible state, vomiting several times in his helmet and in no condition to fight off a serious challenge. No such challenge materialized, however, and he struggled on gamely to finish fifth for two vital Championship points. Carlos – unhappy Carlos – was eighth, out of the points, robbed of the World Championship title he so coveted ... or had he, as so many felt, meekly surrendered the Championship crown?

Now as these words are written Williams Grand Prix Engineering Ltd are working towards their hat-trick of Formula One Constructors' World Championship titles in 1982 – still very much a feared force on the Grand Prix scene, a far cry from the Austin A35, the cobbled-together spare-part F3 Brabham and the Formula One make-weights which helped build the Williams legend...

Alan Jones, Las Vegas 1981. We had become accustomed to leading drivers no longer trying after announcing their impending retirements. Alan proved otherwise with this tigerish drive, to lead from start to finish what he said would be his last ever Grand Prix.

The TAG–Williams race team, 1981. Back row (*left to right*): Tim Hargreaves, Dave Stubbs, Douglas Bebb, John Green, Andreas Richter, Steve Prior, Maureen Hargreaves, Ryngi Nakaya (part hidden), John Jackson, Bob Paxman, Alan Challis, Neil Oatley (part hidden). Front: Bryan Lambert, Alan Jones, Mansour Ojjeh, Charles Crichton-Stuart, Frank Williams (obscuring Patrick Head!), Derrick Jones, Carlos Reutemann.

IV · THIS GRAND PRIX BUSINESS

'The best team will be the one in which every member knows the part
he has to play and plays it without drama, submerging, if necessary, his
own personality and ambitions . . .'

John Wyer: *Motor Racing Management*, 1956.

Inside the WGPE factory at Didcot.

This Grand Prix Business

Motor racing is a complex sport for outsiders to appreciate fully. Anybody can flail a tennis racket, swing a golf club, perhaps strike a cricket ball or kick a football, and grasp much of what those professional games entail. But certainly each has its more obscure level of expert technology . . .

Perhaps racket-string tensions can be important; the carbon shaft club or small ball can make all the difference when shooting for par; a seven-pound bat and the confidence of temple protection may transform a batsman; depending on the weather and pitch, the choice of football studs can be vital . . .

Yet compared to the technology involved in motor racing, such considerations pale into insignificance. Motor racing is the great gasoline sport, a technical exercise in which the drivers may have the glamour and charisma, but their performances are inevitably dictated by the machines into which they are strapped.

Every gleamingly prepared racing car sitting there on the starting grid comprises several thousand lovingly assembled components, the majority of which can spell potential failure, retirement, even disaster.

Behind every driver sitting there in the public eye stands a small army of anonymous aides. Behind every two race mechanics tending a car in a Grand Prix pit are perhaps five, maybe more highly skilled artisans back home, whose hands have crafted the car which their driver is about to wield.

There are the dynamic, brilliant men whose minds have evolved the racing engines, the gearboxes, the systems which feed them oil, fuel, water – the fluids and the electricity which make them work. There are the men who designed the chassis, who spent long days and endless nights researching aerodynamic forms and devices which would give their car a competitive edge. There are the people who developed and tested the cars, their systems and the highly specialized racing tyres upon which they run, and which can totally dictate their ultimate performance – win or lose. And there are the people whose job it is to shuttle the race teams, their cars and equipment, around the world with the least possible aggravation, waste of time and opportunity.

Grand Prix racing as an activity forms a gigantic iceberg, the greater part of which is hidden from public view. The layman may catch an occasional race on television; he sees the action and excitement, the colour and sometimes chaos of what goes on. He glimpses the glittering car liveries, the sponsors' names and slogans stencilled there. The enthusiast at the races or reading the specialist press sees and hears much more – understands more of the finer points. But still the greater part of the activity remains submerged, obscure even to him. The challenge might be understood, but not the way in which it is met – nor the staggeringly intense effort demanded of those who aspire to reach the top.

Any type of race is a challenge made against time. He who takes least to cover the distance will win. Behind the scenes in Formula One, time itself is at a premium. Calendar pressures are intense from January to October every year, with perhaps sixteen races crammed in from South America to South Africa and on into Europe and North America. Competition is ferocious: if you don't develop some clever technical advantage then the next team will. Time is always short. Once the season is at its height, time is even shorter; it can easily be lost, and seldom if ever made up.

To meet such a daunting challenge demands capability, commitment, and money. Some kermudgeons, aware only of Formula One's apparent wealth and its use as a promotional weapon by its big commercial sponsors, claim that it is now more business than sport. It's a moot point. Frank Williams: 'I think at best it's now about fifty-fifty sport versus business, but it is definitely still a sport, because men are competing against one another for competitive reasons. But it is a sport under great commercial influence. Before the flag drops, money plays a very big part. It has to be generated and has to be spent on obtaining the best equipment. But once the flag drops the drivers are racing each other, pure and simple, and all other considerations are no longer relevant. Neither is the best equipment the be-all and end-all, the driver has got to be man enough to compete with it against the others.

'The level of competitiveness in Formula One has increased every year. It has become increasingly difficult to win, and therefore you have to use more and more resources to win, and that means money, and that money has to be generated . . .'

Grand Prix teams have been seeking to generate funds since this type of all-out racing was first introduced in 1906. In those early years major manufacturers took part to publicize their expertise. It took a Madison Avenue advertising man to coin the phrase, 'Win on Sunday, Sell on Monday', but long before its invention the big car companies were already doing just that.

The major oil and tyre companies provided the backbone of Grand Prix racing support way into the late sixties, as the major manufacturers drifted away into competitive obscurity. Then in 1968 the era of 'billboard' sponsorship developed in Formula One, with Team Lotus drawing on American track racing experience of decades to promote a tobacco company with cigarette-packet livery on their cars. By 1970 the old concept of national racing colours – green from Britain, for example – had been thoroughly eroded. French blue and Italian red remained strong but, increasingly, large commercial companies outside the technical world of motoring invested promotional budgets in sponsorship. In effect Formula One swelled to use available funds, and it became more competitive and more complex.

One result was its growing attraction world-wide, and that brought major manufacturers back into contention, as Alfa Romeo, Renault and Talbot joined Fiat – taking increasingly overt interest in their Ferrari part-subsidiary – in tackling the mainly British specialist teams at their own intensely demanding game.

The WGPE team's level of sponsorship in 1981 placed it among the top three or four in Formula One's money table. Ask Frank Williams what Grand Prix racing is all about as a business, and he'll grin and explain that in a perfect world, reduced to its most simple level, '. . . . The idea is that you attract sufficient sponsorship to cover all your expenses for a season, and then all your winnings and bonuses are profit.' It never, ever, works out that way, but the manner in which his team has generated those vital funds explains more clearly how Formula One can work.

The backbone of the team's rise to World Champion status had been the Saudi consortium's sponsorship, augmented for 1980–81 by Leyland Vehicles' more commercial support. From Frank's introduction to Mohammed Al Fawzan of Saudia Airlines in 1977 there grew a complex web of new friends and supporters.

The Saudia deal effectively gave Frank a unique calling-card to help seek further backing from big business in the Arab Kingdom. Once again, old friends came to his help.

'Charlie Crichton-Stuart had been selling cars at H. R. Owen's in London to Prince Sultan, a nephew of Prince Salman, the Governor of Riyadh. Sultan and his brother Fahad were studying in the States and Charlie said, "Let's go and talk to them", so we flew to Denver. Again they listened and liked what we were saying, and said, "Next time you're in Riyadh, be our guest and we'll introduce you to some people you should meet . . ."'

Frank made the trip in January 1978, by which time Patrick and the lads at Didcot had produced their new prototype FW06. At that time only £130,000 or so had been promised firm for the coming season, so the team fell some £250–350,000 short of target.

'What we had in hand would barely have been sufficient to run Alan in the way we had run Neve in the March: just the one car and zero testing. But we had chosen the proper way: a serious season with a spare car and a lot of testing, because we had to progress. It was the right thing to do, and Alan immediately started going very quickly indeed . . .'

In Riyadh the young Princes Sultan and Fahad introduced Frank to several vital contacts, including Prince Mohammed, who ran a company named Albilad which pursued substantial trade with the UK. The Prince was interested in the picture which Frank painted of World Championship racing and of Saudia's participation in his team. He would be in London in February, and would love to inspect the car . . . he liked motor cars, of all kinds.

Between Alan's electrifying drive at Rio and his heroic effort at Kyalami, the Prince arrived in London, and Frank took one of the new FW06s along to Park Lane one Friday evening to show him and his friends. They were impressed. The whole idea of adding further Saudi support to the little team appealed, and Prince Mohammed simply turned and said, 'Frank, we will take care of you . . .'

This was a hugely significant development. Prince Mohammed initially contributed some £200,000 in four monthly payments that first season, while relatives and friends agreed to contribute more. In succeeding months Prince Mohammed was to prove a true inspiration, introducing Frank to business associates who agreed co-sponsorship largely on the Prince's personal enthusiasm.

They ran companies whose names would appear on the cars – names like Dallah Avco, one of the largest airport maintenance concerns in the Kingdom; *Techniques d'Avant Garde*, the mainly aviation high-technology concern, dealing in the Canadair Challenger aircraft amongst others, and with offices in Riyadh and Paris; Baroom, a large steel and cement merchant, was another; Bin Laden, the largest road builders and an old-established trading family; Encotrade, quite a new trading company, agents for many Western concerns working in the Kingdom; Siyanco, a maintenance and engineering consultancy firm . . .

Frank was acutely aware when all this began that his team had next to nothing to sell – other than potential. Al Fawzan's original Saudia Airlines support of the March had amounted to a personal

gesture of faith in Frank Williams, and the team and its Saudi sponsorship consortium were to grow in parallel.

Not that the relationship was entirely smooth. In motor racing at all levels 'right now' is barely soon enough, and in Formula One these pressures are at their most intense. It proved impossible to impress this urgency upon the Saudis. Their word was their bond, utterly rock-solid once promises had been made, but occasionally it would take months for vital funds to arrive. This was the case early in 1979, when Frank was out physically seeking a cheque the night before the team travelled to Long Beach. Four brand-new Cosworth engines were still locked in storage, since the team could not find the cash to pay for them. Alan actually practised at Long Beach with a spare engine borrowed from Fittipaldi . . .

Essentially the team was becoming well sponsored, but with continuous development on the car, expansion in the Didcot plant and continuous testing, they were also spending lavishly – always on essentials. For much of 1978 and on into 1979 Frank was still in that familiar old position of robbing Peter to pay Paul. Despite those secure promises, money was tight.

Among the Saudi consortium Mansour Ojjeh, whose father owned TAG, became one of the team's closest and most ardent supporters. TAG was to assume an increasing share of the consortium's support. When Leyland Vehicles became team co-sponsors with the Saudis in 1980, their individual contribution was larger than any single partner's in the consortium. Into 1981 TAG's contribution exceeded Leyland Vehicles'.

The truck, bus and tractor division of the British motor manufacturing combine had entered the picture as a gesture of faith in its own aggressively enterprising future.

Early in April 1979 Leyland Vehicles' Overseas Marketing Director, Steve Herrick, had been attempting to sell double-deck buses to the Los Angeles RTD operation in California. Unfortunately they had taken their custom elsewhere, and he was left at something of a loose end with time to kill before his flight home. He stopped off at Long Beach to watch practice for the US GP (West), and as he watched, an idea formed in his mind . . .

'Just standing there, watching what was going on and the staggering way in which order suddenly emerges from what is apparently total chaos, I was very struck by the attraction of the cars and the atmosphere of a Grand Prix meeting. It suddenly occurred to me that Formula One could be a very good tool for giving the Leyland Vehicles name wider international exposure . . .'

The company had just closed its Israeli operation and had been removed from the Arab black-list. The Middle-East market had opened up and was attractive. Might there be some possibility of combining with the Saudis to co-sponsor that new Williams team? The new FW07 car had appeared at Long Beach, but was not raced. True, the team had won nothing as yet, but great potential seemed apparent. Herrick mulled over the idea on the long flight home . . .

There he broached his idea to his immediate boss, Bob Morris, the company's Overseas Operations Director. 'I think sponsoring a Formula One team could do wonders for our image and provide a useful sales promotion,' he said. To his astonishment Bob Morris not only agreed enthusiastically but added, 'My wife used to work for Frank Williams, we know him well . . .' Allison Morris had been Frank's secretary during the low years at Bennett Road, and had helped out at Didcot right at the beginning of WGPE.

Morris obviously wanted no part of any decision-making, on account of his personal interest, but he reported to Frank Andrew, LV's Sales and Marketing Director – a tough, shrewd Scot who agreed the idea had merit. He placed it before J. David Abell, LV Managing Director at that time, and the man with ultimate responsibility. Steve Herrick was despatched to research further . . .

Early that summer Sheridan Thynne had lunch with Frank Williams, the London stock-broker and Formula One team chief maintaining their long friendship. During the conversation, Frank mentioned idly that a Leyland Vehicles man was coming to the French Grand Prix at Dijon, 'To see what it's all about'. Sheridan's ears pricked up. For years he had made an annual pilgrimage to the Rouen F2 race, just inland from Le Havre, as his ration of overseas motor racing. Rouen had been cancelled that year, he had nowhere to go. 'Who's going to look after him?' he

asked Frank, who hadn't apparently thought much about that. Sheridan volunteered.

Back in the sixties he had raced his Mini long enough to convince himself he was not going to become World Champion, and in more recent years he had run a Formula Ford Titan for his brother-in-law Richard Cardew. His stock-broker's mind had been grappling with the commercial potential of sponsorship in racing for many years. His annual pilgrimage to Rouen had brought him into contact with Creighton Brown's ICI-sponsored Formula Two team. ICI entertained interested business contacts at these F2 series races, talking plastics, paints, polymers and chemicals over a pleasantly informal luncheon or dinner connected with the event.

Sheridan had discussed the potentialities of motor racing sponsorship at length with David Payne, the ICI executive responsible. Thereafter, more or less as an intellectual exercise, he began to formulate ideas on how to extend motor racing sponsorship beyond its basic billboard concept – using the cars as mobile advertising signs. He batted ideas to and fro with Payne, and a clear picture emerged of the ways in which such enormous commercial concerns work, what type of promotions they will consider, and what aspects of racing or association with it would be anathema to them.

During that luncheon with Frank, Sheridan appreciated that Leyland Vehicles was the sort of company which would require service beyond the billboard syndrome: 'When they join your team – ho, ho – I'll come and look after them for you . . .' At the time neither man thought it was even remotely likely.

So Sheridan accompanied Steve Herrick to Dijon and talked to him as earnestly as only Sheridan can, not only of the Williams team but also of methods to make motor racing work for a major commercial sponsor. Steve Herrick recalled that 'I was serious about the idea, but I'm not sure if the Williams people thought I was, and then we had this great discussion and all the peripherals came up, which had been part of our initial thoughts . . .'

They discussed the necessity not only of finding funds to co-sponsor the team, but also of a support budget to exploit that sponsorship. If it was possible to entertain perhaps sixty influential prospective LV fleet customers at Dijon, how in detail would they arrange it?

One must recall that at that stage none of Frank's cars had won a race, nor even qualified on pole position, but Steve recognized their promise and made a very positive report on his return. And Frank Andrew and David Abell took the enterprising decision for Leyland Vehicles to support the team.

The Saudis were agreeable, and co-sponsorship was arranged for 1980–81 with an option to extend through 1982. It was signed in early October, and Sheridan – to his pleasant surprise – was able to forsake the stock exchange in favour of a cramped desk in one corner of Didcot's front office, 'To look after Leyland . . .' He was to do much more.

At that time BL as a whole was contracting its labour force, its mass-production car lines were in retreat pending release of the Mini-Metro, and the Government-supported group's sponsorship of a Formula One team was likely to prove controversial . . .

But the Leyland Vehicles division was launching its long-awaited Road-Train truck range, and was not afraid of aggressive promotion to sell it.

Steve Herrick: 'We knew we were sticking our necks out and we were rather nervous of media reaction to the announcement, but we were convinced that the only way out of our problems was to adopt an aggressive stance, to damn well stand up and be counted, and to get the Leyland Vehicles name shouted world-wide . . .'

The press announcement was made on 5 January 1980, in a modest reception at London's St Catherine's dock complex, a stone's throw from the City. It was a brisk and businesslike venue, in contrast to the lavish West End hotel and theatre launches favoured by more 'tinsel' sponsors with less technological products, like cigarettes and deodorant.

It went down well. There is no room for what racing people call 'bullshit' in the commercial vehicle world, and patently there is none at Didcot. There you find no extravagant office accommodation . . . deep-pile carpets, rich wood panelling. There you find immense investment in skilled personnel and top-quality machine tools and equipment. No other specialist Formula One team has its own private wind tunnel facility on site, few have such a broad-based engineering team. No expense is spared on racing – WGPE get by on peripherals. It all showed, and media response '. . . was nowhere near as bad as we had expected.'

Within two weeks Alan Jones had won the Argentine Grand Prix in the 'Leyland'-lettered car, and then those few within BL who had opposed the idea began talking about 'our car'. In the many races which followed the point was rammed home to potential big-fleet customers throughout Europe, the USA, Canada, South Africa and Argentina.

Sheridan had toured every European circuit to arrange accommodation and hospitality for an as-yet anonymous sponsor, using a basic block booking of fifty-five. If local LV agencies required more space, they could add to the basic unit. The costs differed wildly between, say, the Österreichring, out in the bucolic pasture-land of Austria, and the super-expensive posers' paradise of Monte Carlo. A nicely converted double-decker bus was to be used as a hospitality centre at the circuits, hung with LV promotional material to put the truck, bus and tractor message across. In some cases the wider group's car interests were also to be promoted.

This extension of the billboard syndrome would see guests arriving on circuit around 9 a.m. with coffee and breakfast in an LV environment at the bus. Local sales people would be on hand. Out to the grandstand seats to watch the supporting races, then back for lunch from 12.30; in the afternoon the Grand Prix, with the white-and-green 'Leyland' cars always in prime contention far into '81, indeed securing their second consecutive team trophy.

During the first World Championship season of 1980, Frank and one of the drivers would appear between morning warm-up and the race to meet the guests, but it was asking rather too much of Alan or Carlos to switch off their personal race preparation. In 1981 a Saturday evening dinner provided a more relaxed atmosphere for all, and allowed the drivers an early night and an uncluttered race-day.

The benefits of this association were numerous and on many levels. Association with such energy and accomplishment had good connotations for the sponsoring company. For example one French haulage operator had stone-walled all LV approaches for years until 1980, when their overtures were suddenly greeted with 'Ah yes, you're the people who've been blowing off Ligier and Renault – come in . . .'

Nor was that all. Such success did its bit in raising company morale. For years much of the labour force had felt British was best; now they were associated with tangible proof – Champions of the World. A car was shown around the factories, great coverage was given to the team's activities in the company newspaper, and Leyland Vehicles' image – buoyed-up by its Road-Train release – could ride still higher on Williams' World Championship.

For any major sponsor with his name or company logos blazoned across his cars, the attraction of a far-flung television audience must be immense. FOCA handle sales of TV rights for World Championship race coverage, and they issue their teams with a chart listing literally dozens of nations which take coverage and the number of minutes' screen-time of each at last count. From Ecuador to Pago-Pago there is a potential TV audience, but Sheridan in his WGPE dealings with prospective sponsors has always been very wary of brandishing it – for coverage of 'your car' cannot be guaranteed.

While Grand Prix racing provides a useful promotional tool or sales adjunct, it remains at heart a high-pressure, quick-reaction laboratory for technological development . . . one of the reasons put forward by the French organizing club for their very first Grand Prix, way back in 1906.

The mighty Mobil oil company has developed progressively closer links with WGPE since 1978. Prince Mohammed is a principal in their Saudi operation, and is involved with them in a large industrial complex sited at Yanbu on the coast. Mobil interest in the team stemmed from him, and they provided modest financial support from 1978–80, and considerably more in 1981, when they added technological support.

In effect the team became an arm of their Research and Development programme, using development lubricants under the watchful eye of Dr Tony Harlow, a British scientist from Mobil's Coryton centre who was to accompany the team to every race.

At one time this form of co-operation between a major oil company and a Grand Prix team would have been entirely normal. But in the commercial sponsorship atmosphere of the 1980s one hears of 'Mobil also pursuing a more conventional association' with posters, windscreen stickers etc on offer at their filling stations and associated advertising, linking their name with Grand Prix success.

Today there is little room for the small-money sponsor in Formula One, although the wealthy enthusiast can still contribute very materially to a top team. In WGPE's case there is the Italian Count Giuseppe Zanon.

Frank Williams: 'For every fifty wealthy enthusiasts who like to own a string of race-horses, there seems to be one who is into racing cars, power boats or aviation. Count Zanon's enthusiasm is Formula One . . .'

With interests in banking and insurance, 'Googie' Zanon preferred to keep his own counsel on the fringes of motor racing rather than in the public eye. He had contributed some private sponsorship to Frank's team in 1971–3; in 1974 he was one of Frank's supporters who bought him a DFV engine, and again in '75. He liked to help Italian drivers on their way to Formula One, and was terribly close to Ronnie Peterson, whose tragic death hurt him keenly. In 1979 he bought WGPE three Cosworth engines, and donated a fourth for 1981. 'Numbers '310', '315' and '320', and then '360,' Frank recites. He also bought himself an ex-team FW06 car, and about three times a year WGPE personnel would take it to Ricard-Castellet for him to drive around. Count Zanon assisted people he had come to like, while his quiet, modest style preserved his personal privacy.

Having generated funds, WGPE dispense them wisely. The engineers pursue their research and development; new ideas are tried, discarded or proven; new designs are carefully considered and drawn up. The factory makes the parts, and the R & D team – which is a separate entity with its own engineer, Frank Dernie, and its own mechanics, car and engines – tests them again, and if successful they enter production to be built on to the race cars. The race team operates the cars, and Team Manager Jeff Hazell and his secretary (Darsi Wickham until early 1981) juggle the logistics of taking the team racing.

Which isn't simple . . .

When the World Championship title was there to be won in Montreal in 1980, WGPE's race team arrived by air with four cars, eight engines, the three leading team engineers, fifteen mechanics – twenty-six people, all told – and no less than five-and-a-half metric tonnes of spares, all of which had to be logged, listed and indexed to allow them to be located rapidly in their RadCon strong-boxes and to pass through Customs without excessive hindrance.

The booking, listing, checking and organizing of such movements became Darsi's speciality – the hidden infra-structure of Formula One, without which each race simply could not take place.

Team Manager Jeff Hazell came to WGPE from Ensign after a memorable occasion in Buenos Aires in '77, when Patrick had found himself staying in the wrong hotel and not knowing about certain last-minute programme changes which had been made. Jeff sold himself to Frank, and by the Guv'nor's admission developed into 'the best in the business'.

Darsi just seemed to be born for her job. As a little girl she was more interested in fixing the family car than combing a doll's hair. She worked for the British Automobile Racing Club before joining Wolf as race team secretary, and then moved to WGPE, where she relieved Gwen Brown of 'the dreaded bookings'. Darsi's husband John managed the March Formula Two team, and if a new circuit appeared on the Grand Prix calendar – as Imola did in recent years – there was F2 experience of local hotels to be drawn upon.

The pressure in the race team office is almost tangible. Packed racks and files and calendar charts tell their own story. Jeff and Darsi plan continuously a minimum three months ahead, a daily job-list is made out, and for every task completed the discipline of 'What's next, what's next, what's next?' has to be applied. Commitment absorbs office staff as much as factory and race team. Darsi: 'I've sat up in bed at 2 a.m. before now and written myself a 39-item job list. If you like to go home and forget your work completely, then racing is not for you . . .'

Hotel bookings form a baseline for the annual calendar. Accommodation for South America, South Africa and Long Beach '81 were reserved in the spring of 1980, and so on through the year.

The team is unusual in that it prefers a policy of keeping to itself, away from the popular circus hotels. To outsiders they won themselves a hard-faced reputation, a remote bunch who did not mix. It was understandable, but they had become a happy and well-balanced team whose members were self-sufficient, got on well together and needed little outside contact. They lived and worked and socialized as a group, and personality clashes within the team were rare, despite the occasional snorer whose room-mates had to be rotated to give them a chance to sleep!

On occasion the team requirement would be too big for one hotel and would be split between two or three. Occasionally one fit for most of the team would not quite match standards expected for drivers or sponsors.

Darsi: 'Frank has always been very particular about the lads' accommodation. They are away for long periods of time and have a right to reasonable rooms. He cares an awful lot about how his mechanics are looked after, and a strip-wash in a bucket after working 'til 2 a.m. is not good enough . . .'

There are occasional 'drop-offs', as Williamsese describes a blunder, but after every race a team meeting is called to iron out all binds and problems. There opinions are expressed firmly, no holds barred. Problems get shaken out before tensions can build up. The Williams management style is extremely open, and it has worked very well. Team members pull their weight and either make the grade or go. Those good enough to stay made the team systems which won races.

For their drivers, Frank and Patrick prefer a post-race debrief, as otherwise they could return home without first-hand knowledge of their thoughts on the cars, Alan living in California, Switzerland or Australia and Carlos in St Jean Cap Ferrat. Unlike so many team principals who helicopter out of a race circuit virtually the instant the chequered flag has fallen, the Williams men like to stay on, and allowance for this is necessary in flight bookings.

Any Formula One team is a conventional travel agents' nightmare. Such a large and active team as WGPE becomes a horror story. For races outside Europe the FOCA agents arrange group air charters, but otherwise Darsi will order tickets as necessary.

It sounds mechanical, an ordered progression through the season, but it's not. The question of whether or not a WGPE airline booking is actually taken up or set aside becomes a major factor, and one which would drive any conventional travel agent hysterical.

For not only is the main team flying to and from its well-planned, long-arranged race meetings, but the R & D team is flitting off to last-minute test sessions, Patrick and his engineers are continually travelling to discuss technology, and Frank spends a major part of his life airborne, visiting sponsors and suppliers and attending meetings and functions.

Frank has often had up to eight alternative travel itineraries planned and booked for the same day, then at the last moment has decided to scrub them all and abruptly booked himself on another flight entirely, to somewhere completely different! Because a meeting doesn't happen, or perhaps he has been delayed, a mass of detailed pre-planning becomes redundant.

Then the team's well-exercised company accountant George Koopman must know which tickets have been used and must therefore be paid, and which have been discarded and may be set aside. Darsi: 'An ordinary company accountant would probably be scared stiff and just get lost in this situation, but George has an interest in everything that's going on and understands why things sometimes get frantic . . .'

George Koopman: 'Like any activity where lots of people are involved, this is as much a planning and logistics exercise as anything. Without plenty of foresight and planning you won't win races, simply because you won't have the right things at the right time.

'Tensions, distractions must not be allowed, because the race team and R & D team and anybody else travelling on our business already has enough on his mind. We're a travel agent's nightmare because we require total flexibility. We are always making last-minute decisions not to go tonight, but to go tomorrow night, or to go right now – this morning – or not to go at all! Then we might decide we want to test somewhere completely different, without

any warning beyond a phone call perhaps from Frank in Los Angeles or Paris. If he rings and wants a car at Snetterton next morning, and the only one we've got is in a million pieces in the 'shop, it will still be there in running order.

'Often, when the team wants a sudden test session, they just go, and we pick up the pieces afterwards . . .

'The airlines in general have got used to us, but a normal High Street agency simply wouldn't have the personal relationship with the airlines which is vital, so we use the regular FOCA men, because they have that relationship and understand the flexibility required by Formula One. The number of unused tickets we turn back to an airline could upset them if it was handled badly, but on the other hand we do provide a lot of business for them . . .'

And with the factory's operations to be handled as well, the accountancy problems of managing a Formula One team's affairs are multiplied: 'If you document everything, and accept that this is just like running a normal business with all the normal forms of expenditure – if all at a frantic pace – and if you are then aware not only of what is going on, but also of *why* it is going on, then you can keep track and see what it's all about.

'We attach great importance to communication, so that everybody knows what everybody else is doing, just what is being made or done in all the various departments, and that way you can keep control. If I just sat at my desk here and looked at bits of paper being passed in with numbers on them, it would all go into a sea, and I'd be lost.

'You can either manage by exception – so that when problems arise you recognize them – or by a "hands-on" philosophy, where you try to build up a good feel for everything that is going on. That involves getting away from your desk and walking around the factory. That's the only way I feel happy. If we were a two-hundred-strong company this would not be possible, but under one hundred it's fine . . .'

In Europe the team equipment and cars are hauled around in their massive Leyland-Yorke transporter. Darsi's office becomes haulage contractor as much as travel agent, juggling cross-Channel bookings and the awesome paperwork demanded by

Customs and highway regulations across the Continent. Carnets have to be acquired, listing in effect everything carried upon the truck to prove – should a belligerent Customs officer ever order a strip and search – that everything brought into that country is indeed about to be taken out again. The *Acquit* documents for France are vital. It is illegal to take a commercial vehicle through France without the properly completed paperwork. The freight department at the port of entry stamp the *Acquit* and all other necessary papers, and the 'incoming' counterfoil is ripped out. If the *Acquit* lists forty-eight wheels incoming, and only forty-seven are found outgoing, woe betide crew and company. At the outgoing Customs post the *Acquit* etc. will be stamped, and their outgoing counterfoils torn off.

Eventually the incoming and outgoing counterfoils will be matched up at that country's Customs centre, and if they do not match then duty can be demanded on all missing parts listed, presumed sold.

When one Carnet from 1978 was returned to Didcot 'undischarged', Darsi had to complete a declaration witnessed by two local PCs to prove the parts in question had been brought back to England . . .

All this paperwork is valid only for a limited period, and demands a banker's guarantee, insurance indemnities and other charges before the various agencies involved will issue it.

What sets a Formula One team apart from a normal haulier – and WGPE are members of the Freight Transport Association – is that local restrictions on heavy traffic can cause them intense pain, where a normal haulier would allow for a weekend's delay and see no great problem. In France it has become illegal to operate a commercial between 10 p.m. Friday and 11 p.m. Sunday unless a special permit has been issued. In 1981 this applied to all routes leaving Paris on Saturdays and Sundays, with virtually no exceptions. It also applied on public holidays, of which there are many at awkward times, and the spectre of the team transporter being immobilized for days, with cars and engines aboard – vitally needed for test, race or rebuild – is a persistent Formula One nightmare.

The truck crew – Ken Sagar and Nick Butler – know the ropes, but the administrators back home have to be aware of all new restrictions in advance to keep them out of trouble.

There is an unwritten Formula One team truck driver rule that if pulled over by the police – especially the French – then you are out of the cab and standing in front of it before they have dismounted. Eye to eye, anxious to discover what you have done wrong – it defuses the situation. Giving them a look around the cars always helps, and team stickers, tee-shirts and general 'goodies' are the most amazing international goodwill currency.

Testing is a major ever-present problem. The R & D team use their own transport, but major test programmes have spilled beyond them to demand the race team's time. Darsi's wall-chart betrays one mind-boggling week in April 1980, with one Williams car and crew testing at Ricard in the South of France simultaneously with a second at Zolder in Belgium, and a third at Jarama in Spain. All three were operating on two days that week, and two drivers were being ferried around all three . . . With such a test programme being planned, the calendar pages are turned back. When did car No. 1 return from its last race? How many days for its necessary strip and rebuild? When would engines be back from rebuild? When could travel and hotels be arranged? 'The dreaded bookings' strike again . . .

In 'spare' moments Jeff and Darsi become involved in ordering new and replacement team uniforms, for every team member has clothing provided. Oil-ruined trousers or torn shirts are to be replaced, waterproofs have failed, the new shirts' sleeves are too tight . . . somebody has dropped-off. And there's the badging: every sponsors' badge or logo has to be applied in the right place, as agreed. It applies to cars as much as clothes, and is a very important part of the business; commitments to sponsors must be met.

And there is the visa problem. Fortunately the team is all-British, apart from two; Carlos' mechanic Ryuji 'Juwie' Nakaya, the Japanese, and Alan's Australian mechanic Wayne Eckersley. Visa requirements vary for different nationalities . . .

No Briton or Japanese requires a visa to visit Spanish territory, but an Australian does. On the trip to Argentina in 1980 every team member was equipped for immigration control at Buenos

Aires, but the team's airliner ran into technical trouble and made an unscheduled landing for repair at Madrid's Barajas Airport. The whole team was allowed entry to pass the time, except the incensed Wayne Eckersley, whose Australian passport had no valid Spanish visa. He was effectively under arrest in solitary for four and a half hours until the plane resumed its journey. Darsi's ear ached on his return, no matter if it was the airline's drop-off and not hers . . .

An irritating effect of visa application is that passports are frozen while Embassies apply their seal. For Brazil '81 Darsi obtained the vital forms from their London Embassy, completed and returned them in good time. The day before departure the Embassy returned the forms, out of date – 1980 not 1981. Darsi had to despatch a van to London for the proper forms, which proved identical save for the date. The new visas materialized just in time. Why did the Embassy wait so long to reject the application? One dare not bawl out a visa clerk – if they proved obstinate the team could miss a race . . .

To keep your head, under pressures which to ordinary people would be insupportable, is a vital feature of a successful Racer . . .

While funds are generated, sponsors serviced and the team's frenetic travelling plans are laid, the Didcot factory makes the tools to do the job.

Dave Neal manages the works. He's an ex-Lola man, having worked for the world's largest production racing car manufacturer, first as a mechanic, then storeman and buyer. He joined WGPE to take responsibility for the everyday running and productivity of the workshops, and maintenance of the whole manufacturing and assembly operation.

For him and most Williams men an average day starts at 8.15 a.m., and they work in theory until 6 p.m. – though often on to eight or nine o'clock at night. Frank is anxious to divide the demands made upon the factory staff from those placed upon, and readily accepted by, the race team crews.

'To give their best you need your highly-skilled artisans in the factory to work virtually normal industrial hours, in comparison to the race team who put in some ferocious time. Most of the race team are relatively young and single, most of the factory blokes are over thirty and have family ties . . .'

The company reckons to pay a good basic rate, sufficient according to Dave Neal 'for normal extra working hours on weekdays to be considered part of the deal; overtime rates only apply at weekends . . .'

Still, by the standards of industry at large, sixty-five hours a week is desperate exploitation. A Williams man doesn't see it that way, or if he does, he doesn't last. He is part of a skilled team with a clear short-term goal in view. They are a happy outfit and they pull together. There are no unions here, neither is the management remote, nor insensitive and decidedly not feeble.

While the factory produces what the design engineers and draughtsmen in the drawing office set down on paper, the race team prepares, maintains and in most respects modifies the cars from race to race.

A Grand Prix car exists in a totally different way to the road cars we all use. We see a road car for sale, we buy it, drive it, garage it and it remains physically the same steel and alloy assembly that we bought – the same bodyshell, engine, transmission, wheels and furnishing. We might fit fresh tyres and change the oil. Barring accidents, that's all that changes.

In comparison a modern Grand Prix car exists mainly as an identity, just a chassis number. Its life as a fully-assembled working racing car is as ephemeral as a mayfly's. Its major parts are given a limited life and are regularly replaced by new ones. Its engine may be removed and replaced by another in as little as ninety minutes or so. And its design is never frozen. Formula One cars are not just completed at the start of a new season and raced in that form until they wear out. Development and modification is a continuous process. The car you see racing in Canada at the end of a season may look superficially the one which commenced the season in Argentina, but if even the basic monocoque chassis has survived that long, it has been very lucky – and was obviously very good to begin with.

Barring serious car-damaging accidents – which the factory copes with on a bush-fire basis like Darsi's sudden flight requirements – by the end of any race day Dave Neal and his assistant Pete

Unsung heroes . . . a few of the factory crew at Didcot. *Left to right:* Peter Ampleford, Bernie Jones, Roger Tipler, Peter Fostekew, John Cadd, Steve Fowler.

Williams Grand Prix Engineering Ltd became the first motor racing team to be honoured with the Queen's Award for Export Achievement, presented here by Sir Ashley Ponsonby, Lord Lieutenant of Oxfordshire, 1981.

Digby will have a clear idea of what parts and services will be required by the race team in the next few days. The Chief Mechanic – Ian Anderson into 1980, Alan Challis in 1981 – will have advised Dave before departure about what components he plans to replace as a matter of course upon the team's return. A card system is used to record the life of major suspension and drive-train components on each car. An item like a suspension wishbone or drive-shaft joint will be allowed a pre-set number of races, or so many hours' use. Once they have expired, it will be discarded as over-age, whether or not it shows signs of incipient failure. The over-age parts will be used for destruction testing to determine possible design improvements or may possibly be assembled into a show car for exhibition.

Team personnel usually fly home Sunday evening from any race in Europe, and by Monday afternoon, or Tuesday at the latest, the transporter will draw into the factory loading bay to disgorge its cars and spares.

Usually by Monday mid-day the team's spares man, Douglas Bebb, will have produced a list of usages in excess of what is required by the existing rebuild list.

The cars are rolled out of the transporter and wheeled into the race team workshop area just as they left the track. They are placed on four corner scales and are precisely weighed. Weight is the enemy of performance. Development, notoriously, adds weight. It is watched with almost anorexic zeal. The mechanics ensure that the last pint of fuel has been drained from the single tank between cockpit and engine. These cars are never to exactly the same specification for more than two races in a row, and they must be kept close to the minimum weight limit.

The rear half of the modern Formula One car is its engine. The unit bolts rigidly to the sheet-metal monocoque chassis which carries the driver and fuel tank and on to which is hung the front suspension. The rear suspension mounts directly to the engine and its gearbox, protruding from the rear.

The active life of a Cosworth engine is some five hundred miles at most if it is to remain competitive. At that point it must be returned to the Cosworth factory in Northampton or to one of their appointed specialist preparation agencies, such as John Judd's in Rugby, where it will be stripped, examined and rebuilt. Components such as pistons, con-rods, valve-springs, cam-drive gears etc. are lifed as rigidly as the cars. Over-age parts are junk. To finish first, you must first finish. 'Lifing' reduces the chance of failure, retirement, losing, but reliability is expensive. During their Championship season in 1980 WGPE had a pool of eighteen available engines, priced new at £22,600 each. Thirteen of them were raced regularly, four were ear-marked primarily for the R & D unit and one was maintained exclusively for experimental purposes.

Once the returning cars have been weighed, the skid-pads which protect the sheet-metal underside of the chassis and the engine castings against damage are unbolted and removed. This leaves the underside clear for the car to be lifted on to a waist-high working trolley and wheeled into its race bay for strip-down. The wheels and body panels are removed, and successively the suspensions are dismounted and dismantled, the gearbox removed and the engine craned out and despatched by Leyland Sherpa or Marina van for rebuild if required. The team's float of engines is in constant rotation, so the van drivers will deliver an old engine and collect a rebuilt one simultaneously.

On the race team, two mechanics are assigned to each car, and they stay with it throughout its life. There are normally two race cars and one spare available at any race meeting, essentially to identical specifications apart from a few minor driver preferences – although all Frank's team drivers have proved very compatible. At times, particularly at a meeting, two floating mechanics pitch in where needed, and in the strip and rebuild process at Didcot a spare mechanic will help out a crew if it encounters problems and lags behind.

After two days' work the cars which had raced on Sunday are as dismantled as they can be, short of being broken up. Bob Torrie's four-man sub-assembly section neighbouring the race bays completely strips down suspension assemblies, the gearbox and drive-train components. Most Cosworth engine users adapt Hewland gearboxes to their own requirements. Mike Hewland's old-established company in Maidenhead is very obliging: if a customer requires something special they will make it. WGPE assemble the basic gearbox with their own selector mechanism, lubrication system and even the side-plates of the casing, which are designed and made at Didcot.

Bob Torrie himself takes virtually sole responsibility for gearbox inspection and assembly, putting them back together with infinite patience and care. A crown-wheel and pinion will normally be time-expired after two thousand miles, or approximately four races plus practice, and the rest of the 'box is evaluated dependent upon conditions.

All suspension components have a roughly similar life limit, around two thousand miles. On the car these parts carry a semi-sheen black finish applied by a hot-dip process called Parco-Lubrising. It looks good, it's a rust preventative and is easily removed for inspection, by bead blasting. Once the components have been blasted back to bare metal, they are minutely examined for incipient cracks, using dyes or a process known as Magnaflux. If they remain usable, the components are then degreased and dipped in the Parco-Lubrising tank, and they emerge, blacked up, for re-assembly.

Radiators tend to change design before they have a chance to reach a life, and normally end up as scrap, with stone or gravel damage. Transit damage will occasionally occur, and body panels in various forms of ultra-lightweight 'glass-fibre' also change design. Most survive no more than three races, by which time they can look rather stone-chipped, crazed and second-hand.

As the cars begin their re-assembly, a secondary inspection is made of all components built into them. If a brand-new engine should appear from Cosworth one of Torrie's crew is ready to 'kit' it, fitting the banjos, fuel connectors, unions etc. which will adapt the basic engine to the Williams car. Once kitted, the engine stays in that form, even being shipped back for rebuild fully-equipped. When an engine returns from rebuild, its kitting is double-checked before it goes off to a car or into the transporter as a race spare.

It has become normal practice to use one engine for qualifying, then fit a fresh one overnight before the race. That engine will then stay with the car – assuming it has remained healthy – for qualifying at the next race.

Fresh components must be available from a carefully managed stores section. Lifed-out components must have replacements available ready to fit. Design is never frozen, development and modification is a continuous process.

New designs emerge from a basic layout penned by Patrick and his engineering team. Working drawings are made, and Patrick follows everything through. Dave Neal: 'Patrick's got his hands on everything we do – he's into everything. Of the race teams I am aware of I really believe we must be the most professional in our attitudes.

'If Patrick and his chaps design a new component and he says, "I want it for that race," I might look at it and say, "We can't possibly produce it in time, but you will have it for the race after with full spares back-up." He'll either look to see if he can change the design to speed up production, or he'll accept that he'll have it for the next race with full spares.

'If there's a gain to be made then we have to have it, but it's always a carefully considered situation. Patrick will say, "Yes, it's worth running" or "No, it's not." We never go out on a limb, but we do have a very fast reaction time, incredibly fast by normal industrial standards . . . that's what this side of Formula One is all about.'

A visitor rapidly appreciates the self-confident energy of the Didcot plant, its staff's mass of accumulated knowledge and experience. Occasionally a different way of making something will be suggested to the designers: 'Patrick's fairly liberal in his allowance for the machine shop or fabrication shop to improve the quality of a component. He very often draws something and says, "I want to see it at such and such a stage, to see if we can modify it." The scrap rate through drawing office error here is very, very small. In the whole of the '07 series we've encountered probably less than five, certainly less than ten . . .'

Out in the factory the nine-strong machine shop staff under Les Wainwright handle a mass of up-to-date computer-controlled machine tools. There are four fabricators under Bernie Jones entirely responsible for chassis construction and repair; five more under Roger Tipler form suspension parts, brackets, pedals . . . the list is enormous.

There is a so-called Pre-Preg shop producing plastic body panels, wings and things, researching alternative methods of construction. There's a model shop attached to the wind tunnel facility just a few doors down the road; the buyers' department; a wheel specialist; and Bob Butterfield the inspector, the ultimate arbiter of precision and acceptability . . .

Meanwhile their end products are being reassembled into the race cars. After perhaps six relatively leisurely working days the cars are ready, often substantially revised and renewed; they are loaded on to the transporter with the carefully indexed and catalogued boxes of spares; the paperwork is double-checked and ready, and the Leyland tractor unit hauls its precious load away towards the docks, the Townsend–Thoresen ferry, and another step on the World Championship ladder.

The standard procedure at the race circuit is for two days of practice and qualifying to precede race-day. Qualifying is all-important, as a driver starting the race from the front row of the normally two-by-two grid has a ready-made advantage over the man starting five or six rows further back.

Friday practice sessions are normally occupied with the race engineers seeking to achieve well-balanced handling and matching the cars to the demands of the circuit, Patrick Head on Alan Jones' car and Neil Oatley on Carlos Reutemann's. The Saturday sessions will often see Carlos tyre-testing and fuel-consumption testing to allow the type of race tyre and the race fuel-load to be decided. Fuel is heavy, there is no point in carrying more than the minimum necessary to survive race distance – and the cars' consumption will vary from engine to engine and circuit to circuit. It has to be predicted very accurately. Meanwhile Alan will be setting up the chassis, choosing springs, anti-roll bars, various settings – the multitude of adjustments available in the modern Formula One car. The drivers are remarkably compatible, turning in very similar times in similarly set-up cars. Each one's findings will apply to the other.

Qualifying reaches its climax in the final Saturday session. The cars are despatched with the minimum fuel load, there is talk of other teams using ultra-lightweight special cars. Frank controls timing, fuel consumption monitoring and tyre choice. Fuel monitoring is vital. If a car runs dry on circuit, the rest of that qualifying section could be lost. Frank tells his drivers, 'If you see the arrow you must come in unless you are on a magic lap. If you are then you can keep going, but it's at your own risk – you might get round, you might not.' If a car becomes stranded, the spare is brought forward with its two mechanics, and they smoothly begin working with whichever driver is in need.

On race morning a final warm-up session allows the cars to be tested in race trim, unless earlier delays have set back the programme or an overnight adjustment has been adopted 'on spec' and has to be tested.

Frank Williams: 'At Ricard in 1980 we were struggling. On the Saturday night Patrick remarked that there was one possibility we hadn't yet tried. I believed we were up to our necks anyway, no way would we beat the Ligiers, so let's try the alternative set-up on Alan's car, put twenty gallons in and give it a go in the morning warm-up. He went straight out and was one and a half seconds quicker than anybody else.

'That worries the other teams. They wonder, "Is he running light on fuel, or is he just effing quick?" People watch Alan, time him. They fear what he can do, just like we watch Piquet or Villeneuve. He can suddenly do something magical – it's demoralizing. After that warm-up we modified Carlos' car to match, and he was quicker too for the race. Alan went to the line with thirty-nine gallons of gas in his car, and it was the first time all weekend he'd driven it in that condition . . .

'At Montreal, in what became the Championship decider, we went to the line not having done full tank tests with Alan and on 13-inch diameter front tyres for the first time. Throughout practice we had suffered a problem, with the car not wanting to turn in crisply to the corners. It was on 15-inch front tyres throughout and because they don't revolve as quickly as the 13s in covering the same distance, they ran too cool and didn't generate enough grip. The 13s weren't perfect, but they were better.

'This is a little bit of brinkmanship, but I'm happy to do it. Patrick has a great and deep understanding of the machines he creates.'

When ex-works FW06 and '07 chassis were sold to private

owners for 1979–80 the factory extended service and parts back-up to them. When Emilio Salazar smashed his '07 chassis worse than the works drivers had ever managed, in a minor race at Monza, Dave Neal recalled: 'It was good practice for us to repair it rapidly, and it kept the chassis shop busy at a time when they were abreast of the team situation . . .'

In Canadian Grand Prix practice at the end of 1980, Kevin Cogan crashed his private RAM Racing '07 heavily over a kerb. 'They phoned me at home on the Saturday night – reversing the charges from Montreal – and asked if we had the labour available to repair the chassis for the American race the following Sunday? It was air-freighted back to London, cleared through Customs on Monday afternoon, and we worked on it all night, through Tuesday into Wednesday, when it was flown back out in time for them to re-assemble it ready for practice at Watkins Glen . . .'

There were their own team dramas as well, like Alan's testing accident at Donington Park in mid-1980: 'Luckily we had a spare chassis ready as a unit, and we built it into a new car. We try to keep a spare monocoque available in emergency. His Dutch practice crash that year was very bad: we shipped out a replacement overnight, but despite the damage it was all repaired in seven days and returned to service. Patrick's chassis is structurally very sound in any case: stiff, robust and elegant. We have to legislate for disaster and have latest-spec spares available for everything. But if we should be unfortunate enough to damage two chassis really badly in one race, that could be a big problem . . .'

No doubt they would meet it. Flexibility, speed of response and a boisterous readiness to 'get after it' permeates the whole business; and the charge is led from the top . . . an object lesson for industry as a whole.

Racer!

V ·APPENDIX: WILLIAMS RACING RECORD

'We had to finish . . . it was no good putting on a flashy show and leading until the last lap, only to blow up or crash. The record books tell the people who matter who won, or who finished in the points. They don't say things like "Graham Hill won but Piers Courage led most of the way." It's results that matter . . .'

Frank Williams, 1981

Key to Abbreviations

DNP   Did not practise

DNQ   Did not qualify

DNS   Did not start

FL   Fastest lap

FR   Qualified on 'front row' (second fastest in practice)

PP   Pole position (fastest in practice)

Rtd   Retired

Unc   Unclassified (too few laps completed although running at finish)

Wdn   Entry withdrawn

Note: Individual car chassis numbers have been verified with the team where possible. Early numbers are taken from contemporary race records.

1967 to 1969

29–10–67	Motor Show '200' F3, Brands Hatch	Piers Courage	Brabham BT21B	*1st* (in heat)
31–3–68	Gran Premio Barcelona F2, Spain	Piers Courage	Brabham BT23C/7	4th
7–4–68	Hockenheim F2, Germany	Piers Courage	Brabham BT23C/7	5th Heat 1/2nd Heat 2 3rd Overall on aggregate
15–4–68	BARC Thruxton Trophy F2	Piers Courage	Brabham BT23C/7	2nd Heat 2/Rtd Final
21–4–68	Eifelrennen, Nürburgring Sudschleife F2	Piers Courage	Brabham BT23C/7	Rtd
28–4–68	Gran Premio Madrid, Jarama F2, Spain	Piers Courage	Brabham BT23C/7	Practice damage, DNS
5–5–68	Limbourg GP, Zolder, Belgium F2	Piers Courage	Brabham BT23C/7	Heat 1 accident
3–6–68	Holts Trophy F2, Crystal Palace	Piers Courage	Brabham BT23C/7	2nd Heat 1/Rtd Final
		Max Mosley*	Brabham BT23C/6	10th Heat 2/DNQ Final
16–6–68	Rhine Cup, Hockenheim, Germany F2	Piers Courage	Brabham BT23C/7	7th
		Max Mosley	Brabham BT23C/6	Race accident
		Jonathan Williams**	Brabham BT23C/7	*1st*
23–6–68	Monza Lottery F2, Italy	Max Mosley	Brabham BT23C/6	8th
14–7–68	Langenlebarn F2, Austria	Piers Courage	Brabham BT23C/7	14th on aggregate
28–7–68	Zandvoort GP F2, Holland	Piers Courage	Brabham BT23C/7	Race accident Final *1st* Heat 2
		Max Mosley	Brabham BT23C/6	Race accident Final 10th Heat 2
25–8–68	Mediterranean GP, Enna, Sicily F2	Piers Courage	Brabham BT23C/7	2nd
		Samuel Brown	Brabham BT23C	DNS practice damage
15–9–68	Trophées de France, Reims, France F2	Piers Courage	Brabham BT23C/7	3rd
20–10–68	Albi Grand Prix, France F2	Piers Courage	Brabham BT23C/1	3rd
27–10–68	Rome GP, Vallelunga, Italy F2	Max Mosley	Brabham BT23C/6	14th Heat 1/15th Heat 2 14th Overall on aggregate
1–12–68	Temporada 1, Buenos Aires, Argentina F2	Piers Courage	Brabham BT23C/1	Rtd
		Carlos Pairetti	Brabham BT23C	DNS burned-out in practice
		Eduardo Copello	Brabham BT23C	Rtd
		J-M Bordeu	Brabham BT23C	7th
8–12–68	Temporada 2, Cordoba, Argentina F2	Piers Courage	Brabham BT23C/1	6th FL
		Eduardo Copello	Brabham BT23C	Rtd
		J-M Bordeu	Brabham BT23C	Unc
15–12–68	Temporada 3, San Juan, Argentina F2	Piers Courage	Brabham BT23C/1	Rtd
		Carlos Pairetti	Brabham BT23C	Rtd
		Eduardo Copello	Brabham BT23C	8th
		J-M Bordeu	Brabham BT23C	10th
22–12–68	Temporada 4, Buenos Aires, Argentina F2	Piers Courage	Brabham BT23C/1	*1st* Overall on aggregate 4th Heat 1/1st Heat 2
		Carlos Reutemann	Brabham BT23C	8th Heat 1/Rtd Heat 2
		Cacho Fangio	Brabham BT23C	17th Heat 1/Rtd Heat 2
		J-M Bordeu	Brabham BT23C	10th Heat 1/10th Heat 2 9th Overall on aggregate

* Car prepared by FWRC ** Deputizing for Piers who had a Formula One BRM drive that day

1969

Date	Event	Driver	Car	Result
4–1–69	New Zealand GP, Pukekohe	Piers Courage	Brabham BT24T/3	3rd
11–1–69	Levin International, New Zealand	Piers Courage	Brabham BT24T/3	Rtd, warm-up Heat 2nd feature race
18–1–69	Lady Wigram Trophy, Christchurch, NZ	Piers Courage	Brabham BT24T/3	4th warm-up Heat 4th feature race
26–1–69	Teretonga Park, Invercargill, NZ	Piers Courage	Brabham BT24T/3	2nd warm-up Heat *1st*/FL feature race
2–2–69	Australian GP, Lakeside, Brisbane	Piers Courage	Brabham BT24T/3	Rtd, collision
9–2–69	Warwick Farm, Sydney, Australia	Piers Courage	Brabham BT24T/3	Rtd, collision
16–2–69	Sandown Park, Melbourne, Australia	Piers Courage	Brabham BT24T/3	Rtd, broken half-shaft
16–3–69	Race of Champions, Brands Hatch F1	Piers Courage	Brabham BT26/1	Rtd, fuel leak
7–4–69	Wills Trophy, Thruxton F2	Piers Courage	Brabham BT23C/16	*1st* Heat 2/7th Final
13–4–69	Hockenheim, Germany F2	Piers Courage	Brabham BT23C/16	3rd Overall
30–4–69	International Trophy, Silverstone F1	Piers Courage	Brabham BT26/1	5th
20–4–69	Pau GP, France F2	Piers Courage	Brabham BT23C/16	3rd
4–5–69	SPANISH GRAND PRIX, BARCELONA	Piers Courage	Brabham BT26/1	Rtd, engine
11–5–69	Gran Premio Madrid, Jarama, Spain F2	Piers Courage	Brabham BT23C/16	3rd
		Malcolm Guthrie	Brabham BT23C	13th
18–5–69	MONACO GRAND PRIX, MONTE CARLO	Piers Courage	Brabham BT26/1	2nd FL*
8–6–69	Limbourg GP, Zolder, Belgium F2	Piers Courage	Brabham BT30/5	4th Heat 1/3rd Heat 2 3rd Overall on aggregate
		Malcolm Guthrie	Brabham BT30/4	10th Heat 1/6th Heat 2 7th Overall on aggregate
21–6–69	DUTCH GRAND PRIX, ZANDVOORT	Piers Courage	Brabham BT26/1	Rtd, clutch
29–6–69	Trophées de France, Reims, France F2	Piers Courage	Brabham BT30/5	3rd FL
6–7–69	FRENCH GRAND PRIX, Clermont-Ferrand	Piers Courage	Brabham BT26/1	Rtd, broken nose mounts
19–7–69	BRITISH GRAND PRIX, Silverstone	Piers Courage	Brabham BT26/1	5th
3–8–69	GERMAN GRAND PRIX, NÜRBURGRING	Piers Courage	Brabham BT26/1	Race accident
	GERMAN GRAND PRIX F2 class	Richard Attwood	Brabham BT30/5	6th Overall/2nd F2
24–8–69	Mediterranean GP, Enna, Sicily F2	Piers Courage	Brabham BT30/5	*1st* Both heats/Overall
7–9–69	ITALIAN GRAND PRIX, MONZA	Piers Courage	Brabham BT26/1	5th
14–9–69	Albi GP, France, F2	Piers Courage	Brabham BT30/5	Rtd, broken fuel line
20–9–69	CANADIAN GRAND PRIX, MOSPORT PARK	Piers Courage	Brabham BT26/1	Rtd, fuel leak
5–10–69	UNITED STATES GRAND PRIX, WATKINS GLEN	Piers Courage	Brabham BT26/1	2nd
12–10–69	Rome GP, Vallelunga, Italy F2	Piers Courage	De Tomaso F2–00298	3rd Heat 1/Rtd Heat 2
		Franco Bernabei	Brabham BT23C/16	6th Heat 1/8th Heat 2 5th Overall on aggregate
19–10–69	MEXICAN GRAND PRIX, MEXICO CITY	Piers Courage	Brabham BT26/1	10th

1970

Date	Event	Driver	Car	Result
7–3–70	SOUTH AFRICAN GRAND PRIX, KYALAMI	Piers Courage	De Tomaso 505–381	Rtd, suspension
19–4–70	SPANISH GRAND PRIX, JARAMA	Piers Courage	De Tomaso 505–381 (2)	DNS, practice damage

* Official time, actually Stewart's Matra was 0.7 sec faster

26–4–70	International Trophy, Silverstone F1	Piers Courage	De Tomaso 505–383	3rd both heats/Overall
10–5–70	MONACO GRAND PRIX, MONTE CARLO	Piers Courage	De Tomaso 505–383	Unc
7–6–70	BELGIAN GRAND PRIX, FRANCORCHAMPS	Piers Courage	De Tomaso 505–382 (4)	Rtd, oil pressure (?)
21–6–70	DUTCH GRAND PRIX, ZANDVOORT	Piers Courage	De Tomaso 505–382 (4)	Fatal race accident
19–7–70	BRITISH GRAND PRIX, BRANDS HATCH	Brian Redman	De Tomaso 505–383	Wdn, hub shaft failure
2–8–70	GERMAN GRAND PRIX, HOCKENHEIM	Brian Redman	De Tomaso 505–383	DNQ
16–8–70	AUSTRIAN GRAND PRIX, ÖSTERREICHRING	Tim Schenken	De Tomaso 505–383	Rtd, engine
6–9–70	ITALIAN GRAND PRIX, MONZA	Tim Schenken	De Tomaso 505–383	Rtd, engine
20–9–70	CANADIAN GRAND PRIX, ST JOVITE	Tim Schenken	De Tomaso 505–383	Unc
4–10–70	UNITED STATES GRAND PRIX, WATKINS GLEN	Tim Schenken	De Tomaso 505–383	Rtd, rear suspension

1971

24–1–71	Argentine GP, Buenos Aires F1	Henri Pescarolo	March 701–06	3rd Heat 1/2nd Heat 2 2nd Overall on aggregate
7–2–71	Gran Premio Colombia, Bogota F2	Henri Pescarolo	March 712M–4	15th Heat 1/DNS Heat 2
		Derek Bell	March 712M–2	13th Heat 1/2nd Heat 2 7th Overall on aggregate
14–2–71	Gran Premio Çiudad de Bogota, F2	Henri Pescarolo	March 712M–4	Rtd, both heats
		Derek Bell	March 712M–2	4th Heat 1/2nd Heat 2 3rd Overall on aggregate
6–3–71	SOUTH AFRICAN GRAND PRIX, KYALAMI	Henri Pescarolo	March 701–06	11th
14–3–71	Mallory Park F2	Henri Pescarolo	March 712M–4	*1st* Both heats and Overall FL shared with Peterson
		Derek Bell	March 712M–2	12th Heat 1/12th Heat 2 12th Overall on aggregate
21–3–71	Race of Champions, Brands Hatch F1	Ronnie Peterson	March 711–3	Rtd, broken brake shaft
		Ray Allen	March 701–06	6th
28–3–71	Questor Grand Prix, Ontario, California, USA F1	Henri Pescarolo	March 711–3	Rtd, Heat 1/15th Heat 2 20th Overall on aggregate
		Derek Bell	March 701–06	13th Heat 1/Rtd Heat 2 15th Overall on aggregate
12–4–71	Rindt Memorial, Thruxton F2	Henri Pescarolo	March 712M–4	*1st* Heat 2/Rtd Final, engine
		Derek Bell	March 712M–2	2nd Heat 1/3rd Final
18–4–71	SPANISH GRAND PRIX, BARCELONA	Henri Pescarolo	March 711–3	Rtd, wing collapsed
9–4–71	Rothmans International Trophy, Oulton Park F1	Cyd Williams	March 701–06	DNS, practice accident
25–4–71	Pau Grand Prix, France F2	Max Jean	March 721M	'11th' NRF
2–5–71	Eifelrennen, Nürburgring Nordschleife F2	Henri Pescarolo	March 712M–4	Rtd, brakes
		Derek Bell	March 712M–2	Rtd, engine
8–5–71	International Trophy, Silverstone F1	Henri Pescarolo	March 711–3	15th Heat 1/5th Heat 2 6th Overall on aggregate
23–5–71	MONACO GRAND PRIX, MONTE CARLO	Henri Pescarolo	March 711–3	8th
31–5–71	Crystal Palace F2	Henri Pescarolo	March 712M–4	Rtd Heat 2/Rtd Final
		Derek Bell	March 712M–2	5th Heat 1/Rtd Final, oil union
13–6–71	Rindt Memorial, Hockenheim, Germany F1	Ray Allen	March 701–06 (2)	Rtd, fuel system

13–6–71	Madunina GP, Vallelunga, Italy F2	Carlos Pace	March 721M–20	2nd Heat 1/3rd Heat 2
				3rd Overall on aggregate
		Andrea de Adamich	March 721M–4	10th Heat 1/6th Heat 2
				7th Overall on aggregate
20–6–71	DUTCH GRAND PRIX, ZANDVOORT	Henri Pescarolo	March 711–3	13th
20–6–71	Monza Lottery GP, Italy F2	Derek Bell	March 712M–2	5th Heat 1/4th Heat 2
				2nd Overall on aggregate
		Carlos Pace	March 721M–20	
		Max Jean	March 721M–4	
27–6–71	Rouen GP, France F2	Carlos Pace	March 712M–20	10th Heat 1/7th Final
		Max Jean	March 712M–4	Race accident Heat 1/DNS Final
		Christian Ethuin	March 712M–2	DNS, practice damage
4–7–71	FRENCH GRAND PRIX, RICARD	Henri Pescarolo	March 711–3	Rtd, gearbox
		Max Jean	March 701–6	14th
17–7–71	BRITISH GRAND PRIX, SILVERSTONE	Henri Pescarolo	March 711–3	4th
25–7–71	Imola GP, Italy, F2	Carlos Pace	March 712M–20	4th Heat 1/1st FL Heat 2
				1st Overall on aggregate
		Giancarlo Naddeo	March 712M–2	8th Heat 1/Rtd, engine Heat 2
1–8–71	GERMAN GRAND PRIX, NÜRBURGRING	Henri Pescarolo	March 711–3	Rtd, suspension
8–8–71	Mantorp Park, Sweden F2	Derek Bell	March 712M–2	17th Heat 1/9th Heat 2
				9th Overall on aggregate
		Carlos Pace	March 712M–20	Rtd, Heat 1, engine blown
15–8–71	AUSTRIAN GRAND PRIX, ÖSTERREICHRING	Henri Pescarolo	March 711–3	6th
22–8–71	Kinekullering, Sweden F2	Carlos Pace	March 712M–20	9th Heat 1/12th Heat 2
				9th Overall on aggregate
21–8–71	Oulton Park Gold Cup F1	Henri Pescarolo	March 711–3	1st Heat 1 = FL/Rtd Heat 2,
				accident
		Tony Trimmer	March 701–06	Rtd Heat 1, race accident
30–8–71	Brands Hatch F2	Henri Pescarolo	March 712M–4	Rtd, engine
		Derek Bell	March 712M–2	DNQ, car completed late
		Carlos Pace	March 712M–20	Rtd, lost fuel filter bowl
5–9–71	ITALIAN GRAND PRIX, MONZA	Henri Pescarolo	March 711–3	Rtd, rear suspension
12–9–71	Tulln-Langenlebarn, Austria F2	Henri Pescarolo	March 712M–2	Rtd Heat 1, clutch
		Carlos Pace	March 712M–20	16th Heat 1/11th Heat 2
				13th Overall on aggregate
		Helmut Marko/		
		Derek Bell	March 712M–2	Wdn
19–9–71	CANADIAN GRAND PRIX, MOSPORT PARK	Henri Pescarolo	March 711–3	DNS, warm-up accident
26–9–71	Albi GP, France F2	Henri Pescarolo	March 712M–4	DNQ electrics/clutch failure
		Derek Bell	March 712M–2	DNQ holed radiator
		Carlos Pace	March 712M–20	DNQ constant misfire
3–10–71	UNITED STATES GRAND PRIX, WATKINS GLEN	Henri Pescarolo	March 711–3	Rtd, camshaft
10–10–71	Rome GP, Vallelunga, Italy F2	Henri Pescarolo	March 712M–4	6th Heat 1/Rtd Heat 2
				'17th' Overall on aggregate
		Derek Bell	March 712M–2	22nd Heat 1, Rtd, engine blown

		Carlos Pace	March 712M–20	18th Heat 1/7th Heat 2
				13th Overall on aggregate
17–10–71	Madunina GP, Vallelunga, Italy F2	Carlos Pace	March 712M–20	Rtd, camshaft
24–10–71	Victory Race, Brands Hatch F1	Henri Pescarolo	March 711–3	Rtd, race collision
31–10–71	Torneio 1, São Paulo, Brazil F2	Henri Pescarolo	March 712M–4	Rtd Heat 1, clutch/DNS Heat 2
		Carlos Pace	March 712M–2	5th Heat 1/Rtd Heat 2
				13th Overall on aggregate
7–11–71	Torneio 2, São Paulo, Brazil F2	Henri Pescarolo	March 712M–4	Rtd Heat 1, DNS Heat 2
		Carlos Pace	March 712M–2	Rtd Heat 1, Rtd Heat 2
4–11–71	Torneio 3, Porto Alegre, Brazil F2	Carlos Pace	March 712M–2	4th Heat 1/3rd Heat 2
				3rd Overall on aggregate
		Claudio Francisci	March 712M–20	DNS, engine in practice
		Arturo Merzario	March 712M–2	10th Heat 1/9th Heat 2
				9th Overall on aggregate
21–11–71	Torneio 4, Cordoba, Argentina F2	Carlos Pace	March 712M–4	3rd Heat 1/Rtd, engine Heat 2
				9th Overall on aggregate
		N. Garcia Veiga	March 712M–2	11th Heat 1/Rtd, fuel pump, Heat 2
		José Dolhem	March 712M–20	DNP

1972

23–1–72	ARGENTINE GRAND PRIX, BUENOS AIRES	Henri Pescarolo	March 721–3	8th
4–3–72	SOUTH AFRICAN GRAND PRIX, KYALAMI	Henri Pescarolo	March 721–3	11th
		Carlos Pace	March 711–'6!'	17th
30–3–72	Brazilian GP, São Paulo, F1	Henri Pescarolo	March 721–3	Rtd, sand in throttle slides
		Carlos Pace	March 711–3	Rtd, sand in throttle slides
23–4–72	International Trophy, Silverstone F1	Henri Pescarolo	March 721–3	Rtd
1–5–72	SPANISH GRAND PRIX, JARAMA	Henri Pescarolo	March 721–3	11th
		Carlos Pace	March 711–3	6th
14–5–72	MONACO GRAND PRIX, MONTE CARLO	Henri Pescarolo	March 721–3	Rtd, accident
		Carlos Pace	March 711–3	17th
4–6–72	BELGIAN GRAND PRIX, NIVELLES	Henri Pescarolo	March 721–3	Unc, '15th'
		Carlos Pace	March 711–3	5th
18–6–72	Republica GP, Vallelunga, Italy F1	Henri Pescarolo	March 711–3	Rtd, broken wishbone
2–7–72	FRENCH GRAND PRIX, CLERMONT-FERRAND	Henri Pescarolo	March 721–3	DNS, practice accident
		Carlos Pace	March 711–3	Rtd, engine
15–7–72	BRITISH GRAND PRIX, BRANDS HATCH	Henri Pescarolo	Politoys FX3/1	Race accident
		Carlos Pace	March 711–3	Rtd, differential
30–7–72	GERMAN GRAND PRIX, NÜRBURGRING	Henri Pescarolo	March 721–3(2)	Race accident
		Carlos Pace	March 711–3	Unc
13–8–72	AUSTRIAN GRAND PRIX, ÖSTERREICHRING	Henri Pescarolo	March 721–3	DNS, practice accident
		Carlos Pace	March 711–3	Unc
28–8–72	Rothmans 50,000 Formule Libre, Brands Hatch	Henri Pescarolo	March 711–3	3rd
10–9–72	ITALIAN GRAND PRIX, MONZA	Henri Pescarolo	March 721–3	DNQ, handling
		Carlos Pace	March 711–3	Race collision

24–9–72	CANADIAN GRAND PRIX, MOSPORT PARK	Henri Pescarolo	March 721–3	13th
		Carlos Pace	March 711–3	9th
8–10–72	UNITED STATES GRAND PRIX, WATKINS GLEN	Henri Pescarolo	March 721–3	14th
		Carlos Pace	March 711–3	Rtd, injection gear
22–10–72	Challenge Trophy Brands Hatch F1	Henri Pescarolo	March 721–3	Rtd, steering
		Chris Amon	Politoys FX3/1	Rtd, misfiring
1973				
28–1–73	ARGENTINE GRAND PRIX, BUENOS AIRES	Howden Ganley	Iso–Marlboro FX3–2	Unc '11th'
		'Nanni' Galli	Iso–Marlboro FX3–1	Rtd, ancillary belt
11–2–73	BRAZILIAN GRAND PRIX, SÃO PAULO	Howden Ganley	Iso–Marlboro FX3B–2	7th
		'Nanni' Galli	Iso–Marlboro FX3B–1	9th
3–3–73	SOUTH AFRICAN GRAND PRIX, KYALAMI	Howden Ganley	Iso–Marlboro FX3B–2	10th
		Jacky Pretorius	Iso–Marlboro FX3B–1	Rtd, overheating
18–3–73	Race of Champions, Brands Hatch F1	Howden Ganley	Iso–Marlboro FX3B–2	Rtd, wheel failure
		Tony Trimmer	Iso–Marlboro FX3B–3	4th
7–4–73	International Trophy, Silverstone F1	Howden Ganley	Iso–Marlboro FX3B–2	Rtd, engine
29–4–73	SPANISH GRAND PRIX, BARCELONA	Howden Ganley	Iso–Marlboro IR–02	Rtd, out of fuel
		'Nanni' Galli	Iso–Marlboro IR–01	11th
20–5–73	BELGIAN GRAND PRIX, ZOLDER	Howden Ganley	Iso–Marlboro IR–02	Race accident
		'Nanni' Galli	Iso–Marlboro IR–01	Rtd, engine
3–6–73	MONACO GRAND PRIX, MONTE CARLO	Howden Ganley	Iso–Marlboro IR–02	Rtd, half-shaft
		'Nanni' Galli	Iso–Marlboro IR–01	Rtd, half-shaft
17–6–73	SWEDISH GRAND PRIX, ANDERSTORP	Howden Ganley	Iso–Marlboro IR–02	11th
		Tom Belso	Iso–Marlboro IR–01	DNS
1–7–73	FRENCH GRAND PRIX, RICARD	Howden Ganley	Iso–Marlboro IR–02	14th
		Henri Pescarolo	Iso–Marlboro IR–01	Rtd, overheating
14–7–73	BRITISH GRAND PRIX, SILVERSTONE	Howden Ganley	Iso–Marlboro IR–02	9th
		Graham McRae	Iso–Marlboro IR–01	Rtd, jammed throttle
29–7–73	DUTCH GRAND PRIX, ZANDVOORT	Howden Ganley	Iso–Marlboro IR–02	9th
		Gijs van Lennep	Iso–Marlboro IR–01	6th
5–8–73	GERMAN GRAND PRIX, NÜRBURGRING	Howden Ganley	Iso–Marlboro IR–02	DNS, practice accident
		Henri Pescarolo	Iso–Marlboro IR–01	10th
19–8–73	AUSTRIAN GRAND PRIX, ÖSTERREICHRING	Howden Ganley	Iso–Marlboro IR–03	Unc '11th'
		Gijs van Lennep	Iso–Marlboro IR–01	9th
9–9–73	ITALIAN GRAND PRIX, MONZA	Howden Ganley	Iso–Marlboro IR–03	'16th', loose bodywork
		Gijs van Lennep	Iso–Marlboro IR–01	Rtd, overheating
23–9–73	CANADIAN GRAND PRIX, MOSPORT PARK	Howden Ganley	Iso–Marlboro IR–03	6th
		Tim Schenken	Iso–Marlboro IR–01	14th
7–10–73	UNITED STATES GRAND PRIX, WATKINS GLEN	Howden Ganley	Iso–Marlboro IR–03	12th
		Jacky Ickx	Iso–Marlboro IR–01	7th
1974				
13–1–74	ARGENTINE GRAND PRIX, BUENOS AIRES	Arturo Merzario	Iso–Marlboro FW–01	Rtd, engine
27–1–74	BRAZILIAN GRAND PRIX, SÃO PAULO	Arturo Merzario	Iso–Marlboro FW–01	Rtd, jammed throttle slide
3–2–74	President Medici GP, Brasilia, Brazil	Arturo Merzario	Iso–Marlboro FW–01	3rd
30–3–74	SOUTH AFRICAN GRAND PRIX, KYALAMI	Arturo Merzario	Iso–Marlboro FW–02	6th
		Tom Belso	Iso–Marlboro FW–01	Rtd, clutch

28-4-74	SPANISH GRAND PRIX, JARAMA	Arturo Merzario	Iso–Marlboro FW–03	Rtd, race accident
		Tom Belso	Iso–Marlboro FW–02	DNQ
12-5-74	BELGIAN GRAND PRIX, NIVELLES	Arturo Merzario	Iso–Marlboro FW–03	Rtd, half-shaft
		Gijs van Lennep	Iso–Marlboro FW–02	14th
26-5-74	MONACO GRAND PRIX, MONTE CARLO	Arturo Merzario	Iso–Marlboro FW–03	Rtd, multiple collision
9-6-74	SWEDISH GRAND PRIX, ANDERSTORP	Tom Belso	Iso–Marlboro FW–02	8th
		Richard Robarts	Iso–Marlboro FW–02	Car taken over by Belso for race after crashing FW–03 in warm-up
23-6-74	DUTCH GRAND PRIX, ZANDVOORT	Arturo Merzario	Iso–Marlboro FW–02	Rtd, 'gearbox'
		Gijs van Lennep	Iso–Marlboro FW–01	DNQ
7-7-74	FRENCH GRAND PRIX, DIJON	Arturo Merzario	Iso–Marlboro FW–02	9th
		J-P Jabouille	Iso–Marlboro FW–01	DNQ
20-7-74	BRITISH GRAND PRIX, BRANDS HATCH	Arturo Merzario	Iso–Marlboro FW–03	Rtd, engine
		Tom Belso	Iso–Marlboro FW–02	DNQ
4-8-74	GERMAN GRAND PRIX, NÜRBURGRING	Arturo Merzario	Iso–Marlboro FW–03	Rtd, throttle linkage
		Jacques Laffite	Iso–Marlboro FW–02	Rtd, collision damage
18-8-74	AUSTRIAN GRAND PRIX, ÖSTERREICHRING	Arturo Merzario	Iso–Marlboro FW–03	Rtd, fuel pressure
		Jacques Laffite	Iso–Marlboro FW–02	Unc
8-9-74	ITALIAN GRAND PRIX, MONZA	Arturo Merzario	Iso–Marlboro FW–03	4th
		Jacques Laffite	Iso–Marlboro FW–02	Rtd, engine
22-9-74	CANADIAN GRAND PRIX, MOSPORT PARK	Arturo Merzario	Iso–Marlboro FW–03	Rtd, 'handling'
		Jacques Laffite	Iso–Marlboro FW–02	'15th', puncture
6-10-74	UNITED STATES GRAND PRIX, WATKINS GLEN	Arturo Merzario	Iso–Marlboro FW–03	Rtd, extinguisher
		Jacques Laffite	Iso–Marlboro FW–02	Rtd, rear wheel

1975

12-1-75	ARGENTINE GRAND PRIX, BUENOS AIRES	Arturo Merzario	Williams FW–03	Unc '15th'
		Jacques Laffite	Williams FW–02	Rtd, holed radiator
26-1-75	BRAZILIAN GRAND PRIX, SÃO PAULO	Arturo Merzario	Williams FW–03	Rtd, metering unit
		Jacques Laffite	Williams FW–02	11th
1-3-75	SOUTH AFRICAN GRAND PRIX, KYALAMI	Arturo Merzario	Williams FW–03	Rtd, engine
		Jacques Laffite	Williams FW–02	Unc '18th'
16-3-75	Race of Champions, Brands Hatch F1	Arturo Merzario	Williams FW–03	7th
		Maurizio Flammini	Williams FW–02	DNS, practice accident
12-4-75	Silverstone, International Trophy F1	Arturo Merzario	Williams FW–03	DNS, engine blown
27-4-75	SPANISH GRAND PRIX, BARCELONA	Arturo Merzario	Williams FW–04	Rtd, driver protest
		Tony Brise	Williams FW–03	7th
11-5-75	MONACO GRAND PRIX, MONTE CARLO	Arturo Merzario	Williams FW–03	DNQ
		Jacques Laffite	Williams FW–04	DNQ
25-5-75	BELGIAN GRAND PRIX, ZOLDER	Arturo Merzario	Williams FW–03	Rtd, clutch
		Jacques Laffite	Williams FW–04	Rtd, gearbox
8-6-75	SWEDISH GRAND PRIX, ANDERSTORP	Damien Magee	Williams FW–03	14th
		Ian Scheckter	Williams FW–04	Rtd, race accident

22–6–75	DUTCH GRAND PRIX, ZANDVOORT	Jacques Laffite	Williams FW–04	Rtd, engine
		Ian Scheckter	Williams FW–03	12th
6–7–75	FRENCH GRAND PRIX, RICARD	Francois Migault	Williams FW–03	DNS, no engine . . .
		Jacques Laffite	Williams FW–04	11th
19–7–75	BRITISH GRAND PRIX, SILVERSTONE	Jacques Laffite	Williams FW–04	Rtd, gearbox
3–8–75	GERMAN GRAND PRIX, NÜRBURGRING	Jacques Laffite	Williams FW–04	*2nd*
		Ian Ashley	Williams FW–03	DNS, practice accident
17–8–75	AUSTRIAN GRAND PRIX, ÖSTERREICHRING	Jacques Laffite	Williams FW–04	Rtd, driver
		Jo Vonlanthen	Williams FW–03	Rtd, engine
24–8–75	Swiss GP, Dijon, France F1	Jacques Laffite	Williams FW–04	10th
		Jo Vonlanthen	Williams FW–03	14th
7–9–75	ITALIAN GRAND PRIX, MONZA	Jacques Laffite	Williams FW–04	Rtd, gearbox
		Renzo Zorzi	Williams FW–02	14th
5–10–75	UNITED STATES GRAND PRIX, WATKINS GLEN	Jacques Laffite	Williams FW–04/2	DNS, driver problem
		Lella Lombardi	Williams FW–04/1	DNS, driver problem

1976

25–1–76	BRAZILIAN GRAND PRIX, SÃO PAULO	Jacky Ickx	Wolf–Williams FW05	8th
		Renzo Zorzi	Wolf–Williams FW–04/1	9th
6–3–76	SOUTH AFRICAN GRAND PRIX, KYALAMI	Jacky Ickx	Wolf–Williams FW05/1	16th
		Michel Leclere	Wolf–Williams FW05/2	13th
14–3–76	Race of Champions, Brands Hatch F1	Jacky Ickx	Wolf–Williams FW05/1	3rd
28–3–76	UNITED STATES GP WEST, LONG BEACH	Jacky Ickx	Wolf–Williams FW05/1	DNQ
		Michel Leclere	Wolf–Williams FW05/2	DNQ
11–4–76	International Trophy, Silverstone F1	Jacky Ickx	Wolf–Williams FW05/1	Rtd, gearbox
		Mario Andretti	Wolf–Williams FW05/2	7th
2–5–76	SPANISH GRAND PRIX, JARAMA	Jacky Ickx	Wolf–Williams FW05/1	7th
		Michel Leclere	Wolf–Williams FW05/2	10th
16–5–76	BELGIAN GRAND PRIX, ZOLDER	Jacky Ickx	Wolf–Williams FW05/1	DNQ
		Michel Leclere	Wolf–Williams FW05/2	11th
30–5–76	MONACO GRAND PRIX, MONTE CARLO	Jacky Ickx	Wolf–Williams FW05/1	DNQ
		Michel Leclere	Wolf–Williams FW05/2	11th
13–6–76	SWEDISH GRAND PRIX, ANDERSTORP	Michel Leclere	Wolf–Williams FW05/2	Rtd, engine
4–7–76	FRENCH GRAND PRIX, RICARD	Jacky Ickx	Wolf–Williams FW05/3	10th
		Michel Leclere	Wolf–Williams FW05/2	13th
18–7–76	BRITISH GRAND PRIX, BRANDS HATCH	Jacky Ickx	Wolf–Williams FW05/3	DNQ
1–8–76	GERMAN GRAND PRIX, NÜRBURGRING	Arturo Merzario	Wolf–Williams FW05/3	Rtd, 'brakes'
15–8–76	AUSTRIAN GRAND PRIX, ÖSTERREICHRING	Arturo Merzario	Wolf–Williams FW05/3	Rtd, race accident
29–8–76	DUTCH GRAND PRIX, ZANDVOORT	Arturo Merzario	Wolf–Williams FW05/3	Rtd, race accident
12–9–76	ITALIAN GRAND PRIX, MONZA	Arturo Merzario	Wolf–Williams FW05/3	Wdn
3–10–76	CANADIAN GRAND PRIX, MOSPORT PARK	Arturo Merzario	Wolf–Williams FW05/3	Rtd, race accident
		Chris Amon	Wolf–Williams FW05/2	DNS, practice collision
10–10–76	UNITED STATES GRAND PRIX, WATKINS GLEN	Arturo Merzario	Wolf–Williams FW05/3	Rtd, 'race collision'
		Warwick Brown	Wolf–Williams FW05/1	14th
24–10–76	JAPANESE GRAND PRIX, MOUNT FUJI	Arturo Merzario	Wolf–Williams FW05/3	Rtd, gearbox
		Hans Binder	Wolf–Williams FW05/1	Rtd, wheel bearing

1977

8–5–77	SPANISH GRAND PRIX, JARAMA	Patrick Neve	March 761-7	12th
5–6–77	BELGIAN GRAND PRIX, ZOLDER	Patrick Neve	March 761-7(2)	10th
19–6–77	SWEDISH GRAND PRIX, ANDERSTORP	Patrick Neve	March 761-7(2)	15th
3–7–77	FRENCH GRAND PRIX, DIJON–PRENOIS	Patrick Neve	March 761-7(2)	DNQ
16–7–77	BRITISH GRAND PRIX, SILVERSTONE	Patrick Neve	March 761-7(2)	10th
31–7–77	GERMAN GRAND PRIX, HOCKENHEIM	Patrick Neve	March 761-7(2)	DNQ
14–8–77	AUSTRIAN GRAND PRIX, ÖSTERREICHRING	Patrick Neve	March 761-7(2)	9th
28–8–77	DUTCH GRAND PRIX, ZANDVOORT	Patrick Neve	March 761-7(2)	DNQ
11–9–77	ITALIAN GRAND PRIX, MONZA	Patrick Neve	March 761-7(2)	7th
2–10–77	UNITED STATES GRAND PRIX, WATKINS GLEN	Patrick Neve	March 761-7(2)	18th
9–10–77	CANADIAN GRAND PRIX, MOSPORT PARK	Patrick Neve	March 761-7(2)	Rtd, oil pressure light

1978

15–1–78	ARGENTINE GRAND PRIX, BUENOS AIRES	Alan Jones	Williams FW06-1	Rtd, fuel vaporization, ran 11th
29–1–78	BRAZILIAN GRAND PRIX, RIO DE JANEIRO	Alan Jones	Williams FW06-1	11th, pit stops, wearing tyres
4–3–78	SOUTH AFRICAN GRAND PRIX, KYALAMI	Alan Jones	Williams FW06-1	4th
2–4–78	UNITED STATES GP WEST, LONG BEACH	Alan Jones	Williams FW06-2	7th, ran 2nd
7–5–78	MONACO GRAND PRIX, MONTE CARLO	Alan Jones	Williams FW06-1	Rtd, oil leak, ran 6th
21–5–78	BELGIAN GRAND PRIX, ZOLDER	Alan Jones	Williams FW06-1	10th, wet race, tyre changes
4–6–78	SPANISH GRAND PRIX, JARAMA	Alan Jones	Williams FW06-2	8th
17–6–78	SWEDISH GRAND PRIX, ANDERSTORP	Alan Jones	Williams FW06-1	Rtd, wheel bearing, ran 4th
2–7–78	FRENCH GRAND PRIX, RICARD	Alan Jones	Williams FW06-1	5th
16–7–78	BRITISH GRAND PRIX, BRANDS HATCH	Alan Jones	Williams FW06-2	Rtd, half-shaft, ran 2nd
30–7–78	GERMAN GRAND PRIX, HOCKENHEIM	Alan Jones	Williams FW06-1	Rtd, fuel vaporization, ran 3rd
13–8–78	AUSTRIAN GRAND PRIX, ÖSTERREICHRING	Alan Jones	Williams FW06-1	Rtd, race accident, 16th
27–8–78	DUTCH GRAND PRIX, ZANDVOORT	Alan Jones	Williams FW06-1	Rtd, throttle cable, ran 8th
10–9–78	ITALIAN GRAND PRIX, MONZA	Alan Jones	Williams FW06-1	13th, tyre changed, ran 5th
1–10–78	UNITED STATES GRAND PRIX, WATKINS GLEN	Alan Jones	Williams FW06-1	2nd
8–10–78	CANADIAN GRAND PRIX, MONTREAL	Alan Jones	Williams FW06-2	9th, puncture, ran 2nd

1979

21–1–79	ARGENTINE GRAND PRIX, BUENOS AIRES	Alan Jones	Williams FW06-5	9th
		Clay Regazzoni	Williams FW06-3	10th
4–2–79	BRAZILIAN GRAND PRIX, SÃO PAULO	Alan Jones	Williams FW06-4	Rtd, fuel pressure, ran 5th
		Clay Regazzoni	Williams FW06-3	15th, ran 11th
3–3–79	SOUTH AFRICAN GRAND PRIX, KYALAMI	Alan Jones	Williams FW06-5	Rtd, rear suspension failure
		Clay Regazzoni	Williams FW06-3	9th
8–4–79	UNITED STATES GP WEST, LONG BEACH	Alan Jones	Williams FW06-4	3rd
		Clay Regazzoni	Williams FW06-3	Rtd, engine
29–4–79	SPANISH GRAND PRIX, JARAMA	Alan Jones	Williams FW07-1	Rtd, gear selection
		Clay Regazzoni	Williams FW07-2	Rtd, engine
13–5–79	BELGIAN GRAND PRIX, ZOLDER	Alan Jones	Williams FW07-1	Rtd, electrics, LED GP
		Clay Regazzoni	Williams FW07-2	Rtd, race collision

Date	Event	Driver	Car	Result
27–5–79	MONACO GRAND PRIX, MONTE CARLO	Alan Jones	Williams FW07–3	Rtd, race accident, ran 5th
		Clay Regazzoni	Williams FW07–2	SECOND
1–7–79	FRENCH GRAND PRIX, DIJON	Alan Jones	Williams FW07–3	4th
		Clay Regazzoni	Williams FW07–2	6th
14–7–79	BRITISH GRAND PRIX, SILVERSTONE	Alan Jones	Williams FW07–1	Rtd, water pump, LED GP
		Clay Regazzoni	Williams FW07–2	FIRST, FL
29–7–79	GERMAN GRAND PRIX, HOCKENHEIM	Alan Jones	Williams FW07–4	FIRST, LED THROUGHOUT
		Clay Regazzoni	Williams FW07–2	SECOND
12–8–79	AUSTRIAN GRAND PRIX, ÖSTERREICHRING	Alan Jones	Williams FW07–4	FIRST
		Clay Regazzoni	Williams FW07–1	5th
26–8–79	DUTCH GRAND PRIX, ZANDVOORT	Alan Jones	Williams FW07–1	FIRST
		Clay Regazzoni	Williams FW07–2	Rtd, race collision
9–9–79	ITALIAN GRAND PRIX, MONZA	Alan Jones	Williams FW07–4	9th, changed battery
		Clay Regazzoni	Williams FW07–1	3rd, FL
30–9–79	CANADIAN GRAND PRIX, MONTREAL	Alan Jones	Williams FW07–4	FIRST, FL
		Clay Regazzoni	Williams FW07–1	3rd
7–10–79	UNITED STATES GRAND PRIX, WATKINS GLEN	Alan Jones	Williams FW07–4	Rtd, lost rear wheel, LED GP
		Clay Regazzoni	Williams FW07–1	Rtd, race collision, ran 3rd

1980

Date	Event	Driver	Car	Result
13–1–80	ARGENTINE GRAND PRIX, BUENOS AIRES	Alan Jones	Williams FW07–4	FIRST, PP, FL
		Carlos Reutemann	Williams FW07B–5	Rtd, engine, ran 4th
27–1–80	BRAZILIAN GRAND PRIX, SÃO PAULO	Alan Jones	Williams FW07B–6	3rd
		Carlos Reutemann	Williams FW07B–5	Rtd, drive-shaft
2–3–80	SOUTH AFRICAN GRAND PRIX, KYALAMI	Alan Jones	Williams FW07B–7	Rtd, gearbox oil leak, ran 3rd
		Carlos Reutemann	Williams FW07B–5	5th, tyre change, ran 4th
30–3–80	UNITED STATES GP (WEST), LONG BEACH	Alan Jones	Williams FW07B–6	Rtd, race collision, ran 2nd
		Carlos Reutemann	Williams FW07B–5	Rtd, driveshaft, ran 6th
4–5–80	BELGIAN GRAND PRIX, ZOLDER	Alan Jones	Williams FW07B–7	SECOND, PP
		Carlos Reutemann	Williams FW07B–5	3rd
18–5–80	MONACO GRAND PRIX, MONTE CARLO	Alan Jones	Williams FW07B–7	Rtd, differential, ran 2nd
		Carlos Reutemann	Williams FW07B–5	FIRST
1–6–80	SPANISH GRAND PRIX, JARAMA*	Alan Jones	Williams FW07B–7	FIRST, FL
		Carlos Reutemann	Williams FW07B–5	Rtd, race collision, LED GP
29–6–80	FRENCH GRAND PRIX, RICARD	Alan Jones	Williams FW07B–7	FIRST, FL
		Carlos Reutemann	Williams FW07B–5	6th
13–7–80	BRITISH GRAND PRIX, BRANDS HATCH	Alan Jones	Williams FW07B–7	FIRST
		Carlos Reutemann	Williams FW07B–5	3rd
10–8–80	GERMAN GRAND PRIX, HOCKENHEIM	Alan Jones	Williams FW07B–9	3rd, PP, FL
		Carlos Reutemann	Williams FW07B–5	SECOND, LED GP, tyre change

* Subsequently demoted from World Championship round status

17–8–80 AUSTRIAN GRAND PRIX, ÖSTERREICHRING	Alan Jones	Williams FW07B–9	SECOND, LED GP – briefly
	Carlos Reutemann	Williams FW07B–8	3rd
31–8–80 DUTCH GRAND PRIX, ZANDVOORT	Alan Jones	Williams FW07B–7	11th, LED GP, skirt damage
	Carlos Reutemann	Williams FW07B–8	4th
14–9–80 ITALIAN GRAND PRIX, IMOLA	Alan Jones	Williams FW07B–9	SECOND, FL
	Carlos Reutemann	Williams FW07B–8	3rd
28–9–80 CANADIAN GRAND PRIX, MONTREAL	Alan Jones	Williams FW07B–9	FIRST
	Carlos Reutemann	Williams FW07B–8	SECOND
5–10–80 UNITED STATES GRAND PRIX, WATKINS GLEN	Alan Jones	Williams FW07B–9	FIRST, FL
	Carlos Reutemann	Williams FW07B–8	SECOND
16–11–80 AUSTRALIAN GRAND PRIX, CALDER F1/5000	Alan Jones	Williams FW07B–7	FIRST, PP, FL

1981

7–2–81 SOUTH AFRICAN GRAND PRIX, KYALAMI*	Alan Jones	Williams FW07B–9	Rtd, skirt damage, ran 3rd
	Carlos Reutemann	Williams FW07B–10	FIRST
15–3–81 UNITED STATES GP WEST, LONG BEACH	Alan Jones	Williams FW07C–11	FIRST, FL
	Carlos Reutemann	Williams FW07C–12	SECOND, LED GP
29–3–81 BRAZILIAN GRAND PRIX, RIO DE JANEIRO	Carlos Reutemann	Williams FW07C–12	FIRST, FR
	Alan Jones	Williams FW07C–11	SECOND
12–4–81 ARGENTINE GRAND PRIX, BUENOS AIRES	Alan Jones	Williams FW07C–11	4th
	Carlos Reutemann	Williams FW07C–12	SECOND
3–5–81 SAN MARINO GRAND PRIX, IMOLA	Alan Jones	Williams FW07C–11	12th
	Carlos Reutemann	Williams FW07C–12	3rd, FR
17–5–81 BELGIAN GRAND PRIX, ZOLDER	Alan Jones	Williams FW07C–11	Accident, LED GP
	Carlos Reutemann	Williams FW07C–12	FIRST, PP, FL
31–5–81 MONACO GRAND PRIX, MONTE CARLO	Alan Jones	Williams FW07C–15	SECOND, LED GP, FL
	Carlos Reutemann	Williams FW07C–12	Rtd
21–6–81 SPANISH GRAND PRIX, JARAMA	Alan Jones	Williams FW07C–15	7th, LED GP, FR, FL
	Carlos Reutemann	Williams FW07C–12	4th
5–7–81 FRENCH GRAND PRIX, DIJON-PRENOIS	Alan Jones	Williams FW07C–11	17th
	Carlos Reutemann	Williams FW07C–12	10th
18–7–81 BRITISH GRAND PRIX, SILVERSTONE	Alan Jones	Williams FW07C–11	Collision
	Carlos Reutemann	Williams FW07C–14	SECOND
2–8–81 GERMAN GRAND PRIX, HOCKENHEIM	Alan Jones	Williams FW07D–16	11th, LED GP, FL
	Carlos Reutemann	Williams FW07C–15	Rtd, engine
16–8–81 AUSTRIAN GRAND PRIX, ÖSTERREICHRING	Alan Jones	Williams FW07D–16	4th (07D was exp. tub)
	Carlos Reutemann	Williams FW07C–14	5th
30–8–81 DUTCH GRAND PRIX, ZANDVOORT	Alan Jones	Williams FW07D–16	3rd, FL
	Carlos Reutemann	Williams FW07C–17	Collision
13–9–81 ITALIAN GRAND PRIX, MONZA	Alan Jones	Williams FW07D–16	SECOND
	Carlos Reutemann	Williams FW07C–17	3rd, FL FR
27–9–81 CANADIAN GRAND PRIX, MONTREAL	Alan Jones	Williams FW07D–16	Rtd, LED GP
	Carlos Reutemann	Williams FW07C–17	10th, FR
17–10–81 CAESAR'S PALACE GRAND PRIX, LAS VEGAS, USA	Alan Jones	Williams FW07D–16	FIRST, FR
	Carlos Reutemann	Williams FW07C–17	8th, PP

* Subsequently demoted from World Championship round status